# EMOTIONAL INTELLIGENCE 2.0

# EMOTIONAL INTELLIGENCE 2.0

*The best guide to develop your EQ, improve social skills, discover the ways emotional intelligence can change your life for the better*

MARK T. COLEMAN PHD

# CONTENTS

# PART 1

# What is Emotional Intelligence ?

## CHAPTER 1

# Introduction

Imagine that you have a large, very important project that you are working on with a team at work. No matter how much you tried to communicate that you could see a problem with the project, people were not listening to you. You tried to point out that the project was doomed to fail if they did not do something different, but everyone seemed to misunderstand you altogether. Finally, the day the final project was supposed to come together, the entire project failed, as you had tried to communicate. Frustrated at what had happened and wishing that people would have heeded your warnings when you first tried raising them, you snapped at everyone around you, telling them that this was all their fault, and ruining relationships with many of your coworkers in one fell swoop.

Your frustration had bubbled and built up over time, and when tensions got high enough, you snapped and exploded. After the fact, you knew you could have handled the whole problem in a far better, more productive manner, but at the moment, you felt powerless to stop yourself from pouring gasoline on the metaphorical dumpster fire that was your situation at the time.

In fact, an incident similar to that may be why you are sitting here reading this book. You may have told yourself that you needed to find a way to control yourself at the moment, or someone may have recommended looking into emotional intelligence to point you in the right direction. Regardless of the reason, you are here, let's look at the situation if you had been someone with a mastery over emotional intelligence in your shoes.

The project at work was still failing, but instead of stressing out about the possibility of failure, you looked for solutions. You still felt just as frustrated as before, but you knew that giving in to the frustration would do more harm than good. Instead, you pointed out the problems you could see with the project, and because you are more skilled at communicating in ways that people pay attention to, you are able to get your coworkers to listen to you. Together, you and your coworkers are able to brainstorm ways to fix the project before it is too late, and you all manage to do so, long before it becomes a problem with work performance. Your coworkers happily went along with your suggestions as they realized that you seem to know what you are doing and approach the situation with integrity and empathy, and one of them even mentioned to your supervisor just how integral you were to the team in completing this project. The end result was successful progress, better workplace relationships, and even some recognition from your boss for being a good leader in the face of adversity.

You can see just how drastically different the results where when the problem at hand was handled tactfully and with better communication skills that come naturally to those with higher levels of emotional intelligence. While the person was still the same both times and still had similar feelings of frustration, they took that frustration and handled it in two vastly different ways. The higher levels of emotional intelligence exhibited were more conducive to success due to enhanced problem-solving skills.

If you tend to identify more with the person who made the situation worse, you are in the right place. This book will guide you through the ins and outs of what emotional intelligence is, why it matters, and the ways emotional intelligence can change your life for the better.

## CHAPTER 2

# What is Emotional Intelligence?

Emotional intelligence defines everything about you and your interactions with the world. It is how you manage your feelings, how you interact with other people, and how you respond to adversity or challenges. It directly impacts our relationships, our wellbeing, and can even leave a lasting mark on how successful you will be in life. Considering that it is a form of intelligence, it should be no surprise that it varies from person to person, with some people being quite gifted while others struggle greatly. The good news is that your EQ is not fixed—it is a series of skills that create intelligence, and those skills can be practiced and mastered to make you better versed in social interactions.

## *Defining Emotional Intelligence*

If emotional intelligence needed a definition, it would be the ability to be aware of, regulate, and express emotions, as well as the ability to handle interpersonal relationships with empathy, compassion, and fairness. There are two key parts of emotional intelligence: the ability to recognize, understand, and regulate your own emotions, and the ability to recognize, understand, and influence the emotions of those around you.

Practically speaking, this means that an emotionally intelligent individual is able to understand how their own emotions influence themselves and others, and that individual is able to manage those emotions in order to get better control over him or herself. This is particularly important during moments of stress or tension, as when emotions run high, they tend to cause behaviors that often come with unintended consequences, such as the example of the individual blowing up at work after failing to communicate effectively.

In practice, consider the example of if you had had higher emotional intelligence when faced with your hypothetical problem at work. You were able to identify your own emotions, recognizing the frustration for what it was, which is recognizing your own emotions. You understood that the emotion was not conducive to solving the problem causing it. You controlled yourself so your emotions did not create further problems, managing your emotional reactions. That is the first half of emotional intelligence. You then recognized the emotions of your coworkers, communicating in a way that made sense to them and helped them see your perspective. This enabled you to influence their behaviors in order to get the result you needed. The entire interaction never blew up or escalated, and everyone ended up better off due to your own emotional intelligence.

## *History of Emotional Intelligence*

Though the term has been found as far back as in 1964 in a paper written by Michael Beldoch, emotional intelligence saw its rise to fame starting in 1990: Peter Salovey and John D. Mayer used the term "emotional intelligence" to refer to what they called, *"a form of social intelligence that involves the ability to monitor one's own and others' feelings and emotions, to discriminate among them, and to use this information to guide one's thinking and action."* Broken down, this means that emotional intelligence focuses on the ability to read social situations, and how emotions impact those social situations. It is the ability to be able to look at a situation, see what emotions are playing out, and understand exactly how those will cause certain behaviors to play out, as well as being able to look at the emotions surrounding the individual and understand how to alter his or her own behavior in order to influence the situation at hand.

Upon identifying this form of intelligence, they started research programs that would allow them to develop ways to quantify emotional intelligence, as well as to see just how significant it actually was within society. They performed research in a wide range of situations to discover how widely emotional intelligence seemed to reach and just how influential it was. Unsurprisingly, it reached out far and wide, and the reach of emotional intelligence is still being studied today.

Salovey and Mayer eventually settled on what is known today as the ability model to describe emotional intelligence. They believed that their emotional intelligence consisted of four specific abilities:

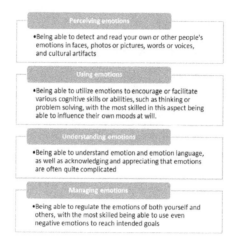

After Salovey and Mayer had their run at emotional intelligence, it was pushed even further into the limelight by Daniel Goleman, who published *Emotional Intelligence—Why it can matter more than IQ* in 1995. This book is largely known as the real stepping stone the term used to make its way into daily language.

Goleman came up with his own concept of emotional intelligence, recognizing five key constructs as coming together to comprise the skill or ability of emotional intelligence: Self-awareness, self-regulation, social skills, empathy, and motivation. His model for understanding emotional intelligence is referred to as the mixed model, and it includes the following:

**Self-Awareness**
- Knowing one's own emotions, values, goals, strengths, and weaknesses, and acknowledging the impact of their own emotion-driven behaviors on other people

**Self-Regulation**
- Being able to manage or redirect disruptive impulses or feelings and being flexible and able to cope with change

**Social Skills**
- Being able to manage relationships positively and successfully

**Empathy**
- Having consideration for other people's feelings, especially in regards to considering how one's own decisions will impact them

**Motivation**
- Having the drive to succeed simply for the sake of succeeding

Each of those constructs encompasses a series of skills related to each, and being competent in the series of skills leads to competence in that particular construct. For example, self-awareness as a skillset involves being able to know your own emotions, goals, strengths and weaknesses, and values. Each of those factors to know is considered a separate skill, and when you have mastered knowing and recognizing all of those, you are said to have a mastery over self-awareness.

So, stemming from the five main constructs for emotional intelligence, Goleman identifies several skills or competencies that fit within each domain. These emotional competencies are skills that are developed over time, as opposed to being innate and fixed values. Goleman believed that we as people are born with a certain level of general emotional intelligence. This level of general emotional intelligence was believed to be a wide range of potential for that particular individual's total EQ, recognizing that the number could move within that range based on practice or dedication to changing the behaviors, though this belief has been criticized by others.

## *The science behind Emotional Intelligence*

The science of emotional intelligence comes from a combination of emotions, feelings, and reasoning (or rationality—the two will be used interchangeably). Neuroscientists have found that these three concepts are quite interrelated, and they are used as the scientific backing for emotional intelligence.

### Emotions are evolutionarily primitive

The science behind this assumption comes from the fact that the areas of the brain that trigger emotion is largely in the more primitive areas. These parts of the brain, the limbic system, are associated with the fight-or-flight response. This part of the brain is quite primitive, existing in the center of the brain. It is newer than the "lizard brain" that people refer to being the reflexive part, which is tasked with keeping you alive. This implies that the development of emotions came after the development of reflexes, but before rationality and higher-level thinking. It also implies that emotions are an important foundation for higher-level thinking as well. Evolutionarily speaking, it is believed that this area of the brain developed along the way, creating layers of emotions with different purposes. It is believed to have started with primal emotions developing as necessary for survival, such as fear. The part of the brain that creates fear, the amygdala, is located deep within the brain. From there, filial emotions are believed to develop next, when ancient mammals seemed to develop the capacity for love toward their offspring, which is necessary for mammals to nurture their young. From there, social emotions are believed to have developed among social primates. Interestingly enough, sometimes, further development of the brain overrides the older part dedicated to regulating emotion, such as the cortex has the ability to moderate the amygdala's fear response. This means that the fear response developed first, and eventually, the cortex developed the ability to override that fear response.

The range of emotions that humans experience come together to create a system that is tailored to being able to survive in small groups or bands of people. Each of the emotions felt by humans helps adapt them to surviving in a social group without constantly stepping on each other's toes.

### The reasoning is relatively new evolutionarily

Just as emotions are ancient, the reasoning seems to have come along relatively recently, with the development of the frontal lobe. Even in children, you can see that reasoning capacity develops slowly, not really becoming mature until several years into adulthood, as opposed to emotions being instinctive and noticeably present from a very early age.

Human reasoning develops overtime to keep us alive. It involves our capacity to learn from the world around us and make inferences, as well as to create sorts of moral codes that enable us to live with others and follow rules. It involves being able to plan, judge situations, and have self-awareness. This part of the brain helps us control impulses and handle social situations with tact and skill.

### Feelings and emotions are different

Feelings and emotions involve two entirely different processes within the brain, and although they are closely related within common speech, they are not scientifically. Emotions are the activation of the brain, and frequently, that particular activation of the brain is over by the time that the brain consciously recognizes the emotion, which creates the feeling.

### How they all intertwine

If you want to be able to control your emotions, you must be able to be conscious of them. This requires the feeling to come as well, as the feeling is the conscious awareness of the emotion. In order for reasoning to take over and mitigate the impact of emotion, the individual must be conscious of the emotion in the first place, which will only happen once the feeling has registered.

This has the implication that emotional intelligence, or rationality and the ability to control or influence one's emotions, is entirely dependent on feelings happening first. Without the feelings to cue the rational part of the brain that something has happened externally and warranted an emotional response, the rational part of the mind would never know it was supposed to kick into action. This would imply that, without emotions at all, we would not be responsive to the world around us, as our responses are triggered by emotions.

.

## CHAPTER 3

# Components of Emotional Intelligence

Emotional intelligence is complicated! While the general idea may be easy enough to comprehend, there are several components that are important to understand if you hope to develop a strong grasp of the concept as a whole. The whole picture, with the parts of emotional intelligence broken down and conceptualized, becomes easier to understand. When you know exactly how your own emotions or temperament can combine and interact with your emotional intelligence to influence your behavior, you begin to have an easier time truly grasping what is happening in real-time. Just as naming and understanding something can make it less intimidating, being able to name and understand what is happening in your mind can make your emotions seem less powerful, granting you the control over yourself that emotional intelligence seeks to create.

Your behavior is a result of your emotions, empathy, and temperament all interacting with your emotional intelligence. Your emotions, empathy, and temperament create your gut instincts and reactions while your emotional intelligence acts as a sort of filter for them, only allowing the constructive ideas, impulses, and behaviors to actually be acted upon. This filter, when functioning correctly and strongly, keeps your actions acceptable and conducive to success and happiness while encouraging you to develop effective leadership and interpersonal skills.

## Emotions

Nearly everyone feels emotions. They can be pleasant, annoying, distracting, or completely unwanted, but they seem to come and go on whims without any real input from us. Before we are aware it has started, the emotion has already been triggered and feelings have been felt, almost with no warning. Before we get into the interactions of empathy, emotions, and temperament too much, you must start to understand the individual components. Emotions are one of those concepts that we all know, but struggle to define when prompted to do so.

### Defining Emotions

Emotions are tricky to define. It is one of those concepts that everyone understands, but struggle to really explain without the proper vocabulary developed over time. It is an instinctive state of mind that is directly influenced by the circumstances, mood, relationships, or other environmental stimuli present in that particular moment. This rather convoluted sentence gives you the general idea of what emotions are, but that concept can be further broken down into easily understood bits.

Your emotions are instinctive—this means that they come naturally to you, much in the way that eating is natural when you are hungry, or sleep is natural when you are tired. They are natural and automatic, happening without your own conscious effort as reflexive responses to things that are happening around or to you. They are directly influenced by several things that are fluid and constantly changing based on your own current surroundings. This correctly implies that emotions are not consistent. Something that makes you happy in one context may annoy you in another or deeply upset you in yet another. This makes them fickle—they are so dependent on everything around you, or even your own innermost thoughts, that they are hardly reliable judges. With that in mind, you may find it tempting to believe that they are not important. This is wrong—they are incredibly important and they do deserve attention, but they should also not be allowed to influence your behavior freely without your intervention.

### The Cause of Emotions

There is no one agreed-upon theory for what causes emotions. While psychologists have a general idea of where they originate, there is not one accepted answer for exactly how they are created. There are, however, three basic theories that are widely accepted as likely answers. These are the James-Lange theory, the Cannon-Bard theory, and the Schacter-Singer model. Each of these has slightly different understandings of the formation of emotions as we know and understand them.

- **James-Lange Theory:** Within this theory, emotions start physiological reactions to an external source. The physiological reaction is then interpreted, and the body feels the appropriate emotional response. For example, imagine you are driving along on the freeway. You are going at least 60 MPH when suddenly, a car cuts you off without a blinker. You have to slam on your breaks in order to narrowly avoid crashing into it, and by some miracle, the car behind you was far enough away that they were able to avoid crashing into you as well. Now, let's consider how this would cause emotions. Using the James-Lange theory, first, you would see the car that cut you off suddenly and unexpectedly in front of you. You would then tense up in anticipation of crashing into the car as you slammed onto the breaks, with your heart rate increasing and your body pumping adrenaline through your veins in anticipation of injury and pain. Your brain reacts to the stimulus and the physical response, or arousal, and translates that into fear.

- **Cannon-Bard Theory:** Within the Cannon-Bard Theory, it is believed that both emotions and the physiological response to the emotions occur at the same time in two different parts of the brain in response to a stimulus. The hypothalamus is responsible for the physical reaction you feel to the stimulus while the cortex or the front part of your brain is responsible for the emotional response. For example, when you see the car cut you off, you immediately tense up and your heart pounds, and at the same time, you feel fear. The two are believed to be concurrent rather than sequential.

- **Schacter-Singer Model:** This explanation for emotions is a two-step process as opposed to the previous two. Within the Schacter-Singer model, emotion is created when physiological response and cognition combine in response to a stimulus. For example, if you see the car coming toward you, you automatically feel your heart pound and you tense up, while also consciously thinking, "I am scared!" which creates the feeling of fear.

## Purpose of Emotions

There are several different theories that attempt to explain why we feel emotions. If they are as unreliable as they seem to be at first glance, they must be important for something. If they should not be trusted as reliable judgments of what is happening around you, then they seem as though they should be disregarded and rationality should be favored.

The problem with that line of thinking, however, is that it seeks to deny your very biology. You are biologically wired to feel emotions in order to aid with your survival. Each emotion you feel has a biological purpose that sought to keep you alive back when humans ran wild and had to struggle to survive against the wilderness instead of being able to walk into the local supermarket to buy food. Each of your four primary emotions, happiness, sadness, anger, and fear helped to keep your ancestors alive long enough to reproduce and keep the human race around.

Think about what kind of species humans are—we are social. We live in groups with other people and depend on each other for survival. We develop close bonds to those around us, especially within our own family or tribe units, and we seek to keep those within our inner circles alive and well at all costs. Especially since human children are so needy and take so long to rear into adolescence and adulthood, we have to be able to support each other in order to survive. Being able to support each other and know what the other needs at a glance then becomes important. This is where emotions come in.

Emotions work twofold to keep you alive. On one level, they motivate you to do things that keep you alive, and on the other, they provide an intricate, wordless method of communication between you and other humans around you. Each emotion implies to your body that you need to take a certain action or that you need to meet a specific need. If you feel happy, you know that your needs are met, whereas sadness implies that something terrible has happened and that someone in your circle was lost or injured.

Emotions, along with empathy, created a wordless communication system, in which we can see the emotional state of others through their expressions and body language and can respond in an appropriate manner. This communication ensures that people are able to take care of each other in an efficient manner. Empathy, simply put, is the ability to understand and feel the emotions of others as if they were your own. Because, at a glance, you can read the emotions of and empathize with someone, you will feel the desire to help mitigate those feelings, especially if they are negative and the person feeling them is someone to whom you are particularly close.

### The relevance of Emotions to Emotional Intelligence

Emotions, as you would infer, are a critical component of emotional intelligence. Without them, you would not need a form of emotional intelligence at all. Your emotions and rationality are constantly battling for control over your body, and those with lower EQs typically are swayed by their emotions. It is only with the ability to identify your emotions as they occur and manage them to ensure your behavior remains productive that rationality can occur. Rationality is important during moments of high emotion, and those who can practice it are typically able to respond to tough situations more effectively. Consider if you were to go into surgery—would you want a surgeon who is levelheaded, even when things go wrong, or would you want a surgeon who is happy, easy to relate to, but passionate and easily overwhelmed by emotions?

The levelheadedness of the surgeon comes from emotional intelligence. The surgeon likely still feels the claws of panic gripping at his throat when something goes wrong but is in control of himself enough to ignore the claws and use the desire to avoid the situation to think quickly and calmly about the situation in order to stop you from bleeding out and solve the problem.

While the vast majority of people will never be in the shoes of a surgeon struggling to save a life, they will experience their own emotional conflicts throughout life. Think of the mother who sees her adult child struggling to make good decisions no matter how hard she tries to encourage him to and rationally has to let go of her feelings of guilt or blame, or consider the man who has struggled in his marriage and has ultimately decided that he wants a divorce. His emotional side of his brain may be screaming at him to stay, whether to keep status quo or because he does not want to lose time with children, while the rational side says that it would be the best for everyone for the marriage to dissolve. These sort of conflicts arise, and when the emotions and the rational side of the brain are in conflict with one another, you can run into cognitive dissonance or the sensation of your emotional thoughts and rational beliefs not quite lining up. Emotional intelligence allows for the emotions to be heard and justified while still acting in a way that will be the most beneficial to everyone involved.

## Temperament

Temperament, while it has an impact on emotions, is not quite the same thing. Temperament is the individual person's nature, which means it has an impact on the individual's base mood. This is typically created through a mixture of nature and nurture, in the sense that part of it is genetics and physical ability or characteristics, while the other part is influenced through life experience and the environment in which a person was raised. Temperament would be the general words someone would choose to describe you if asked to do so.

### Defining Temperament

Within a dictionary, temperament is defined as something along the lines of a person's nature, particularly when it permanently affects their behavior. Temperament creates the tendency to react in certain ways to certain situations, but a temperamental tendency toward one emotion is not a guarantee. Consider these traits:

- **Outgoing:** This person likely enjoys the attention and thrives when spending time with others or in social situations. They love going to parties and socializing with other people and never shy away from an invite to go out and meet new people. Novelty is exciting and they are always happy to try new things, especially if those new things involve new people as well.
- **Easygoing:** This person is likely quite laid back. Very little ruffles her feathers, and she is typically incredibly patient and willing to put up with a lot more nonsense than most others. She likely goes with the flow and is very flexible when it comes to making decisions, allowing others in the groups to voice their preferences because she doesn't mind either way.
- **Caring:** This person is likely to be particularly in tune with other people's emotions or thoughts, and he frequently seeks to make sure everyone's needs are met at all times. He frequently puts himself last to ensure that everyone else is happy, and he gets great satisfaction in being able to take care of other people.
- **Argumentative:** This person is likely quite stubborn and refuses to admit fault or wrongdoing wherever possible. Many people would call her hard-headed or frustrating to be around. She may push the blame onto other people or refuse to back down from an argument, even when the other person wants to agree to disagree.

- **Charismatic:** This person is a natural leader—whatever he says is listened to attentively and he is usually quite influential. People may naturally gravitate toward this kind of person and seek out interactions with him whenever possible. He revels in this sort of attention and enjoys that he gets it.

Notice how each of the examples of temperament is all adjectives that could be used to describe a person, and they all tell you key features of the person's personality. The actions and tendency described are not necessarily always followed, and while it may be out of character for the caring person to act selfishly or the easygoing person to lose her temper, it can and does happen, especially if emotional intelligence or rationality has a chance to intervene before emotional impulses are acted upon.

### The Cause of Temperament

Temperament is part nature and part nurture—half of its influencers are internal and fixed whereas the other two are external forces onto the individual. Genetics, physical characteristics and limitations, life experiences, and environment all mesh together to create a person's temperament. The external forces typically take place in early childhood, acting upon predispositions that come from genetics. For example, someone with a genetic predisposition toward a depressed, or pessimistic, personality that goes through some sort of trauma or difficult situation is more likely to develop into that particular temperament than someone who is predisposed toward optimism. Likewise, someone who has a predisposition toward being quite easygoing may develop a hardheaded, strict, or even obsessive temperament if they go through a traumatic event. Consider someone who was quite easygoing to a fault being robbed one night due to not locking doors—his nature is likely to shift toward anxious or needing to feel in control after something like that.

Once temperament is developed, it is typically somewhat fixed, though it can be impacted by traumatic events, or overridden through diligence and developing a high emotional intelligence and constantly correcting the impulse toward unproductive behaviors before they can be acted upon.

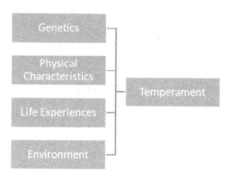

### Purpose of Temperament

Temperament is what creates your base personality. It is your natural tendency toward certain preferences or behaviors, tells whether you like social situations, and explains what makes up who you are. This is the basic foundation for who you are and is an almost endless collection of traits that combine in a unique way to create an individual person. Your temperament could be a tendency toward shyness or extroversion or could say that you are submissive or hardheaded.

Understanding your temperament is important to understand what kinds of situations and relationships you will be happiest within. For example, someone who does not enjoy social settings likely does not want to be a public relations manager for a famous band, and someone who does not like attention or being in the spotlight probably would prefer not to be a movie star. Someone outgoing who thrives on attention and praise, however, would be great on stage or in the public eye. However, just because you may not have the right temperament for certain jobs does not mean you cannot do that particular job. Even someone who struggles with stage fright or is introverted could learn to thrive on stage, performing for others. Someone who prefers to follow and be submissive in most relationships may actually be a fantastic leader, particularly if he has charisma and empathy that makes him consider the needs of others more than some of the other options for the leadership roles.

Remember, you cannot necessarily change your temperament on your own, though you can guide your reactions to it. If you think about your temperament as a guide to your behavior rather than a predictor, you will better understand the relationship. It will also help you remember that your temperament or predisposition to certain behaviors, such as the hardheaded individual's proclivity for arguments, is not an excuse for poor behavior. Even if you have a negative temperament, you still cannot behave negatively and expect those around you to not say anything about it or complain.

### The relevance of Temperament to Emotional Intelligence

When you struggle with your emotional intelligence, typically your temperament and emotions together are influencing your behaviors. You often respond instinctually, going with gut reactions. For example, imagine that you are hardheaded. Your friend gently tells you that you are wrong about a fact you brought up in a conversation and pulls up a source on her phone to back up what she is saying. Instead of accepting what your friend has to say, you double down and insist that the source is wrong and that you cannot believe everything you read on the internet—even though the thing that you had mentioned was read on the internet. You quickly grow angry at her attempts to convince you otherwise, and she gives up and tries to change the subject. Instead of allowing her to, you go on a tirade about fake news and how everything on the internet is meant to keep you dumb and distracted. Your own tendency toward being unable to admit you are wrong and your anger at being called out cause you to lash out at your friend, and she decides to leave instead of putting up with your rants. In this case, you lacked the emotional intelligence necessary to separate your temperament's gut reaction from appropriate behaviors.

Consider this graphic:

This depicts how your emotions and temperament combine. Your emotional intelligence interacts with the impulses created by your emotions and temperament, and the three of them together create the behaviors that you exhibit toward other people. When your EQ is not high enough to be an effective filter, all of the negative impulses manage to get through into your behavior.

When your EQ *is* high enough to filter out the negative impulses, you are often able to override many of the impulses your temperament and emotions push. You may still be hardheaded, but you are empathetic and self-aware enough to recognize that pushing the point is not conducive to a good relationship, and you choose to live with the discomfort of admitting your mistake rather than ruining your relationship with a friend. You are able to recognize and acknowledge your own feelings and tendencies, but still work to interact with others in an effective, rational way. For this reason, people with higher EQs tend to be more successful in relationships, less impulsive, and generally less stressed than their lower EQ peers.

## CHAPTER 4

# Components of Emotional Intelligence

Emotional intelligence is one concept built upon five separate skillsets. Altogether, these five skill sets create a person who can function well emotionally and socially. The skills within these five skillsets combine to give you the tools you will need to cope with adversity, stress, or conflict, and create a natural leader. If you are tired of feeling stressed, overwhelmed, or just running into conflict with other people, try taking a look at the five skill sets of emotional intelligence and trying to practice and implement the specific skills included within each. The five skillsets you will be introduced to are sorted into two separate categories: Personal competencies and social competencies.

The five skills are:

- *Self-awareness*
- *Self-regulation or self-management*
- *Self-motivation*
- *Social awareness*
- *Social or relationship management skills*

## *Personal Competencies*

As you may have guessed, personal competencies are all about being aware of yourself. It involves self-awareness, emotional awareness, being able to assess your own skills, and being confident in who you are. These skills create the foundation for emotional intelligence, and without this, you are likely to struggle mastering skills in the other categories. Personal competencies include self-awareness, self-regulation, and self-motivation.

### Self-Awareness

Self-awareness is your ability to accurately identify your own emotions, as well as seeing how they impact other people. This particular skill is the most fundamental within the entire emotional intelligence system—without self-awareness, the rest of the skills crumble. You *must* be self-aware to manage yourself or be successful in social settings. Self-awareness is often broken into a handful of traits and skills on its own:

- **Emotional Awareness:** The most fundamental part of emotional intelligence. This is the ability to recognize your emotions as they occur within you accurately and efficiently. Those who are skilled at emotional awareness know the nuances between similar emotions, whereas those who struggle with emotional awareness are likely to struggle to put names to their emotions at the moment beyond identifying good or bad. If you feel as though you struggle with this skill, try looking up a feelings wheel online to see a wide range of emotions and how they branch out from each other.

- **Accurate Self-Assessment:** Being able to self-assess accurately helps you be conscientious of your own strengths and weaknesses. Because you know where your strengths and weaknesses lie, you are more likely to learn from experience, especially if you know it is related to a weakness of yours. People who excel at self-assessment frequently welcome constructive criticism and enjoy hearing new perspectives, recognizing that they can always improve themselves. They often are able to make jokes about themselves. Those who struggle with making accurate self-assessments, on the other hand, do not understand their strengths and weaknesses, and often feel threatened when they are criticized, responding defensively to even the most well-intentioned constructive criticisms.

- **Self-Confidence:** To have self-confidence, you must have an accurate, solid sense of your own self-worth and your own abilities. Those with a mastery of self-confidence typically know their own values that guide them. These are the individual's morals, and those morals will guide the individual's actions, even if they lead to unpopular actions. The individual with self-confidence does not care about going against the grain if he believes he is truly right. Further, those skilled in self-confidence have developed the ability to make snap decisions that they are confident in, even under pressure. They believe that they have control over how their lives go, and act accordingly, constantly striving for things that line up with their beliefs. On the other hand, those struggling with self-confidence flounder when expected to make important decisions. They may not yet know their true calling or what they truly believe in, and often feel as though their lives are spinning out of control.

### Self-management

The competencies that makeup self-management provide you with the skills you need in order to regulate yourself. You understand that you are able to manage your emotions, and strive to do so because you see the value in stopping impulsive actions or behaviors. You recognize that emotions are important, but that they should not dictate what you are doing at any given moment, or how you should respond, particularly in stressful situations.

- **Self-Control:** This is the ability to maintain your composure, no matter what you are currently feeling. This ability entails being able to manage impulses and strong emotions well, which allows you to remain calm, and even optimistic in the face of adversity. These skills enable you to think clearly, even when you are under immense stress or pressure. On the other hand, those who struggle with this competency are typically impulsive and easily swayed by their emotions.
- **Trustworthiness:** Those who are trustworthy follow through with their promises. You understand that those around you are counting on you to be true to your word, so you make it a point to do so. You typically act ethically and attempt to avoid disappointing those around you. You build trust through earning it, constantly being there when you say you will, and you are willing to admit when you have made a mistake. If you feel that someone else is behaving in an unethical way, you are likely to call them out for it, even if doing so is an unpopular opinion. You stay true to your own values and beliefs, regardless of what other people think about them. Those who struggle with trustworthiness, however, frequently let other people down or often fall back on their word. They may be morally ambiguous, and not seem to follow any particular moral compass. They may instead always go with what is popular, even if they disagree on some level.
- **Conscientiousness:** To be conscientious is to be thorough and to have a desire for whatever you are doing well. You approach your

tasks with vigilance and make a special effort to ensure that you do the task thoroughly and well in a timely manner. Those who are conscientious keep their promises and make it a point to complete their commitments. They hold themselves accountable and are self-driven to complete their goals or tasks. Those who struggle, however, often find themselves falling short on promises, doing the bare minimum to squeak by, or even failing to complete the tasks at hand at all. They are typically unorganized and often try to shift blame away from themselves.

- **Adaptability:** Adaptability is the capability of being able to cope with changes by making appropriate adjustments in your own behaviors to accommodate. Those who are adaptable are typically quite flexible—they are able to handle changing priorities, juggling multiple demands at once, and can make adaptions to their own priorities to ensure that demands are met. They usually have a wide range of ways to complete their work, and will pick and choose which skills to use accordingly. Those who struggle with adaptability, however, typically struggle to be flexible, and get frustrated when plans or priorities change. They are quite rigid and struggle to accommodate or cope when their finely tuned plans are suddenly disregarded.

- **Innovativeness:** Along with adaptability, innovativeness requires a certain degree of flexibility. While adaptability is the ability to cope with change, innovativeness is the ability to come up with new solutions to the changing demands around you. Those who are skilled at innovation are typically quite creative and can think outside the box when faced with a new, unexpected problem. They do not get caught up when they run into a roadblock that they are unprepared for, and instead, they tackle the problem head-on. Those who struggle with innovativeness, however, struggle to come up with solutions to their problems. They do better following rather than leading, preferring having that guidance present, and are unlikely to be able to cope with surprise complications, especially if they happen regularly

### Self-Motivation

Self-motivation is the ability to keep yourself moving forward, without needing outside influences forcing you to proceed. Those who are self-motivated do not require external forces to keep them on track. Instead, they are driven to succeed simply because that is what they want. Self-motivation consists of the achievement drive, commitment, initiative, and optimism.

- **Achievement Drive:** Those with an achievement drive are motivated to strive for excellence. They have goals in mind and seek to excel at them for no reason other than striving for anything less than excellence seems like a waste of time. If you possess an achievement drive, you likely set yourself goals that are challenging, knowing that they will better you, and you will frequently refer back to those goals to see how your progress is going. You are motivated to get what you need to succeed without needing someone else reminding you or keeping you on task, and you are typically quite efficient at using your time. On the other hand, if you do not possess an achievement drive, you may frequently procrastinate, especially if the task at hand is something you are not passionate about. You may complete your work lazily, or fall behind.

- **Commitment:** This competency involves ensuring that you make sure that your own goals are aligned with the goals of whatever group or organization you are working with. If you are set to be the lead on a project for work, for example, you make sure that your personal goals during that time line up with the expectations of your superiors. Those who are skilled in commitment typically have a good idea of what their superiors are expecting and make it a point to meet and exceed expectations wherever possible. They make sure that their projects are things they generally agree to. Those who struggle with commitment may disagree with what they are doing, but do it because they were told to do so, or may struggle to meet expectations.

- **Initiative:** Taking the initiative means that you are willing to take the lead. You have no problems being responsible for the project at hand, including being the leader in problem-solving and conflict resolution. You also recognize that it is your job to try to prevent any problems from arising. You frequently seek out new ideas, come up with new ideas to problems, take new perspectives, and constantly look for ways to better your ways of doing things. Those who struggle to take initiative find that they struggle within leadership roles in the first place. They do not do well being in charge or having the burden of making sure everything runs smoothly.

- **Optimism:** This competency could be named persistence as well—it is the ability to continue moving forward, even if you have reached an obstacle or failed the first time you tried something. People skilled in this competency frequently are persistent in trying, even after failing. They see failures as learning opportunities, and no matter how many times they fail, they continue to get back up and try to complete the task at hand. People who struggle with remaining optimistic frequently give up easily or get discouraged when met with challenges.

## Social Competencies

The social competencies, social awareness, and social or relationship management skills, focus on your ability to interact with other people. These skills typically come after developing personal competencies, as you cannot hope to understand or influence other people if you cannot even understand your own emotions.

### Social Awareness

Social awareness is your ability to understand the emotions and actions of those around you. You learn to read situations because you can empathize with those around you and understand their motivations or reasons for doing what they do. These are typically considered general people skills and are necessary for getting along with other people in social settings.

- **Empathy:** Empathy is the ability to understand what those around you are feeling. If you are empathetic, you are typically an active listener who cares about the people around you. You often listen and ask questions when necessary to really understand what other people are trying to say, and can usually tell a person's emotional state through reading body language alone. You understand how their own behaviors and words may impact those around you. If you struggle with empathy, however, you may find yourself constantly clashing with other people or misunderstanding them when interacting. In lacking empathy, you may not care much about what the other people think or feel.

- **Service Orientation:** Think of service orientation as being the stereotypical customer service attitude—you are interested in serving other people and ensuring their needs are met as thoroughly as you can manage. You look for ways to go above and beyond to make sure those around you are happy and put the other people's desires and needs in front of your own. If you struggle with service orientation, however, you may be selfish or unable to put others' needs before your own. You may be unconcerned with other people or just unable to read the situations well enough to understand what is needed.

- **Facilitating Others:** This competency involves you making it a point to act in ways that meet other people's needs or feelings. This means you actively listen to what other people are saying that they need and seek to meet those needs as they come up. You seek to put the needs of yourself on the backburner temporarily so you can cater to the needs of those around you. Those who struggle with this find it difficult to fully disengage from their own wants or needs, or they may not be effective at guiding the group or the people around them.

- **Leveraging from Diversity:** This competency gives you the ability to view the differences within a group of people as an asset. Rather than seeing people's weaknesses, you focus on the way each person brings a different skill to the table. You see that one person may be good at public speaking, but struggles to write, while another is good at writing, but has terrible stage fright. You see that these two people are a perfect complementary match for each other and seek to use their skills to better both people. Further, you can see how different cultures or backgrounds allow you to get different views on any problems your group may face, and you genuinely value all input you get from all group members, even if you may not necessarily agree with it; it all gets the same consideration. Those who struggle with this skill do not see the benefit of diversity. They may hear someone say something they disagree with and completely shut it down, even if there is value in what they have to say.

- **Politically Aware:** This competency's name is deceiving—it does not have to do with government politics. Political awareness in the context of emotional intelligence refers to being able to read emotional undercurrents within a group of people. You understand the group's culture, hierarchy, wants, and needs, even when it is not verbalized or made overt. You can read the tone in the group or room, and you use that to your advantage. Those who can both read political situations within a group and continue to act with integrity are able to navigate through group situations with ease. Those who struggle with political awareness, however, struggle to understand the undertones in the room. Instead of being able to navigate easily, they may make mistakes or cultural faux-pas, so to speak, such as bringing a smelly tuna sandwich to lunch when there is an unwritten rule about avoiding strong-smelling foods into the workplace.

### Social and Relationship Management Skills

This skillset is all about managing relationships and social groups. Those who are skilled with these competencies frequently make good leaders. These skills allow for effective influencing (but not manipulating) of other people. With all of these skills mastered, people will be far more likely to follow your lead and listen to what you have to say or request of them.

- **Influence:** The quintessential leadership skill, if you are skilled at influencing others, you are skilled at persuading people to do what you ask. Typically, those who are influential are adept at their self-awareness and self-management skills, while also managing empathy and innovation, and they are able to get others to follow them. You are persuasive and engaging, and those around you feel inspired to follow through with what you are suggesting, with suggestions being the keyword here. You do not order people around, but instead, ask or suggest, using your own empathy skills to understand when the best time to ask is. Those who struggle to be influential may think that they have authority due to a position in the work hierarchy, even if that was never earned, and think that they can order people around. They also may not be empathetic enough or may struggle with their own self-awareness or self-management skills, and that is enough to make them just not effective at influencing others.

- **Communication:** The most effective leaders are skilled in communication. If you have mastered this skill, you can listen to both good and bad news. You are just as happy to hear some sort of criticism as you are to hear that you did well, as either is feedback and offer you an idea of what to do next—with bad news, you know something has to change while good news tells you that you are on the right track. Further, you are great at choosing words tactfully and effectively to get the results you want or need, and you are skilled at listening as well. If you struggle with this competency, however, you likely are not very open to listening to criticisms. You also may struggle to listen and really understand what people around you are saying, or you may frequently choose words or ways of phrasing things that are inflammatory, even if unintentionally.

- **Act as the Catalyst of Change:** The best leaders are not afraid of being the catalyst for change, no matter how drastic or shocking the change might be, and no matter how unpopular the idea might be. If you are a change catalyst, you inspire people around you to make noticeable changes in their behaviors in hopes of changing the entire system. You are willing to poke holes in the current system or to question current ideals to determine if it is time for a culture change. As the change catalyst, you recognize that change is necessary for one reason or another, and seek to remove the barriers to those changes. In a simple, low-risk example, consider that you want to change the office dress code, as do those around you, but no one wants to approach the boss and ask. You would be the one to go out of your way to open up the discussion on changing the dress code, presenting the group's arguments. If you struggle with this competency, however, you likely are intimidated by the idea of change, or you struggle to identify when change is necessary.

- **Conflict Management:** Being skilled in conflict management means that you can see when a situation is starting to trend toward conflict and trying to resolve it before it ever actually becomes a conflict at all. You seek to avoid conflicts at all costs, as they only detract from achieving the goals you are working toward. If you are skilled at this, you are likely good at listening and encouraging discussions between two conflicting people in order to find a good middle ground before things get messy. If you struggle with this, however, you may fail to identify when conflicts are impending, and you may even struggle with the act of mediating between the parties.

- **Facilitating Relationships:** This competency involves making a large network of friends, acquaintances, coworkers, colleagues, and peers in a way that is mutually beneficial. You never ask yourself what the other person can do for you; instead, you look at it as what can you do for each other. You never expect to receive without first giving. You are good at meeting new people and creating new relationships with a wide range of people from a wide range of backgrounds and careers, giving you a wide range of perspectives. If you struggle with this competency, you may not have wide networks, instead possibly having only a few trusted confidantes. While this can be good for personal situations or settings, in a leadership role, you want as many connections as you can possibly get, as you never know when you will need them.

- **Improving Team Capabilities and Facilitating Cooperation:** This is a two-pronged skill, involving first encouraging bonds between coworkers or team members, and then identifying the ways to encourage them to work well together, playing on strengths and weaknesses to make the most effective team dynamic you can. This means you want to encourage your team to get along and see each other as assets and a team rather than as competition. You want everyone working together for the same benefit, rather than trying to outdo one another, and once everyone is working together, you can then move toward identifying skills within the group that complements each other. This way, you can make sure people are working together in ways that best showcase their best talents and individual skills. Those who struggle with this skill may foster competition instead of camaraderie, or they may pair people together poorly. The team likely does not work well together when led by someone who struggles in this regard.

## CHAPTER 5

# EQ versus IQ

Book versus street smarts is a common trope seen in media. You have the stereotypical nerd who knows everything in the encyclopedia but cannot manage to have a normal conversation with those around him, and in contrast, you have the street-smart person who may not know very much about science or history about an obscure war, but is charismatic and able to work up to a leadership role just through charisma alone. In the war between EQ and IQ, typically, the one with the higher EQ comes out on top, but what does that mean? Is the emotional intelligence of an individual really more valuable than regular intelligence? In order to answer this question, we must first delve into the intricacies of both quotients.

## What is IQ?

IQ, or intelligence quotient, is all about testing cognitive abilities. It seeks to test skills associated with traditional intelligence, such as spatial processing, reasoning skills, and general logic. The questions rarely require much background knowledge, such as knowing the quadratic equation, history of the state of Alabama, or understanding the etymologies behind words and are instead interested in seeing if you can identify patterns or analogies and work with basic knowledge to create inferences and expectations through your capacity for logic and reasoning.

The IQ seeks to quantify intelligence into a standard form of measurement that allows for it to be compared from person to person. When taking an IQ test, you are given a series of questions to answer, which is then scored. On the original IQ tests, mental age is calculated based on the percentage of questions you got correct, and your mental age would then be divided by your chronological age and multiplied by 100. So, if your mental age is M and your chronological age is C, the equation would look like (M/C) 100.

While anyone can learn, and people can generally raise general intelligence, it is incredibly difficult to raise an IQ score. Because the IQ score looks at reasoning abilities rather than learning, there is not much preparation that can be done or skills that can be improved upon, to raise an IQ. The questions will primarily be hypothetical logical problems, such as being presented with a series of seemingly unrelated numbers and being asked to choose the next in the sequence.

Today, however, your IQ score is determined by comparing your score to averages found within your same age group. Those who perform better than average have higher IQ scores, with the average being somewhere between 85 and 110. These scores are used in a broad capacity, with schools using them to identify students who need extra support or those who are gifted, and the military has used them to determine roles suitable for individuals based on their IQ. .

### What is EQ?

EQ, or emotional intelligence quotient, aims to quantify emotional intelligence rather than cognitive intelligence. These tests seek to quantify how skilled someone is at navigating a wide range of emotional situations, ranging from identifying one's own emotions to being able to influence a crowd with a speech. It wants to evaluate how well you can comprehend, regulate, influence, understand, identify, and communicate emotions of both your own and others. It serves to identify just how empathetic you can be and whether you are able to recognize the nuances of human interaction.

Like IQ, EQ is typically tested through a series of multiple-choice questions meant to be answered as honestly as possible about a wide range of topics, and then a score is calculated, similarly to IQ. These tests will typically offer some sort of guidance to your general emotional intelligence skills, at which point, you can begin working to fill in any gaps. Unlike IQ, however, EQ scores are based on concrete skills that can be strengthened, therefore raising the EQ.

EQ is becoming an increasingly popular way to compare the qualifications or skills of people, including in comparing two applicants for the same job.

## IQ vs. EQ: Which Matters More?

Once upon a time, IQ was believed to rule. It was seen as the primary predictor of success. It was assumed that those with higher IQs are more likely to achieve success and accomplishment. Everyone wanted a higher IQ, but it seemed limited by biology and genetics. No matter how much people were taught, they could not quite budge their IQs, although their knowledge had definitely expanded. This is because IQ is so much more than just working knowledge—it is the ability to problem-solve and think rationally about what is in front of you.

Over time, however, critics recognized that high intelligence guaranteed nothing. There are plenty of people with high IQs that struggle to succeed, particularly when they struggle with interacting with other people or integrating themselves with society. It became clear that reasoning and problem solving alone were not enough to really determine just how successful someone might be. It turned out that there was more to being successful than being functionally book smart. In fact, those who had higher IQs sometimes struggled in workplaces and groups, even more so than those with lower IQs but higher EQs.

It has become clear that while higher IQs can aid in getting you through school and university, and may aid in initially landing you the job of your dreams, ultimately, a higher EQ is what will help you navigate through life.

The skills associated with emotional intelligence are far better suited to working in groups or being effective, fair, and as leaders. These skills, such as being empathetic and able to influence behaviors, allow for those with higher EQ to navigate complicated, difficult social settings that may cause someone with high IQ to clam up. Humans are emotional creatures, and being able to understand emotions is critical to being able to understand the people that you will work with. For this reason, higher EQ is believed to be more valuable in the workplace. You could be the smartest person in the room, but if you struggle to read the undertones of the conversation, or you cannot see how what you have said or done is harmful emotionally to the people around you, you are not going to be a well-liked or productive member of the team.

Consider the following—you are a high EQ and average IQ individual. You may have to work harder to get the job done, but you are driven to do so by your own emotional intelligence competencies. Even though the work is tough and you may spend more hours in the day dedicating yourself to your job than the person in the cubicle next to you, the fact that you excel in the social situations makes you a better employee overall. Speed is not the most important part of being effective, and your coworkers and supervisors commend you for your problem solving and conflict resolution skills. The person in the cubicle next to you, on the other hand, has a higher IQ with minor EQ deficits. He flies through the work quicker than anyone else in the office, and his work is always immaculate, but when it comes to being asked to make a correction or to work in teams, he tends to clam up. While he works well on his own, he struggles in groups as he is frequently taking offense when he feels others have implied that he is wrong or that his work was subpar.

Within the workplace, you may be the more popular choice to lead projects. Your skills in understanding people and being able to identify the skillsets of those around you make you far more efficient at management because you recognize the inherent differences around you and want to make the best possible use of those differences in ways that could benefit you and those around you.

On the other hand, the person with low EQ and high IQ is going to struggle to lead projects. Especially if he lacks empathy, he is going to struggle to see other people's strengths and weaknesses separately from his own. He may assume that everyone is going to work similarly to each other and that each should have the same skillset if they are working with the same team on the same project, and may not consider the value differences in the team. He would struggle to put together a cohesive team that works well together with respect to their differences to one another.

These differences are critical—the person with higher EQ is far more effective at being a leader, though the person with a higher IQ is better at technical skills. Jobs that require involvement with people in any sort of capacity, or require someone to be a team player, are going to be better filled by someone who has the emotional ability to work well with others. For this reason, workplaces are often searching for higher EQ employees. Questions meant to judge EQ are common occurrences within job interviews. They may ask how you would solve a specific social problem, or ask about a time where you had to solve a conflict between yourself and another individual. The answers you provide are typically used to determine whether you would be a better fit for the team. No one wants to hire someone who may be a liability in the office, and would instead prefer to find someone who will make waves in a positive manner instead of in a way that will derail the office and reduce productivity to the detriment of the company. Ultimately, intelligence is important, but emotional intelligence is more so in terms of being a successful, functioning, an integral part of the workplace dynamic.

## CHAPTER 6

# The Importance of EQ

EQ, as established, is essential in nearly every aspect of your life. There is not a single interpersonal interaction you will have in your life that goes unaffected by your emotional intelligence— or lack thereof. Everything you do, from your behaviors to how you speak to other people is all impacted by your EQ. Your ability or inability to control yourself or handle stressful situations is determined by just how skilled at social interactions you are. Remember, your temperament and emotions come together, and that combination is essentially filtered by your emotional intelligence to create your behaviors. This can make or break your performance in a wide range of situations, and either strengthen or weaken several different relationships. Consider how an individual's interaction with several people plays out within the following examples to see just how critical developing a high EQ can be.

### EQ in the Workplace

Imagine that you work as a car sales representative. The vast majority of your pay comes from commission, and you are well aware of that fact. The more cars you sell, and the more expensive the cars you sell are, the more money you bring in. It has been a particularly dead month, and sales are down, meaning your pay is down from what you normally average. As you sit there, waiting for someone to stop in, you see a young couple with a child in tow, looking stressed out as they approach the lot. Immediately, you jump to attention, sizing up the couple and trying to get an idea of what to expect from them and what they are going to be interested in. You approach them, and they quietly tell you the amount they can afford to pay per month, which happens to just barely be what the cheapest car on the lot would be, after you negotiate the price down. Consider two different situations: One in which you have a lower EQ and one in which you have a higher EQ.

### Proceeding with a Low EQ

As a lower EQ individual, you may think over the information you have been presented with and try to upsell. You earn a percentage of every sale you make, and you directly benefit from raising the bar a little bit. You see that they have a child with them, and from that information, you infer that they absolutely need a car to get around and that they will likely trust whatever you say in terms of how much you can help them.

Because you may not be very good at reading body language, you do not see that they seem awfully uncomfortable, and you may not tune into the fact that they may barely be able to afford the amount they had said they could. After all, cars are basic necessities in today's society, especially in towns that do not have well-developed public transit. You may suggest to the people that they buy a car that is not the cheapest on the lot, pointing out how it is a nice SUV, which would make taking a child and all the equipment that follows out and about simpler, and tell them that the price per month is only about 15% more than what they had said they could afford. You make no mention of the cheaper car that you know is sitting in the back of the lot.

They seem uncomfortable and glance between each other before shaking their heads and asking if there is anything cheaper. You tell them no, that is the best you can do, and they thank you and leave without buying anything.

In this instance, you did not pay much attention to their needs, instead of focusing on your own desires and needs, and it backfired on you. Your attempt to convince them to buy something out of their price range was unconvincing, unwarranted, and selfish. You failed at the most basic customer service skills—service orientation. This time, that failure cost you any commission at all. Because they did not buy, you got nothing for your time.

### Proceeding with a High EQ

With a higher EQ, you probably took the time to try to understand what the other people were thinking or feeling. You knew that the key to getting that sale was ensuring that you went above and beyond to find the perfect fit for the people in front of you, no matter what that commission might calculate out. After all, if you are on a budget yourself, you recognize that it is even more likely that someone else, especially with a young child, likely is as well. Instead of immediately attempting to upsell, you decide to work with what the people provided. If they could only afford the cheapest car on the lot, then that was good enough for you. A sale is a sale, and that is what is important, along with the sense of having helped a family with a meager budget for a car that they likely really needed.

You offer them the cheapest car on the lot, mentioning that it is a compact sedan, but it will do the job and it runs well. The family seems grateful and agrees to test drive. You tweak the price a bit with the discretion you have to negotiate to ensure that the price falls within their budget and you lock in the sale. The couple's entire demeanor shifts from concerned about how everything would work and worry about being judged for asking for the cheapest car on the lot to being relieved and happy that things were working out. They happily sign all of the paperwork and drive away from the lot, completely content with what had happened, and promising to recommend you to anyone they know who is looking to buy a car.

In this case, your EQ benefitted you greatly. You landed the sale, built rapport, had the added benefit of feeling better for helping some people in need and providing excellent customer service, and now have a family who will be recommending you to others. You may have gotten a lower commission than you would have preferred, but some commission is better than no commission, and you may be able to land more sales in the future from people who were referred to you. Overall, the situation went much better. Your concern for the other party and your attention to their emotional states meant that you were interested in meeting their needs, which in turn served you as well.

## EQ in the Family

In family, you can see EQ play out with similar results. Imagine that you have an eight-year-old daughter named Ellie. Ellie loves to make messes and get her hands dirty. She will not think twice about the consequences of digging in a pot of soil for a houseplant or mixing said soil with water and soap in the bathroom sink to see what happens. While she is very experiment-motivated and interested in seeing what will happen if she tries something, she often does not worry about what might happen. Imagine that you walk into the bathroom in time to see her newest concoction clogging up the sink. It will not drain at all, and you cannot even see the bottom of the sink underneath the murky mess. The reaction to your surprise is dependent on your own emotional intelligence, and the results between responding with low and high EQ are extreme.

### Proceeding with a Low EQ

You immediately feel your frustration and exasperation bubbling up, and before you know it, you are shouting for your daughter to get in the bathroom. She runs over, knowing that tone in your voice and looking up at you sheepishly. You ask her what the mess in the sink is, snapping at her and telling her she should have known better than to dig up a houseplant and put the soil in the sink. You tell her she is too old for such nonsense and that she is not a toddler that needs constant supervision. You ask what she was possibly thinking, and how she could have thought that was a good idea.

Immediately, she breaks down, crying. Unfortunately, this only makes the situation worse, and you tell her to stop being a baby and that she shouldn't be making messes, both metaphorical and literal, that she could not manage on her own. The more she cries, the angrier you get, until you eventually tell her to get out of your sight while you clean up her mess.

As you scrub down the sink, attempting to scoop up as much of the dirt as you can, you may realize your mistake—you were swayed by your emotions. Your child did not deserve to be yelled at or belittled, and you recognize that just as you were frustrated that she did not control her emotions, she is likely feeling the same. You failed to consider her perspective or feelings at the moment, instead of continuing to yell and making her shut down, which effectively damaged the trust your daughter had in you. She now thinks that you will snap at her if she ever makes a mistake, which really only serves to make her more reclusive and desperate to hide mistakes from you in order to avoid setting you off.

### Proceeding with a High EQ

Now, consider how this interaction would have occurred with strong emotional intelligence skills. Upon seeing the mess in your sink, you still would have felt annoyed and frustrated, but you would have had the self-control to take a moment to steady yourself and get your emotions under control before reacting. Using your self-management skills, you would have taken a deep breath and calmly called for your daughter.

She would have come running over happily until she saw you standing in front of the sink with your arms crossed. You ask her what this mess is, keeping your voice steady and calm. She shrugs her shoulders and mumbles something about wanting to see what would happen.

Instead of getting irritated further by her response, you nod your head and reaffirm what you know—that your daughter is always curious and interested in seeing what would happen next. She brightens up a bit, realizing that you are not about to yell at her. You tell her that as glad that you are that she had fun experimenting and learning, you are also frustrated that she left such a big mess in your sink for you to deal with. Keeping your voice calm, you mention that you had just cleaned the sink earlier that day, and now it no longer even drains. You ask if she has any ideas for what she could do to help you fix the mess, and she suggests that you should try using a cup to dump all the water down the toilet so you can then clean out the dirt without it constantly just washing away.

Before you can even ask, she runs off to get a cup on her own and helps you work through the mess, apologizing for leaving it for you and doing most of the dumping work and scooping out the muddy mess at the bottom while you go get the chemicals you will need to unclog the drain. The two of you manage to get through the mess relatively quickly, making jokes about the dirt, and your relationship feels stronger. Your child learns that she can go to you if she makes a mistake, and that is a big aspect of parenting—you need that trust to be effective. The two of you turn the mess and mistake into a problem-solving session, and no harm is done.

## EQ in Romantic Relationships

Consider you have a romantic partner, Alex. Alex loves spending time with you, but also needs space at the end of the day to unwind sometimes. During this time, Alex prefers to be alone and play some video games, away from you. This is not due to disliking you or wanting to be away from you, but rather because Alex needs that time to unpack the day and relax before bed. You dislike this about Alex, as you would prefer to spend that time cuddling together. You crave that physical connection at the end of the day to relax while Alex wants a physical disconnect, at least for a little while.

### Proceeding with a Low EQ

If you were to approach this situation with Alex while struggling with EQ, you may not think to consider Alex's feelings. By not approaching the situation with empathy, you do not consider what your partner needs and instead focus only on yourself. You know that you need that physical connection to feel loved, and when you do not get it, you worry that Alex does not want to be with you anymore. You latch onto that concept and allow it to make you feel unworthy or unvalued in your relationship, and that insecurity feeds into your discomfort.

Unable to resist, you storm over to where Alex is playing video games and ask why cuddling with you or spending time with you is so undesirable. Alex seems surprised by this accusation and disagrees with your assessment, saying that cuddling is fine, but sometimes, alone time is needed too. You refuse to believe this, and soon, you find yourself arguing with Alex. Now tensions are higher and you tell Alex that your own needs are not being met within the relationship.

The argument escalates, and eventually, the two of you storm off in opposite directions within the home, seething with anger and contemplating ending the relationship. Your inability to recognize that maybe all Alex needed was 30 minutes alone before spending time with you caused you to look at the whole situation in a selfish manner. Those selfish desires going unmet combined with not being very good at managing your own emotions created a toxic situation that did both of you a disservice.

### Proceeding with a High EQ

However, if you had approached the situation with a higher EQ, you would have sought to understand how Alex felt and recognize what Alex needed before meeting your own needs. You would have made it a point to assume that all Alex wanted was a bit of space before tending to your needs, and you would have been able to acknowledge and respect that need.

By granting that need, you likely would have found Alex coming to bed a bit later and enjoying spending some time with you as well before

bed. The two of you could have talked over your feelings, day, and anything else that came to mind without worrying about stepping on each
other's toes. Your empathy and ability to see things from Alex's point of
view helped calm you down when you felt your own insecurities beginning to prey on you.

Further, your self-control skills would have kept you from lashing
out at Alex for wanting space. You would have waited patiently for Alex
to come to you, and that patients would have been rewarded. Your relationship would have felt stronger, as you did not need to speak to learn
what Alex's needs at that moment were. Likewise, you felt loved and valued because Alex came to you after taking alone time. Both of you had
your needs met in an effective manner and no resentment was allowed
to build.

### EQ in Friendships

Consider a friendship you have had in which both you and your
friend have conflicting viewpoints. You are firmly liberal while your
friend is firmly conservative. While politics are rarely mentioned within
your relationship, they do come up from time to time, especially during
elections. While the two of you make it a point to avoid political conversations, sometimes you have no choice but to face your differences head-
on.

Perhaps the two of you have gone out for lunch, and hear another
person very loudly talking about a hot political topic at the moment. It
could be anything, so long as it is a controversial topic. You can clearly
hear the conversation from your seat in the restaurant, and even though
you try, you cannot quite drown it out. You can see your friend in front
of you, squirming uncomfortably as she listens to a political view she
does not share being loudly discussed, as well as a few choice words
about people who disagree with the loudspeaker.

### Proceeding with a Low EQ

As someone with a lower EQ, you may feel as though you should tell
your friend to suck it up and deal with it, especially if it is your own

belief that is being loudly discussed nearby. Because you agree with the belief, you do not pay much attention to the fact that your friend is uncomfortable, as truthfully, you do believe that your friend is wrong on her stance. If she continues to be bothered, you may snap that she should not be bothered being around someone who has those views, and points out that you, yourself also share them.

If she continues to voice her displeasure at the situation, rather than picking on your political standpoint, you may feel the need to defend your own beliefs. Perhaps you are uncomfortable because you feel that anyone that disagrees with you is a direct threat to your own values, so you feel the need to defend those values as adamantly as you can.

Struggling to communicate tactfully, you quickly find that you and your friend both seem to be a victim to rising tensions. Your friend tries to disengage, but you continue to push the point, wanting to make sure that you ultimately assert that you are right. The entire situation implodes, and may even end in yelling, at which point, both of you are asked to leave the restaurant. Your lack of communication skills, empathy, and tact added fuel to the fire and you felt as though the entire situation was a wash. You may even have considered ending the friendship altogether due to irreconcilable differences. You lack the skills to defuse the situation, and the entire thing becomes far too overwhelming and difficult for you.

### Proceeding with a High EQ

Now, imagine if you had had a higher EQ. You would have seen how uncomfortable your friend was getting at the political talk, and recognized that no matter how hard the two of you were trying, you could not quite drown out the shouts about how the other political party is filthy, lacks morals, or is corrupt. Instead of allowing the situation to escalate, you may ask the waiter if there is any way for you and your friend to move to another table, away from the loud person.

You and your friend move over, but still, find no reprieve from the constant political talk. Seeing your friend grow even more uncomfortable, you ask if she would prefer that the two of you take your food to go and head back to your home for a movie or something instead of staying there. Your friend graciously agrees, and the two of you head out. You specifically avoid talking about politics because you and your friend have a wonderful agree to disagree policy that you would prefer not to violate. You know that your friend is so much more than her political beliefs, and the two of you genuinely like each other for who you are, and because of that, you choose to just avoid the political topics altogether.

Your empathy helped you identify that your friend was in need of protection. Your problem-solving skills and flexibility enabled you to see a solution to your problem. Your communication skills and tact helped you understand how to navigate through the delicate situation without offending or upsetting your friend, and your friendship was stronger because of it.

## EQ as a Leader

As a leader, if you want to be effective, you need to have a high EQ. The best leaders are typically incredibly emotionally intelligent, and they use it to their advantage. Every adversity is seen as a challenge to be conquered and better the situation. Effective leaders are charismatic, inspiring, and get people to follow them without having to rely on dirty tactics like threats or manipulation. The effective leader is able to persuade and influence people to follow along just through being persuasive in general. This charisma makes people want to listen to them.

Further, leaders need empathy to be persuasive. People have to feel like a leader really understands them in order to convince them to give their support and loyalty to that particular leader. If the leader wants one thing but the rest of the people want another completely different result, the leader is not going to be very effective in convincing the people to do as requested. The empathy needed to understand what the people want and need, as well as the ability to read the undertones of the crowd. Leaders need to know what the people want and balance it with what they need and how to get it.

A leader who struggles with EQ likely will not remain in a leadership role for very long. They will quickly find themselves disliked or unable to convince people around them to do what they are asking. Likewise, because they will struggle to understand what people want and need, they likely will not be very effective. If they fail to manage their own feelings and behaviors, they will find themselves making missteps while in the very public eyes of the people, and that can be particularly dangerous when it comes to their reputation. They may even begin making selfish decisions that do nothing to better the situation but meet their own desires.

## *EQ for Problem-Solving*

Because EQ is crucial to maintaining composure when stressed or in the face of adversity, it is integral to problem-solving. You cannot hope to effectively tackle a problem if you are unable to think clearly or see the bigger picture beyond your initial gut reactions. You need to be able to disconnect from those impulses and analyze the situation calmly and with a level head in order to find the answers to your problems. Consider someone whose child has just fallen off of a playground and has broken his arm. A parent with a lower EQ is likely to panic himself, seeing his child in pain and not knowing what to do. He may freeze up and require another bystander to handle the situation or to call 911 and get paramedics over as quickly as possible.

On the other hand, if the parent has a higher EQ, he is far more likely to be able to see past the fear coursing through him in order to think clearly about what his child needs at that moment. He will be able to effectively assess the situation and see the easiest way to get what is needed, which, at that moment, would be medical care. If that means getting an ambulance, he will call for one, or if he thinks the best course of action is to drive the child to the hospital himself, he can do that as well.

In the heat of the moment, EQ drastically sways how an individual reacts. Those with higher EQ are more effective at handling the unexpected or emergencies due to their ability to look past emotions and to keep their emotions from ruling them.

## Traits of a High EQ Individual

- You have a fantastic emotional vocabulary
- You are a flexible and welcome change
- You understand perfection is unattainable
- You are interested in the people around you
- You are rarely offended
- You are aware of your strengths and weaknesses
- You do not hold grudges
- You are good at judging other people's moral character
- You are willing to forgive (but not forget) mistakes
- You try to avoid toxic situations or defuse the toxic situations that are unavoidable
- You control your negative thoughts and keep them from ruling your mind

## CHAPTER 7

# The Importance of Developing EQ Skills

Just as EQ is an integral part of all relationships within your life, it has an impact on developing several skills within your life. Those who are seeking to develop several skills in their life, such as teamwork, leadership, conversation or social skills, or relationship skills, are likely to benefit from developing their EQ, as EQ competencies are at the heart of all of those. A person who is struggling with their EQ is likely to struggle with all of the listed skills as well, and likewise, someone who is skilled at EQ likely feels teamwork, leadership, conversations, and relationships come naturally.

## EQ and Improving Teamwork

Within the context of teamwork, emotional intelligence is a social lubricant. Emotional intelligence allows for the team to work together well, settling any disputes that may come up quickly and efficiently, and providing several different points of view which can be used to brainstorm more with a wider range of results. This is achieved because the underlying emotional intelligence competencies keep everything moving smoothly and quickly smooth over any bumps that may be encountered. While all components of EQ are important, the following EQ competencies are particularly crucial to working within a team.

### Trustworthy

When the members of your team are all trustworthy, the need to micro-manage disappears. Everyone is trusted to complete their own roles, and everyone feels comfortable asking for help from those around them if it is needed. When people are trustworthy, they always follow through with their end of the bargain, and within teams is no exception. They make it a point to do everything possible to ensure they do not let others down.

Work on making yourself trustworthy through making it a point to follow through when you say you will do something. One common way to do this is to under-promise, but over-deliver, meaning you may say you can have something done by Friday, but really have it finished up by Wednesday again. You may have known that you could have it done by then, but chose to give yourself some leniency just in case you struggled unexpectedly.

### Self-motivated

When you are self-motivated, you do not need extrinsic promises to fuel you to complete work. You want to complete it for the sake of having completed it, no matter what the challenge may be. You enjoy the challenge of it rather than seeking out a reward, and you use that motivation to ensure that you complete the task at hand as thoroughly and as well as you possibly can. You do not cut corners to complete your task quicker, ensuring that you will complete your share of the work.

If you need to work on keeping yourself motivated, try looking at the results that are attainable if you dedicate yourself. Find something about the job you are doing that is enjoyable for yourself, or that you feel lines up with your own values. Once you can assign a value to something, it becomes easier to keep yourself interested in the task at hand. For example, if the job you are working on at work will be involved working together to design a new building, relate that to something you are passionate about—maybe you love or appreciate something about another building, and you can use that love to inspire yourself so you begin working on the project as a passion project instead of just as another work assignment you must do to get paid.

### Problem/Conflict solving

By being skilled at navigating problems and conflicts, you are able to keep them from growing out of proportion if you do encounter them. The goal is always to avoid conflicts within teams, but it is an inevitable part of working with other people. There will always be conflicts at some point, and for that reason, being skilled in solving them is essential. It keeps the team working together smoothly if conflicts are able to be solved before they can really get overwhelming.

If you struggle with problem-solving or conflict solving, try revisiting your social skills. You may have a deficiency in understanding how other people are feeling or reacting, and that can make it harder to understand how to solve the conflict. Likewise, you may struggle with communication, and need to brush up on how to interact with others in ways that are persuasive and genuine.

### Self-management skills

Managing your own reactions and emotions is crucial to being able to work in a team. You cannot be impulsive when other people are involved and must be able to consider how other people will be impacted by your behaviors. You cannot act emotionally when trying to work with other people, as you could have unintended consequences or make any problems you may already be having worse.

If you struggle with managing your own emotions, you may need to revisit the basics. Take a look at your self-awareness skills and really work to bolster your ability to understand your emotions and how they impact your behaviors.

### If You Are Struggling with Teamwork Skills

If you find yourself struggling with teamwork skills as a whole, your best bet is to go back to the basics: Start by working on your personal competencies. Oftentimes, a deficiency in those fundamental personal competencies can lead to struggles when other people are added into the equation. Understanding your own emotions and developing self-management skills will help you keep yourself under control so you can start focusing on how you interact with other people. After all, you will not understand how they are feeling and acting if you cannot control how you are feeling and acting.

## *EQ and Improving Leadership Skills*

If EQ was important in teamwork skills, it is even more so when in the leadership role. The leader takes responsibility for the group; it is the leader's job to ensure that everything gets done smoothly and any conflict is mitigated before it can get out of hand or completely derail the project altogether. The major competencies make a return here, with self-awareness, self-regulation, motivation, and empathy being absolutely crucial here.

### Self-awareness skills and leadership

Leaders must be self-aware. If they are not aware of their own emotions, they cannot hope to be aware of their group's, which means they cannot effectively ensure that their group is taken care of. Further, self-awareness enables you to see your own strengths and weaknesses in an accurate manner, which will enable you to understand which aspects of your life may require more attention. Being self-aware also enables you to behave with humility, ensuring that you are seeking to serve your people rather than yourself, which makes you a more desirable leader in general. Developing self-awareness is crucial if you hope to be an effective leader, and without it, you are likely to fail at your tasks or lose the following you are trying to develop.

To work on your self-awareness, try keeping a journal to help you understand your feelings and how they arise. Even just a few minutes a day will be enough to help you work on your own self-awareness. You will be able to identify repeated failures through journaling, which can help you understand your weaknesses.

### Self-regulation skills and leadership

A leader that is good at regulation is typically even-tempered when interacting with others. This means that their interactions are typically pleasant, even when dealing with tough subjects or listening to problems. This particular trait also lends itself to a leader's ability to be flexible in the face of adversity, as well as the ability to hold him or herself accountable for the behaviors of himself and the group he may oversee. The entire purpose of this is competency is to remain in control of yourself, and using that control over yourself to influence those around you.

If you need to develop this skill, try to make it a point to hold yourself accountable for everything and anything. If you drop a cup and it shatters, apologize and clean up your mess. Don't try to blame it on the cup being greasy or flimsy, or push it off onto anyone else. Admit to the mistake and learn from it.

You can also focus on your own values to understand what motivates you. If you know where your personal values lie, you will know when to compromise and when you refuse to. Understanding where your passions are is important, and if you are in tune with those, you will be able to make decisions, even under stress.

Pausing before reacting can further help you develop this skill, allowing you to take a moment to compose yourself before responding to the stimuli around you. This allows you to take control, rather than allowing your gut instincts to determine your behavior.

### Motivation and leadership

Leaders that are motivated constantly feel that drive to work toward what they hope to achieve. They hold themselves, and those around them, to high standards, especially when it relates to things they are passionate about. This motivation helps them to constantly strive for bettering their situation, and being aware of their values allows for them to be the catalyst for change when it is better for everyone.

If you struggle with motivation, you should try reevaluating why you are doing what you are doing. If your answer is you are doing it for the money, then ask yourself why you were passionate about the job in the first place. What do you enjoy about it? You can also make it a point to find something to focus on that is optimistic—whether it is the results of your efforts or the journey along the way. For example, if you work in insurance and are feeling unmotivated, ask yourself what you enjoy about the job. Maybe it is being able to help others in moments of needing help, such as immediately after a car accident. Identifying that and recognizing that you are helping dozens of people each day may be enough to return your intrinsic motivation.

### Empathy and leadership

Empathy is perhaps one of the most important skills in relation to leadership. You need to be empathetic in order to be an effective and desirable leader, whether of a country or of a small group at work. A leader with empathy is able to insert herself into someone else's shoes, so to speak, and can identify how that other person is likely feeling or doing. This invaluable skill enables her to develop the people on her team, pointing out the strengths and weaknesses she can see in other people, confront those who are being unfair without tipping into the zone of being unfair herself and are able to provide constructive criticisms or feedback. All of these create a leader who is looking out for her people, ensuring needs are met, people are happy, and conflicts are minimized.

If you struggle with empathy in regards to leadership, try practicing empathy with individuals. Try to understand what other people are going through by imagining how you would feel if the roles were reversed. You can also pay special attention to body language in hopes of getting extra feedback toward that particular person's state of mind. You should also try to respond well to other people's feelings. For example, if your partner has made a mistake on his share of the project and you have to ask him to correct the majority of his share in the next two days to meet the deadline, you may see him look disappointed with what you have said, though he agrees to make the corrections. Try telling him how much you respect his dedication to his job, and to let you know if he needs any extra support to help him get through it. By responding compassionately and empathetically to emotions, you create better workplace relationships that correspond to better leadership relationships.

## *EQ and Improving Communication Skills*

Communication is something that comes up everywhere. Whether verbal or nonverbal, any time you are around other people, you are communicating. Sometimes, it is conscious, such as speaking your mind or having a conversation, but others, it is conveyed through body language. Nonverbal communication is so integral to humanity that it is something that transcends language barriers, with the same base emotions and body languages being recognizable by people of any culture. Everyone has the same expression of happiness, sadness, anger, fear, and other basic emotions.

This should be good news—it means that you should be able to communicate with people with ease, right? Wrong. You need to be able to read other people to be able to understand those instinctive nonverbal cues. This involves emotional intelligence. In order to read other people, you must first have a good grasp over-identifying emotions. Once you can identify emotions, you can begin reading the body language of others.

This can be a bit tricky for someone unaware of the nuances of body language, especially since many emotions can have similar body language, but learning how to read other people is crucial. When you learn to read body language, verbal language follows suit. Typically, however, emotional intelligence is what determines your capacity to understand that body language. If you struggle with your EQ, then you may struggle to read other people, which means you are often reacting in inappropriate or disproportionate manners.

Body language and verbal communication together make up an actual conversation or communication skills. If you want to really understand what someone is saying, you must take their instinctive body language along with their verbal communication. This creates the whole picture of what is trying to be conveyed, and with your own empathy and listening skills, you will be able to communicate and act accordingly.

If you struggle with your communication skills, there are a few things you can do to help strengthen them. The first would be revisiting emotions of others. You can look at pictures of various body language and attempt to identify what is being conveyed. Once you learn what various emotions look like, you can begin trying to identify them as you go out and about, seeking to identify the emotions of those around you and adjusting your own behaviors and body language to see how it influences others.

When you think you have a good grasp over how to read other people's body language and how to adjust yours appropriately, you can begin using those skills in real life. Ultimately, the best way to bolster your communication skills is to practice, over and over again, until you get it down. Those you are close to are likely to be a bit more patient with you as you practice your skills, and they can have open and honest conversations when you do attempt to read them. You can ask them if your interpretation was correct, and if it was not, attempt to identify why you were wrong and correct whatever misconception caused you to misread the situation.

### *EQ and Improving Relationship and Dating Skills*

Very little is as full of personal emotions as being in a relationship with another person. Because romantic relationships and dating are so packed with emotions, it should come as no surprise that emotional intelligence one of the most desirable skills you can have in the dating and relationship playing field. Romance is guided by the heart, which is guided by emotions rather than rationality, and because of that, emotional proficiency is the most important skill you can have.

Consider this: If you are guided only by your heart when trying to make decisions, you may be led astray by physical attraction first—you will usually first notice physical chemistry with someone, usually related to lust or desire, or potentially infatuation. This can lead you to an unhealthy relationship for the wrong reason—you would stay because your heart says you want this person, even if you may not connect very well anywhere other than the bedroom.

Consider now if you were guided by your mind instead, turning off your heart altogether. You may find a partner that looks good in theory; perhaps he is a rich doctor and quite physically attractive. However, in practice, you may share very little in common. While he may be great for living a comfortable, secure life, and he may never hurt or betray you, you might not actually share an emotional connection to make the relationship feel fulfilling or worthwhile.

Instead of being ruled by either your heart or your mind, what if you allowed those skills to intermingle? This is the concept of emotional intelligence—you identify what you want and how you feel about someone, and then allow the rational side to identify whether it makes sense or not. You could be physically attracted to someone with whom you share little interest, and your mind would be there to remind you that that person would be a bad marriage prospect due to that lack of commonality.

Beyond being useful just in finding someone to date, emotional intelligence also allows you to control your own behaviors within a relationship. If you are emotionally intelligent, you will not let those impulsive text messages get sent in the heat of the moment when you are angry.

With a higher EQ, you will also be able to be more supportive because you will not be swayed by negative emotions that will pop up, no matter how perfectly matched you and your partner may be. You will empathize with your partner, offering support when necessary, and avoiding invalidating emotions because you understand just how important those emotions can be.

Overall, those with higher EQs are far more successful in the dating pool, and they make themselves more desirable because of their tendencies toward being supportive and emotionally in tune with both themselves and those around them. If you struggle with your EQ, particularly involving relationships, try focusing on your empathy and self-regulation skills. These are two of the most crucial parts of emotional intelligence in regards to relationships, as they make sure you do not exacerbate negative situations, and that you will support your partner.

## CHAPTER 8

# The Importance of Empathy

Empathy has been mentioned repeatedly throughout this book. It is a defining factor of emotional intelligence and is so significant that it gets its own dedicated chapter, as opposed to a small section within a chapter. To empathize with another is to really understand them as if you yourself were experiencing what they are with the same intensity. It is an ability that leads to great, compassionate relationships and creates a good, reliable leader.

## Defining Empathy

In the simplest terms, empathy is defined as the ability to put yourself in another person's situation in a way that is meaningful and provides you with insight into that particular person's experiences. This is something we start teaching children at a young age when we ask them how they would feel if someone did to them what they did to someone else, and the skill develops and grows into adulthood. Empathy allows you to communicate emotions through understanding what the other person is feeling, and is a crucial part of understanding body language. The importance of this, then, is that when we are able to empathize with others, we intimately understand what they need at that moment, and emotional intelligence enables us to provide that. There are five distinct components to empathy: These are understanding others, developing others, service orientation, leveraging diversity, and political awareness.

Understanding Others
•Sensing others' feelings and sharing concerns and needs

Developing Others
•Acting in ways to meet others' needs or emotions

Service Orientation
•Putting others first and attempting to go out of your way to aid other people

Leveraging Diversity
•Recognizing differences between individual's skills and the value diversity brings to groups

Political Awareness
•Responding to a group's emotional states and being able to understand undertones or hierarchies within a group

## The Purpose of Empathy

Empathy is there so we are able to understand others. This lets you look at someone else and understand what they are really going through at that given moment, which you can use to understand how best to support another member of your group, better ensuring the survival of your group. While we may no longer be in hunter-gatherer groups that need to convey immediate needs wordlessly and effectively to literally survive, understanding each other is still an incredibly important skill to have.

Along with ensuring survival through being able to read body language cues, such as fear when running from a predator, or sadness when in need of support or help, empathy serves another role in today's societies. It allows groups to assign different roles for individuals to best play on each other's strengths and weaknesses. Consider leveraging diversity—it involves understanding how our differences in personality, temperament, backgrounds, experiences, and skills could lead to a betterment of our group. If one person has a bad leg and struggles to do anything physically intensive because of that, but is fantastic at crafting with cloth, that person could best serve a group's survival by creating clothing that is used to keep warm, whereas someone who may not be particularly intelligent or crafty, but is very adept at physical activities may be an ideal hunter or soldier to protect the group or provide food.

Of course, in today's society, things often work a little differently. Nonetheless, if you find yourself heading a group project at work, you would be well-served if you could tell the difference between people's skills and match them up accordingly. If you have one person who is skilled at grammar and assuring that all the words on the paper make sense grammatically, but struggles with writing actual content, you could be best served by having her be the editor over the final draft of the project, while someone who may struggle with grammar, but still manages to write in convincing, inspiring ways may best serve the group by providing the writing, typos and all. Another person may be particularly gifted with numbers and could be tasked with designing all of the charts for the project, while another is great at research and is tasked with research. By breaking up the work and assigning it in accordance to personal skills, you have empathetically divided up the workload.

## Empathy versus Sympathy

Empathy and sympathy are closely related but still different. You can be sympathetic without being empathetic, and vice versa. While empathy is understanding someone's situation intimately, as if you, yourself, are experiencing it at the moment, sympathy is feeling bad for someone. Empathy can lead to sympathy, but the two do not necessarily entail each other.

For example, imagine you are on your way to work and see a homeless beggar. You could look at him and feel sympathy without having any real understanding of what he may be going through. You simply feel bad because he is hungry, and offer him a couple of dollars because you felt bad. This is sympathy without empathy.

Likewise, you could see the homeless man and understand his plight and having an understanding of how you would feel if you had lost your home, but choosing not to feel badly because you believe that the homeless person should just get a job if he would like to live a normal life. Your opinion of the homeless person keeps you from feeling sympathetic, although you do feel empathy for him. You then choose to do nothing, because while you feel for the man, you believe he brought the problem upon himself.

When empathy and sympathy combine, however, you create **compassion**. Compassion has four crucial components to it:

- Awareness of the other person's suffering (Empathy)
- A deep concern for that person's suffering (Sympathy)
- Wishing to see the other person's suffering relieved
- Choosing to act in a way that helps to relieve the suffering

Compassion is an important aspect of emotional intelligence as well, particularly for those who are hoping to better their relationship management skills. It enables them to be driven to better the situation of those around them in order to alleviate suffering.

### Empathy and Emotional Intelligence

The empathy you feel for other people creates a sort of unspoken bond between yourself and others. It enables you to understand what people around you feel intimate, which creates a sort of camaraderie between yourself and the other people. This is a driving factor in emotional intelligence, as you must be able to relate to those around you and understand their feelings in order to be able to influence them or manage the relationships between yourself and the others around you.

Consider arriving to work and discovering that you have a new coworker who knows absolutely no one there. You see her sitting at her desk, looking somewhat uncomfortable as she tries to get her personal belongings organized while waiting for the work computer in front of her to load up. You can tell that she feels out of place by how tense she appears and how she tries to keep her eyes down so as to not pry into other people's business. You understand her feelings—you were new there once, too, and you remember how tough your first day was. Because of that understanding, you decide to go up to her and introduce her to break the ice. You are the first in the office to do this, and she seems to greatly appreciate this.

This is acting upon your empathetic intuition on the situation in order to influence the behavior of another person. You saw that the person was feeling nervous and uncomfortable, understood her feelings, and chose to act kindly in order to encourage her feelings of discomfort to shift. It worked, and soon, the new coworker was chatting with everyone due to the ice being broken.

That ability, to see a situation and influence it, is a key tenet of emotional intelligence. Considering a large portion of emotional intelligence involves identifying emotions and influencing those around you, the fact that empathy is so important is no surprise. It is essentially the most fundamental, basic way you are able to influence others. Without understanding someone else's mindset, you would struggle to change their feelings on matters.

## Strengthening Empathy Skills

If you struggle with empathy, you are not alone, though you will find it hindering you on a regular basis, particularly in regards to emotional intelligence. Empathy, though, is a skill that can be developed and learned through time and practice. Just because you never learned how to be empathetic as a child, or you struggle with it today does not mean you need to continue to struggle with it next year. If you do struggle with empathy, you will likely find that many of your relationships seem to struggle as well. Here are eight ways you could improve your capacity to empathize with others.

### Challenging Yourself

There are times you need to get out and push yourself out of your comfort zone. Doing so is a surefire way to leave you feeling humble, which can aid in your ability to feel empathy. Through humbling your-self through struggling with a new skill, you can learn newfound respect for people who are new to situations, especially if it has been a while since you have had something challenge you in such a profound way.

### Expose yourself to new environments

If you can, travel somewhere else. You will learn new perspectives that may be different than anything you have ever considered before. You can see diversity in action, which can give you a new respect for dif-ferent opinions, and you may learn to think about things in a new light. Think of how many different cultures there are out there—they all have differing views of society and different ways of doing things. This can aid you in problem-solving in the future.

Even if money or time off from work is an issue, you would be sur-prised at just how different leaving your usual neighborhood to go to the one over could be. Even neighborhoods within the same town can have different cultures based on the demographics, and sometimes, that is enough to gain a newfound respect for diversity or different abilities, opportunities, or thought processes.

### Ask others for Feedback

Sometimes, it may be hard to see where you are falling short in rela-tionships. You may need to ask someone else about how your relation-ships appear from the outside to identify any weaknesses you may have. You can ask anyone, friends, family, or coworkers, to ask what you could do better within your relationships, as well as where you are really suc-ceeding. This feedback gives you a solid baseline that you can use as a guide to determine where you should focus your efforts on developing yourself.

Even after you have done this once, try to do so again periodically. This can provide feedback to determine if the changes you have been trying to implement are having an impact on your relationships, as well as whether you have created any new problems that may need attention.

By asking others to identify your weaknesses and tell you what you are doing well, you are developing your ability to understand how your own behaviors influence other people—a key feature of being empathetic.

### Learn how to listen—and practice it often

Active listening is different than just hearing those around you, and knowing when to turn on active listening is an effective way to boost empathy. There are three situations that typically imply that you should begin active listening:

- When the other person is conveying an emotionally-charged thought or message
- When someone is struggling to clearly communicate
- When you are uncertain you completely understand the other person

When you have identified that active listening is warranted, it is time to begin ACTIVE listening. This is an acronym for the five steps of active listening.

- Attention
- Concentration
- Total
- Interested
- Valuing
- Empathetic

Remembering this acronym can help you remember the steps. You should put down your phone, electronics, or any other distractions to give the other person your undivided attention, and really concentrate on the words that are being said. Make sure that you are as undistracted as possible and understand the message that is being said. Make it a point to ask clarifying questions or to reword what is being said to you in order to ensure you are understanding and to show that you have been paying attention. Validate the emotions behind the message—make sure you never voice that you think the emotions are wrong. Lastly, make sure you try to empathize with the other person as well. You should make it clear that you are understanding the situation and may even find it useful to provide a time when you felt similarly to show that you understand.

### Stop judgment before it can happen

It happens sometimes—you are talking to someone and you feel the urge to voice how you disagree with the situation at hand. Instead of passing judgment, stop and consider the other person's perspective. Try to create an argument from the other person's side in order to get a fuller idea of how their mind works and to identify what motivates them. For example, if you are talking to someone, who voices that they are in support of some obscure cult-like organization, and you immediately feel the need to voice how much you disagree with that choice, you should take a moment to pause, wonder what would have attracted that person to that choice in the first place, and at worst, agree to disagree with their decision and move on to something else. You can even try asking questions if necessary to really understand their perspective. If you really cannot pass on the desire to criticize or declare your dissent, at least ask if the other person is interested in hearing your opinion before doing so. Remember, advice or opinions are only useful if they are wanted and welcomed.

### Practice emotional awareness

If you still struggle with empathy, try revisiting your self-awareness! Ensure that your own understanding of your own emotions is strong enough to support attempting to understand and comprehend other people's emotions as well. If you struggle with your own emotions, of course, you struggle with other people. Practice self-reflection when you can in order to begin further understanding your own emotions. As you teach your brain to create emotional labels that it uses for itself, it will begin to fill in the blanks for other people as well. Stop and understand how you are feeling at least two or three times a day, particularly when emotions run high, and you will find yourself more fluent in emotions soon.

### Teach yourself to quiet your own mind

The better you get at silencing your own mind, the better you will be able to hear and understand other people's perspectives. With your mind no longer preoccupied with yourself or whatever narration you have happened at that moment, you will find focusing on understanding what other people are feeling significantly easier. In order to do this, find ways to ground yourself, such as quietly identifying the things around you, or picking up meditation. Anything that can calm and quiet your mind is good enough here. Once you master quieting your mind, you can begin observing your surroundings and trying to empathize with other people as well.

### Teach yourself to remember and use other people's names

This may seem like an odd way to encourage empathy, but by remembering another person's name and using it, even if it is someone you rarely see, you personify that person—providing him or her with an identity in your mind. While all people are human and deserve that recognition and consideration, your mind focuses better on people that it can identify by name or some other defining feature.

Further, by calling people by name, you are making it clear to that other person that they matter to you. You acknowledge that they are there, important, and influential. Using their names on a regular basis allows you to foster a bond between the two of you, which also encourages empathy. Empathy develops more easily for people we already share a bond to, likely due to trying to keep those we care about or acknowledge alive. Even if you struggle with names, do your best to remember them, and if you cannot remember, there is no shame in asking for a reminder!

## CHAPTER 9

# 7 Practical Steps to Boost Your Emotional Intelligence Skills

Emotional intelligence is all about skills. Skills build upon skills to create emotional intelligence, and you can strengthen your emotional intelligence through skills meant to strengthen your skills. Confused yet? Don't be! This chapter will provide you with seven practical steps that, if implemented and used consistently, can enable you to boost the competencies of emotional intelligence. With these skills, you will find yourself able to practice and understand how to better impact your own emotional intelligence skill level. Through utilizing these seven steps, you will manage to change your life for the better—as you master these steps, your emotional intelligence should begin to increase as a result.

### *Understand Where You Are*

At its simplest, this step involves recognizing your current emotional or mental states—not where you are physically at that moment! You should take the time to observe how you are feeling within that particular moment. Knowing how you are feeling at any given time is essential to any of the other steps on this list. You need to be able to understand how you feel before you are able to begin working on other areas of emotional intelligence.

In order to know where you stand, take a moment to stop what you are doing and really listen to yourself. You want to know exactly how you are feeling as specifically as possible. Use the most creative words you can to describe your current mental state in order to move forward. If you need to, look up an emotion wheel and go through that to choose specific words if you are unsure what the word that you need is.

Once you have identified the feeling you have at the moment, you should then take the time to reflect on your physical feelings as well to create an understanding of how your mental state is relevant to your body language. Try to analyze every bit of your body language and see how you are coming across.

From there, you should try to identify your behaviors or the impulses toward specific behaviors, and seek to understand how they are related to each other. This step may take some more introspection as you try to understand what kind of behaviors you have a tendency to feel a desire to do.

In order to wrap this all up, consider a time you felt overwhelmed with emotions. Perhaps you were at work with a deadline looming over your head, and you did not know if you could actually meet it. You stopped to take a moment to understand how you were feeling in that moment, noticing that your emotions were starting to get out of control, and realize that, at the core of everything, you felt overwhelmingly afraid and ashamed that you could not meet expectations, and in response to that fear and shame, you also felt anger toward letting yourself and your supervisor down.

After identifying where your emotions are, you next decide to reflect on your body. You can feel the tension in your body, and notice how you keep your hands close. You feel how your heart rate is quicker than normal and that you seem to feel on edge. All of these, you realize, can be explained by your emotional state in that particular moment. Realizing just how strongly you're emotional and physical states seemed to be linked, you take a moment to take a deep breath, and then start to focus on what you feel inclined to do at that moment.

You realize that more than anything, you want to run away. You want to stop trying and give up because you feel that you will fail anyway. You do not see the point in continuing, and for that reason, it seems like there will be no difference between deciding to continue with the project, or just stopping and alleviating your stress. This provided valuable insight to you—you realized that your fear of failure was impacting your physical state and making you physically uneasy, and your natural inclination at that moment was to run away from the problem altogether because giving up would not necessarily be any different than failing in your book.

### Managing Your Negative Emotions

This step involves limiting how much control over your behaviors you allow your negative emotions to have. By managing the negative feelings, you are able to keep from getting stuck in a negative feedback loop, as you did in the previous example. Negativity breeds negativity, just as positivity breeds positivity. Recognizing that loop makes mitigating negativity that much more important.

While this does not mean that you should attempt to eliminate negative emotions altogether, as they serve important biological purposes, you should seek to make sure you do not allow your negative feelings too much sway over your actions. If you were to react negatively to an already negative situation, the end result will almost always be you continuing to feel negative, making it a useless endeavor.

In order to manage your emotions, making it a habit to stop and think before acting, especially when your emotions are running high. The next time you feel the desire to run away from your problems, as in the previous example, take a deep breath before diving into the impulse. Stop yourself and ask yourself how doing that would benefit you in any way. Would it bring you joy? Would you still be happy about it in a day? A week? A year? If it would not do anything to eliminate the negative feelings you are trying to run from, why would you do it in the first place?

Again, consider that you are overwhelmed by your project at work. You begin to pack up your belongings to leave for the day, essentially giving up before finishing the project, but before you finish, you stop yourself. You acknowledged your feelings already—but would run away really mitigate them? Taking a deep breath, you consider how your actions would impact both you and those around you the next day. Your coworkers would be let down by you failing to complete your end of the bargain. Your supervisor would be angry or upset with you for not completing the work you are paid to do. You could even lose your job, which would bring a whole new slew of problems on its own.

As tempting as acting on that negative impulse felt, you find the desire to run away slowly fading as you realize just how many negative implications there would be if you left without completing your assignment. Instead of running away, you power through the remaining part, and though you struggled, you manage to get it finished up minutes before the deadline. Congratulations! You just interrupted your negative emotions and prevented them from ruining your career!

### Practicing Empathy

Yet again, empathy is an integral focus of the book. In this instance, you should practice empathizing with those around you in order to strengthen your emotional intelligence. Remember how important empathy is too emotional intelligence, and how integral emotional intelligence is to social interactions. Practicing empathy is definitely one of those skills that should be used again and again, ad nauseum, until it is mastered.

Because empathy is so important, you should make it a point to practice it wherever you go. Even with those around you, like your cashiers or that random person walking down the street that you will likely never see again, you should try to empathize with them. If you see someone in a bad mood, try to identify why they seem to be annoyed. If you see an elderly lady struggling to get her bags of groceries up the stairs to her building, offer to carry them in for her. If you see a child whose ball got stuck in a tree and you can reach it, pull it out. By empathizing with others, you create a better relationship between yourself and those around you.

Imagine that you are on your way home from the grocery store after a late-night trip. You stopped in late at night in order to pick up some necessities on your way home from a late night at the office. As you finish putting your groceries into the trunk of your car, you notice another person closing up their own trunk and pushing their cart back to the corral before getting into the car. The person seems to be sitting in the car for a minute, checking something on his phone.

You push your cart back to the corral and notice that there is a wallet sitting in the child basket seat of one of the carts in the corral. You pick it up and open it to see who it belongs to and notice that it is full of cash. You have two options here—you can pocket the cash and turn in the wallet to customer service, saying you found it, or you can run-up to the car and give the owner the wallet back.

Very briefly, you consider keeping it. You are tight on money and struggling to make ends meet, and the cash would be a lifesaver. After a split second, however, you recognize how you would have felt if someone else had taken your money because you had made a mistake and forgotten your wallet for less than a minute. Knowing that feeling of being financially ruined by such a careless mistake, you instead speed-walk to the individual in the car, who is still browsing something on his phone. You wave at the person and hold out his wallet. Immediately, he recognizes it as his, and he takes it, checking inside and thanking you profusely for being honest and giving it back to him.

Even though, in this case, being selfish and keeping the wallet that had been forgotten would have led to a better financial position, you chose to act empathetically and bring the wallet back. You practiced putting yourself in someone else's shoes and identifying how you would feel in that particular situation. This is thinking with emotional intelligence.

## *Using a Positive Style of Communication*

Remember how negative thoughts create negative behaviors? Negative communication also creates negative thoughts and behaviors. In order to avoid the negativity feedback loop, you should instead seek to always communicate positively. This also keeps your mind in an optimistic mindset, which is crucial to being successful.

When you communicate with others, always seek to use positive words when possible, and when you do have to speak negatively, make sure you are doing so in the most tactful, least offensive way possible, and try wording it in such a way that you add good into cushion the bad. For example, if you have to criticize someone at work, you should try to acknowledge something that the person is doing well, and then say the part that could use some work, and then lastly, add another positive element. This keeps the overall net emotion in your situation positive, as the positive outweighed the negative, and you still got your point across carefully.

For example, imagine that your coworker's work recently has been somewhat sloppy—files are ending up in the wrong place and you can never find what you are looking for because of it. If you had to confront her, you could do so by first saying that you have noticed just how hard she has been working lately and that you see that she is often the first one at the office and the last to leave. Then, you could mention how you have also noticed, however, that some of the files that she has been responsible for have ended up in the wrong places. Finish it up with saying that you did, however, notice just how complete the notes within the files were when you did finally find them. Notice how by using kind language and sandwiching the criticism between to compliments, the entire message felt more positive in general.

When you are on the receiving end of bad news or criticism, you should also aim to keep the mood positive. Even if you may have disagreed with the criticism, you should accept the opinion as valid, and thank the other person for bringing the issue to your attention in the first place. Instead of feeling frustrated or annoyed, welcome it as a learning experience and an opportunity to do better than you have been do-ing.

### Create a Positive Environment and Bounce Back from Adversity

Similar to the previous sections, you want to keep your environment generally positive, as a negative one will do nothing but drag you down. Keep yourself surrounded by people you enjoy and trust, while trying to limit forced interaction with people who always bring you down. Within your environment, always emphasize the positive. This does not make you naïve—it makes you smart. By focusing on a positive environment, you are going to be more productive, as will those around you. Positivity is conducive to success, and you want to keep that at all costs. You can do this by ensuring that meaningless criticism is discouraged, and language needs to be kept as professional as possible.

Not if, but when you do face the inevitable adversity, you should see it as a learning experience. Think about it this way—if you fall, you only have one way to go from there: Up. Pick yourself up when you fail, dust yourself off, take a moment to compose yourself, and continue on your way with trying to succeed. You need to remain perseverant if you want to succeed, especially at tasks or skills that may be more difficult, but your perseverance and positivity will be rewarded when you finally do succeed.

Remember, success is not created overnight, and many of those big names you see as influential authors, inventors, innovators, and other household name success stories, such as JK Rowling, created their suc-cess from failures. Rowling submitted her writing to several publishers, all of whom rejected her until one took a chance.

### Desire to Help Others Succeed and Succeed Yourself

Part of empathy involves being invested in whether other people suc-ceed. When you are invested in other people, particularly when they are on a team with you, such as at work, you want those people to succeed, even if it involves you being involved in the process. Even if you have to guide them, suggest ways to better their situations, or even hold their hand through the process of fixing the problem, you are happy to do so. You do not mind, as them succeeding can only be good for you as well. You see their successes, especially if they are on a team with you, as a success for yourself too, but not in a narcissistic way. If your teammate is able to succeed, you see the benefit of that too. Your department performs better, your project is better received, or your department may even see more work, which means more money. Your teammates are an integral part of your team, and you recognize that.

By making it a point to guide your teammates to success with you, you ensure that the entire group is taken care of. You should always seek to make sure that your teammates are doing okay as well, as their failure is also your failure if it means that your projects never get finished on time.

If you make it a point to help others within your group, you will begin seeing the return. Though that return should not be your motivator, it is present. Those you help will be far more likely to help you if you ever find yourself in need of help as well. If both you and your team value the art of working together and recognize that you have to aid each other, you are far more likely to get the best results.

## *Being Motivated*

Being motivated by yourself is a difficult thing to manage, particularly within the context of your job. However, if you can manage to self-motivate, you will find that doing the job hardly seems like work. If you are working on a project that matters to you, or within a career that you love, your work will have intrinsic motivations—that means that you will feel the need and desire to complete your work for your own satisfaction rather than for a paycheck or to avoid being nagged at by supervisors.

If you lack this intrinsic motivation, you will struggle to feel any drive to complete your work, improve upon what you are doing, or to remain resilient, even in the face of adversity. This can be lost if you find yourself becoming burnt out with your job, or you simply lose sight of what had drawn you to that particular job in the first place. If you are able to identify what it was that called you to the job in the first place, you may be able to rekindle that self-motivation and reap the benefits that come with it.

For example, assume for the moment that you are a nurse. You got into the nursing field because you are truly passionate about helping people and you believe that all people deserve the best possible care that can be given, no matter how much money they have or lack. Because of that value, you decided to become an emergency room nurse in an underprivileged area within your city. This has the unfortunate consequence of meaning that you are frequently run ragged, with too many patients and not enough time, as the doctors try to get them in and out as quickly as possible to prevent a jam-up of the ER in case of a true emergency.

Many of the people you find yourself treating are homeless, poor, or lacking health insurance, and the number of people on drugs, alcohol, or that are mentally ill that you see is staggering. Many of them get angry at you if you are not quick enough, despite the fact that you are over-burdened, and they may also yell at you if you apologize and tell them that you cannot prescribe any of the drugs they are asking for.

The longer this goes on, the more jaded you become. Eventually, that capacity for compassion and the passion for helping other people that you had, to begin with, is completely burnt out. You cannot keep up with the demand on your mental health any longer, and instead, decide to do the bare minimum and keep things as professional as possible. You stopped going above and beyond because you were sick of being treated poorly. As a result, you lost your passion. You lost touch with the value that had drawn you to your job, and you find yourself dreading going to work most days.

Instead of quitting, you should stop and reflect on what drew you to it in the first place. If you stop and remember your reason for becoming a nurse in the first place, which was inspired by seeing how compassionately one had treated your younger sister when she was seriously ill and in the emergency room due to not having insurance or money for a regular doctor, you may rekindle that passion. Thinking about that instance again, you may remember that your original goal was to be that person for others who arrive, scared, hurt, sick or even just cold some nights; the person who supports them and treats them with compassion and like humans, no matter the reason they are there or how much money they have. This passion being rekindled brings back the intrinsic motivation, and once again, you find yourself wanting to give it all to your job, even if you go unappreciated sometimes because you know that some people do appreciate you.

## CHAPTER 10

# Practical Ways to Use Emotional Intelligence to Improve Your Life

*8 Practical Ways Strong Emotional Intelligence Will Improve Your Self-Management*

1. By being able.to identify your internal core values, you will be able to better align your goals, career, projects, and general life with those values, ensuring you are always motivated to continue working to better your situation. You will always want to do better if what you are working on is something you are passionate about. For example, someone passionate about trying to eliminate the performance gap between financially sound children and children from low-income families in schools may make it a point to work in public schools in underprivileged areas so he is always able to work toward that goal.

2. Because those with higher EQs are far more resilient than those without it and are far more able to cope with the unexpected, you will be far more likely to continue trying, even when facing adversity. Though others may be easily daunted by what you have found yourself facing, you know you can roll with the punches

and come out of the situation better than when you started. For example, if you are trying to bake a cake with your children and the whole thing falls apart when you try to remove it from the pan, instead of getting upset, you decide to make cake pops with your children instead.

3. With a higher EQ, you are far more likely to be able to keep your mindset positive, meaning that the little negative thoughts, feelings, or fears that may come up when you are working will not be able to derail you from working toward your success. For example, if you are a naturally anxious person, and you hear that little nagging voice in the back of your mind telling you that there is no way for you to succeed, you know that you can ignore that voice and replace it something positive.

4. Because you care about the impact of your behaviors on other people, you will be more likely to remain diligent and true to your values if it means that it benefits someone else, especially if that someone else is someone closer to you. You want to establish yourself as trustworthy, and that desire to be trustworthy keeps you motivated. For example, if you promise to build a giant Lego tower with your son after work, even though you come home exhausted, you still build it because you know not doing so would disappoint him and prove to him that you are not trustworthy.

5. Your ability to understand your own emotions and how they impact your behaviors allows you to keep those behaviors in line. You know that your emotion-driven behaviors are rarely productive or conducive to positive results, especially when those emotions are negative. For example, if you are angry at your spouse and really want to scream and punch a wall to vent your anger, you recognize that neither screaming nor punching the wall would really better your situation, and would actually probably frighten your spouse, so you override that impulse altogether and instead decide to go to work out to vent your frustration.

6. Your ability to understand that you always have a choice in your behavior, no matter how strongly you may feel an impulse toward

a specific action, enables you to acknowledge that emotional be-havior is often faulty or flawed. You understand that you are to blame if you blow up at someone, not your emotions. For exam-ple, if you were to punch the wall in anger, you would have to ad-mit that you punched the wall because you wanted to punch the wall, not because your anger made you do it.

7. Along the same lines as #6, you understand that you are not your emotions; you are able to separate yourself and your identity from the emotions you may feel. For example, even if you are feeling short-tempered that particular day that does not necessarily mean that being short-tempered has to be a defining feature, or that you have to act upon it.

8. Because you are aware of your own strengths and weaknesses, you are able to acknowledge when you have bitten off more than you can chew, and though it may be embarrassing, you have no prob-lems asking for help, if that is what you need at the moment. For example, if you signed up for part of a project, but halfway through realized you were entirely clueless on what it entailed, you would be comfortable asking someone else for help.

## 8 Practical Ways Strong Emotional Intelligence Will Support Decision-Making

1. Because you know exactly what your values are, you are able to make snap decisions that line up with them. You know what you believe, and you are willing to make decisions that line up with that belief, even if the belief is not necessarily the popular opin-ion. You are determined to do what you think is right. For exam-ple, if you have a belief that fairness and equality are not the same things, you may push to have an office that is fair, but not equal, even if some people complained about not getting their handheld while other people got extra support, even if they did not need the support, to begin with.

2. Because you are confident in yourself and your beliefs and values, you are able to identify when you think there needs to be a change, and you are not afraid of being the person to bring about that change, even if people may not agree at that moment that change is necessary. You accept being a change catalyst, and will gladly poke holes in current status quos if you think you notice discrepancies or if you feel that the status quo is unethical or morally wrong. For example, if your belief that things should be fair at work is disregarded for equality, you would not hesitate to point out that making sure that everyone has what they need to work effectively is hardly a bad thing or worth making waves about. Extra support and accommodations are given in school, and there is no reason they cannot be given in the workplace as well.

3. Because you are not afraid of making mistakes or admitting when you have made a mistake, you are more likely to take risks. You know that you will bounce back if you made the wrong choice, and you will gladly own up to that mistake. Knowing that you are comfortable being wrong, you are more likely to take chances, especially if you think that chance you are taking is the right choice. For example, if you want to try out a new structure for group projects within your team, you may implement it not knowing how it will work. When it fails, you have no problems taking the blame and letting the supervisors know that all blame for the project being late is on you.

4. Because you are driven to ensure those around you succeed, you are happy to make decisions that you think will facilitate that. You recognize that your entire group succeeding is more important than individual successes, and you will make decisions that allow your group to decide.

5. The ability to balance both emotional impulses and rationality allows for you to see a clear picture, even in the throes of emotion, and you will use that rationality to make decisions on the best possible solutions whatever is causing you negative emotions at

that moment. For example, if you accidentally deleted a huge, important program on your work server, your impulse may be to panic and then run and deny it was your fault. The rational part of your brain, however, overrides that impulse and you instead decide to call IT, who is able to fix the mistake relatively quickly

6. Your ability to balance emotional impulses and rationality allows you to understand that your emotions are not the best decision-makers, and grants your rational part of your brain more say over your decisions while still heeding the emotions you felt as cuing you to your needs. For example, if you are interacting with a coworker and you get that feeling that something is wrong, you may choose to continue interacting and finish up whatever it was that you were working on, but make it a point to keep a closer eye on that particular person within the workplace because you had an intuitive feeling that something was off.

7. Your ability to empathize with your team at work enables you to identify and decide upon the best ways to divide up workloads for team assignments and give each person an assignment that works well with his or her individual skills and abilities. You are able to make sure that everyone within the group contributes something meaningful. For example, if you know that one person is skilled at the organization, another is skilled at math, and another can write really compelling reports, you give them assignments accordingly.

8. Your ability to empathize with those around you enables you to identify and decide when to walk away from an argument because you are able to recognize when it will not get any further. For example, if a friend of a friend keeps insisting you are wrong about something important to you, you may eventually decide just to walk away from the entire argument altogether in order to protect your own mental health.

## 8 Practical Ways Strong Emotional Intelligence Will Improve Your Communication

1. Your emotional intelligence will enable you to understand what those you are communicating with and what they are feeling in the moment, which allows you to approach situations and communication with tact and skill, ensuring the maximum amount of communication with minimal conflict.

2. Your ability to understand the emotions of those around you enables you to become much more skilled at leading through your words. You are able to persuade people to act in certain ways just through talking to them and convincing them it is the right way.

3. Your ability to communicate well with others enables you to catch misunderstandings before they can get bad enough to cause problems for you and those around you. This means that conflicts happen less frequently, and you are trusted by those around you to notice and communicate any issues or misunderstandings.

4. Your ability to be in tune with your own emotions means you are able to better recognize when you need to be more cautious with what you say. You understand how your emotions fluctuate and know that impulses can be quite persuasive when you are caught up in the moment with emotions flying. This means that you communicate more carefully.

5. Your ability to understand what others are feeling means you will be able to communicate in a way that supports and validates those around you, which encourages them to keep going and builds rapport between you and those you are supporting.

6. Your self-awareness and attention to your own needs enable you to identify and set boundaries necessary to communicate effectively. You are not afraid to call someone out for addressing you inappropriately and are able to stand up for yourself calmly and assertively in order to defuse the situation and stop the conflict from escalating.

7. Because you are more flexible than someone who struggles with emotional intelligence, you are far more likely to take criticism well, no matter how it is worded by the person who said it to you. You will be able to hear the value within the other person's words and seek to use that value to benefit you later.

8. You are able to build up trust and keep communication open between yourself and your teammates through building rapport using empathy and social awareness skills.

## *8 Practical Ways Strong Emotional Intelligence Will Better Your Relationships of All Kinds*

1. Your empathetic skills enable you to be a fantastic listener, which strengthens relationships. Because you understand how to listen attentively and actively, you are able to support the other person and encourage trust and bonding between the two of you. For example, if your spouse comes home, stressed about work, you are able to disengage from everything that would distract you and sit and really listen to what your spouse has to say.

2. Your empathy means that you are always in tune with what the other person needs, and you are often eager to make sure they get whatever it is that they need. This means that the other person feels supported, and once again fosters trust in you. It encourages a reciprocal nature for a relationship as well. For example, if you see that your friend is stressing because she has a big work project due soon, but her children have been making her preparations difficulty, you may offer to babysit while your friend works, insisting that it is no hassle and that your own children would love a play date.

3. Your flexibility and perseverance mean that change does not intimidate you, meaning that you will be able to adapt to the changes that happen over the natural course of a relationship. As people age, they often mature and change as well, and if you are flexible, you are far more likely to be able to cope with this than

someone who is more rigid and may be intimidated or afraid of the prospect of his or her friend or partner changing. For example, a couple who got together as immature teenagers may have drastically different values, hobbies, and interests as middle-aged adults, and if they both possess higher levels of emotional intelligence, they found themselves able to look past the changes and see that the person they fell in love with is still there.

4. Because you are better at communicating and are more resilient than most, you are able to listen to criticisms that come from your partner. Do you snore too much? Maybe they dislike the way you do dishes. Whatever the criticism, emotional intelligence will make you far better equipped to handle it than someone who struggles with their EQ. For example, when your spouse comes to you to tell you that you have been too lenient with the children and their television time and implies that you are being lazy, you do not get offended and shrug off the criticism, hearing just the message behind the words and not the frustrated undertones. You then change your behavior accordingly to keep that from becoming a problem again.

5. Since those with higher EQs frequently keep their mindsets positive, you are able to see the good in the other person, even in the midst of a fight or argument of some sort. You know that the bad will pass and recognize that even a serious fight or disagreement can be a learning experience for the two of you. You welcome the lesson and hope to use it to better your relationship instead of seeing it as a sign the relationship is doomed. For example, if you and your spouse have a big blow out where words are said that were not meant, you are able to see that those words were spoken in anger and should not be taken seriously. Instead, you focus on your love for your spouse and that generally, the two of you are quite happy together.

6. Because you will likely have better communication skills if you have a higher EQ, you are more likely to get what you want. Because you will know how to communicate effectively, as well as

how to compromise to make sure the needs of both sides are taken care of, you are more likely to convince the other person to give you whatever it is that you are asking for, whether it is a prime shower time, or getting the other person to quiet down in the mornings.

7. Your empathy will give you the ability to be more mindful about the other person's thoughts, feelings, and behaviors. Because you know how the other person is likely to react, you try to avoid any serious triggers to avoid conflict if necessary. If you know that your partner likes to sleep in on Saturdays, for example, you would try to avoid scheduling date-type activities Saturday morning.

8. Your own empathy and self-awareness skills can combine to make you a much more patient person. Your patience will aid in solving conflicts between yourself and the other person and will encourage you to try to do things differently if the old way has not been working for the two of you, such as a chore rotation that has fallen apart because neither person is really free when they are assigned the chores.

## *8 Practical Ways Strong Emotional Intelligence Will Improve Your Workplace*

1. Workers with high emotional intelligence levels are more likely to cooperate well with other people. They understand that their feelings are not the only ones that matter and try to acknowledge that to make the lives of everyone easier. They understand that cooperation is key to a successful team at work, and seek to cooperate whenever is possible. For example, if they are asked what their opinion on something that they are relatively indifferent about is, they are more inclined to go with the majority opinion.

2. By being more even-tempered in general thanks to your great self-regulation skills, you are able to manage, or even reduce, workplace stress with the hopes of keeping the peace and keeping

everyone efficient. You know that stress will be detrimental to work and try to resolve any problems that are causing stress before they can derail everything. For example, if you are feeling the tensions of a looming deadline, you may try to up your team morale with bringing donuts and coffee to work, while complimenting everyone and thanking them for their hard work.

3. With better communication skills, those with higher EQs run into fewer misunderstandings and arguments at work. They and their coworkers are able to communicate in ways that keep conflicts to a minimum. Because they are skilled at communicating, typically they talk through miscommunication long before it gets bad enough to create a conflict. For example, if they can sense that conflict is looming, they may swoop in and disarm it quickly and early before it is on the radar of other people within the group.

4. When conflict is encountered in the workplace, higher emotional intelligence levels mean it is solved quickly and tastefully without any hard feelings or grudges held. People with higher EQs accept the conflict, accept the results, and move on. For example, if two people disagree on how to do a certain part of their work project, they may quietly discuss the matter, and eventually defer to whatever the group leader asks them to, and never speak of the matter again. They are not offended by the conflict with each other and do not take it personally.

5. When mistakes are made, those with higher EQs are more likely to see it as a way to make their work even better. They see the mistake and the solution and see discovering the solution as a way to learn how to do better the next time they are attempting a similar project. For example, if they learned that trying to use a computer program a certain way would cause it to crash and dump all of the work they had put into their project, they would file that information away for the next time they had to use that particular software.

6. Employees with higher EQs are typically self-motivated and will keep themselves on task with very little management needed from

other people. They are driven by their own ambition, which keeps them working, even when no one is looking or paying attention. For example, someone working on a project for work who genuinely likes the research he is doing will likely continue to work, and try to get the best possible result while paying meticulous attention to detail in order to make it as high quality as possible simply because of his own passion and ambition as opposed to any external factors.

7. Workplaces with people with higher EQs are typically far more positive. Because criticism and mistakes do not bring down morale, they are able to work past it without damage to the emotional undertones of the workplace. This positive attitude boosts production, which also keeping those with a positive mindset far more creative and engaged than those who are discouraged by adversity. For example, if there have been conflicts within the workplace recently, they are not memorialized or even really discussed as much of anything but a small hiccup and a learning experience. The conflict did not ruin any relationships, and there were no hard feelings or grudges held.

8. When everyone within an office has a solid foundation of emotional intelligence, criticism no longer becomes something to be tiptoed around—the entire office or team will be interested in hearing any criticisms so they know how to further improve themselves. Driven by their own ambition and internal values, they want to do the best they can, even if it means hearing something negative to learn where they can still improve in the future. For example, in an office dynamic where criticism is seen as helpful and welcomed, one person may quickly pull another aside to let them know that they had noticed a problem within their work that needs to be addressed quickly because it is interfering with another part of the job. The person who made the mistake would thank the other person for bringing it to attention and go off to fix the problem without making a fuss about it.

## 8 Practical Ways Strong Emotional Intelligence Will Improve Healthcare

1. Patient outcomes are improved when the team working on the patient has a higher EQ. EQ is one of the key features that define successful healthcare settings. Because the physician-patient relationship is improved and strengthened when the physician has a higher EQ, the patient outcome is better. The physician is more in tune with the patient's general wellbeing and the patient feels more trust for the physician, meaning the patient will be far more likely to follow the physician's instructions exactly as provided. Together, this raises the chances of the patient making a full recovery.

2. When the staff has higher EQs, they are far better at recognizing that the patient also has emotional needs that need to be met as well to encourage and foster proper healing. Those with higher EQs are more attentive to the person behind the injury or illness, and seek to really listen to the patient's complaints rather than attempting to diagnose and treat without patient input.

3. When there is a higher EQ within the healthcare system, the entire system flows more smoothly. Communication is heightened and everyone sees their roles, ensuring that the entire system does its job effectively.

4. When doctors have higher EQs, they can react effectively when things take a sudden, unexpected turn for the worst. Because they are skilled at self-management, they are able to work past the heightened emotions in life or death situations and handle the situation tactfully and skillfully. Skill and effectiveness do not suffer during these heightened emotions. For example, a surgeon during a teaching session may be guiding a surgical resident through the procedure, but the resident accidentally nicks a vein. The surgeon, instead of blowing up at the resident, no matter how frustrated the surgeon may feel in that moment, instead uses it as a teaching opportunity as she patches up the wound and walks the resident through the steps of fixing the problem, while pointing out what had gone wrong so the resident can learn from the mistake. Despite her feelings, her

hands were still perfectly steady and she was able to get through the process without her mental clarity compromised.

5. When doctors and nurses have higher EQs they are able to better cope with the bad outcomes when they inevitably occur. There is no way for the medical profession to save every single person who comes in for treatment, and those with higher EQ are better able to cope when medicine simply cannot save someone, no matter how hard they may try to do so. Even when they fail to save someone, they try to find a way to learn from the loss to try and avoid similar results repeating in the future.

6. The best doctors and nurses are able to read a person's body language and tone and understand the undertones behind it. They are able to adjust their own behaviors and tones in order to be assuring and calming to the patient with which they are interacting. This ability is a key feature of emotional intelligence. For example, if the patient is a child, the doctor is able to adjust vocabulary down to a child's level and display open, welcoming, and warm behaviors meant to engage the child and earn trust.

7. When medical professionals understand their strengths and weaknesses, a key factor in being emotionally intelligent, they are able to recognize when to walk away from a patient and send someone better equipped to help instead. They can acknowledge when they are not able to help someone, and will honestly admit that to the patient in hopes of getting the best possible patient outcome. For example, if a doctor began treating a regular illness within his specialty but then learned that the illness actually needed a specialist, the doctor would refer the patient out instead of continuing to treat the issue, recognizing that he was no longer the right choice for the job.

8. Along the same lines as #7, doctors and nurses value their integrity, which lines up with their core values and beliefs, along with their desire to help and heal. They would much rather admit that they are ill-equipped for a situation than accidentally harm a patient trying to stroke their own egos proving that they could handle a situation that they had no business handling. They take their oath to do no harm quite seriously.

## CHAPTER 11

# Conclusion

The information you were provided within this part will hopefully benefit you as you continue on your journey toward developing an understanding and mastery of your own emotional intelligence. This part sought to provide you with the information necessary to develop a foundation of knowledge intended to help you understand your interactions with your own and with other people's emotions, as those interactions and understandings are some of the most integral interactions you will ever face.

As you move on to this book and aiming to better your EQ, do not forget the information found within these pages. Your working definition of emotional intelligence, including what it entails and how it works, will benefit you greatly as you seek to strengthen it. Do not forget the importance of the five components of emotional intelligence—these hold the skills that you will need to master in order to better yourself and your own emotional intelligence. These five skillsets, self-awareness, self-regulation, self-motivation, social awareness, and social and relationship skills, each represent one prong of emotional intelligence, and understanding what each entails will be crucial to learn what your own emotional intelligence is.

Remember just how important your emotional intelligence is. If you ever feel discouraged, weak, or incapable, remind yourself what you are working toward. In this case, you are working toward developing your EQ skills so you can better interact with other people in hopes of creating a happier, healthier life and with the intention of learning how to manage both yourself and other people. These skills are priceless, and they will carry you far as you continue through life. Emotional intelligence will either help or hurt you in a wide range of situations, depending on how high or low your EQ is.

Lastly, as you continue your journey, never forget the emphasis that must be placed on empathy, and just how crucial that skill of being able to look at someone and understand how they are feeling at a glance is. This is the foundation to all of your interactions with other people—without understanding how other people are feeling, you will never consciously be able to change your own behaviors to encourage changes in their own behavior. You will not be likely to be as effective as a leader. You are not likely to inspire others if you cannot even manage to understand those who you would like to inspire are feeling.

If you desire to be an effective leader, or to at the very least, have positive social interactions with those around you, you must develop your emotional intelligence. As you work toward your endeavors, do not forget the ways that emotional intelligence can guide you! Remember every way that it can build up your capacity for social interactions, and seek to add those changes into your own life to encourage better social skills.

You have officially reached the end of this part, and it is time for you to decide where to go from here. Do you wish to learn to master your emotional intelligence? Move on to the Emotional Intelligence Practical Guide part and take the emotional intelligence assessment included within it. Do you wish you could parent in an emotionally intelligent manner to teach your child all of the skills you may currently be struggling to master? Move on to the Emotional Intelligence for Kids part. Both of the parts would be fantastic stepping stones as you continue on your journey. With your newfound knowledge on the subject of emotional intelligence, you are prepared to move forward and learn how to make the most out of your social interactions in order to better your relationships and increase happiness.

Good luck on your journey!

# PART 2

# Emotional Intelligence Practical Guide

## CHAPTER 12

# Introduction

Have you ever had a time where you reacted poorly in an emotionally charged situation, and your reaction resulted in a situation that you wish was different? Perhaps you have had a bad day at work, and when you got home, you lashed out at your spouse and children out of frustration when they played a game just a bit too loudly for your taste.

Though they were having a blast playing together, they annoyed you, and you said things you regret. As a result, your children went to bed upset with you after calling you a meanie-head and saying they wished you were still at work, and you angered your spouse, who chose to sleep on the couch instead of in bed with you. After your outburst, you are left with the guilt weighing on your conscience, a wish to change on your mind, and the assumption that the kind of change you would like to see is an impossibility in your heart. You may feel as though you are not the person your family deserves due to your inability to deal with emotional situations.

The reason you reacted so poorly to the situation is due to a low level of emotional intelligence. Emotional intelligence is believed to be one of the most accurate predictors of success and happiness in life, and those who are lacking average or high levels of emotional intelligence often find themselves struggling socially, especially when emotions are running high. We all have natural levels of emotional intelligence, influenced by upbringing and general temperament, much like how we have natural levels of intelligence, but unlike intelligence, emotional intelligence levels are flexible.

You can build your emotional intelligence and influence your ability to read and react to emotional situations. This means that you can improve your EQ (emotional quotient; the measurement of your emotional intelligence), and improve your social skills and relationships, though it will take effort.

Imagine if you had a higher EQ in the above situation: You would have come home from work angry, but instead of lashing out at your family, you took a deep breath, recognized that your family was having fun, and went to take a quiet drive around town for fifteen minutes to yourself to unwind before returning home and joining in on playtime and your children's bedtime routines. Instead of them being upset and angry at you, your children told you they love you, told you that you are the best, and went to bed happily. You then were able to spend time with your spouse, calmly explaining the situation and why you were angry, which gained you the emotional support of your spouse as well. Ultimately, you were able to handle the situation tactfully, and despite the anger you felt, you bettered your relationships with your spouse and children.

With the help of this part, you will be provided the skills you will need to bolster your EQ and develop the ability to handle social situations with tact. You will be guided through the basics of EQ, provided tests to see where your current EQ levels are, and then given plenty of tips to improve on your EQ levels. You are not destined to remain at low levels of EQ forever; putting in the effort to boost your skills is entirely possible, and you can achieve the high EQ you and those around you deserve.

## CHAPTER 13

# The Emotional Intelligence Framework

Emotional intelligence is composed of several different skills that make you capable of understanding and appraising emotions, regardless of whether they are your own or belonging to other people. People with higher EQ are typically much more effective at controlling and regulating their feelings, which enables individuals to better control behaviors.

### Breaking down Emotional Intelligence

Emotional intelligence is better understood by breaking it down beyond understanding what it is as a whole. The entirety of emotional intelligence is comprised of five separate realms of emotional intelligence, which are further organized into four quadrants that affect each other. Understanding these ways of breaking down and organizing emotional intelligence is useful in understanding where you stand and what the purpose of each of the skills is.

### Realms of Emotional Intelligence

The skills of emotional intelligence can be broken down into five separate realms or behaviors and skills:

- *Understanding your emotions*
- *Regulating your emotions*
- *Keeping yourself motivated*
- *Understanding and recognizing the emotions of other people*
- *Managing relationships* (managing the emotions of other people)

Each of these realms of emotional intelligence is important, but being strong in one does not necessarily mean you are emotionally intelligent, nor does it mean that you will be particularly effective in social situations. In order to be emotionally intelligent, you must be proficient in all five realms. Someone who understands and controls his emotions with no regard for other people's emotions is not going to be emotionally intelligent; everything he does will be to ensure that his own needs are met. Likewise, someone who is skilled at understanding and recognizing other people's emotions but is awful at self-regulation of emotions is going to be selfless to a fault and find that her needs are never met. All five realms come together to create one well-rounded, emotionally intelligent person.

### Quadrants of Emotional Intelligence

The four quadrants or domains of emotional intelligence are:

- *Self-Awareness*
- *Self-Management*
- *Social Awareness*
- *Relationship Management*

As you can see, each of these closely relates to one of the realms of emotional intelligence. Each of these skills can be sorted onto a chart to represent a different combination of self or social-relational and awareness or regulation.

Each quadrant of emotional intelligence relates closely to the others. A high self-awareness typically lends itself to higher social awareness and self-management. When you have higher social awareness and self-management, you are more likely to have stronger relationship management skills. When all four quadrants are strongly developed, that person is believed to be very emotionally intelligent.

**Self-Awareness**

Within emotional intelligence, self-awareness involves developing a deeper understanding of your own emotions. It involves knowing yourself and understanding what you are feeling or need. If you are able to identify and meet the needs of yourself, you are far more likely to be able to understand and meet the needs of other people. For this reason, the foundation of emotional intelligence begins with self-awareness.

Some traits associated with self-awareness include the following:

- Being self-confident because you understand yourself
- Being aware of your own strengths and weaknesses
- Being conscious of your current emotional state
- Understanding how your actions affect other people
- Understanding and being conscious of how other people or situations influence your own emotional state

By having a deep understanding of yourself, you have the foundation to understanding others. After all, if you could not identify when you are sad, how could you possibly hope to recognize sadness in another person? Without the most fundamental basics of emotions and how they impact you, you will struggle to ever truly relate to other people.

## Low Self-Awareness

There are several signs that may point that you have a low self-awareness quotient. If you feel like you have any of these signs, you may need to work on your self-awareness.

- Easily stressed: When you are not in control of your emotions and not doing what is necessary to cope with the negative ones, you may find yourself easily stressed out by things that would not be a big deal to someone with a higher EQ. If you are not addressing your emotions as they come up due to a lack of knowledge to do so, you are going to see it build up and stress you out.
- Difficulty being assertive: People lacking the EQ necessary often struggle to handle conflict in a productive manner. Instead, they resort to passive or aggressive behavior to allow the conflict to pass.
- Struggle to describe emotional states: People who cannot label specific emotions as they feel them struggle to handle them. For example, while they may be able to identify that they feel bad, they cannot label whether what they are feeling is anxiety, frustration, or sadness.
- Operate on assumptions: People lacking in EQ often make a snap decision or assumption and then fall victim to the fallacy of confirmation bias; they will accept any evidence supporting their opinion while ignoring the evidence that contradicts it.
- Hold grudges: Grudges come from stress responses, and people lacking in EQ struggle to cope with that stress.
- Lock onto mistakes: People with lower EQs frequently lock onto their mistakes and refuse to look past them, or they forget about them, dooming them to repeat the same mistakes over and over again.

- Feeling misunderstood: People with lower EQs cannot clearly convey their own emotions because they do not understand them themselves, leaving plenty of room for misinterpretation.
- Lack of understanding what your emotional triggers are: Everyone has some sort of trigger—something that immediately causes strong, and often irrational responses to some sort of stimulus. Those lacking in EQ often do not know what theirs are.
- Hiding emotions: People with lower EQs tend to see negative emotions poorly and instead prefer to keep them hidden behind positive ones. This means that their needs are never being addressed because they are never using their negative emotions.
- Blaming others for how they make you feel: People with lower EQs see other people as responsible for triggering their own emotional responses instead of recognizing that no one is responsible for their emotional states.
- Being easily offended: Those with lower EQ typically lack the self-confidence those with higher EQs have. They also lack the understanding of their own strengths and weaknesses, which makes them a little more self-conscious when called out for them.

### Self-Management

Self-management involves the ability to dictate your own thoughts, feelings, and behaviors. This quadrant of emotional intelligence focuses on your ability to manage yourself. It includes your responses to those around you and the situations you may find yourself in, as well as expressing your positive emotions while controlling negative reactions. While negative emotions are acceptable to feel, they should never be in control of you as a person. You should be able to manage feeling negative feelings while still not harming others or lashing out. It involves using self-awareness to keep those negative feelings within your control, as you are able to identify what they are and why you are feeling them.

Some of the frequently seen abilities in people with high self-management include:

- Keeping control of emotions: The ability to recognize and feel emotions without letting them dictate behaviors.
- Trustworthy: These people are reliable and often make it a point to follow through with what they have agreed to do.
- Flexible: The ability to roll with change when it is unexpectedly coming up without it ruining the plans or stopping the individual from meeting other goals.
- Optimistic: Negative feelings are not enough to discourage him or her from attempting to achieve desired results.
- Motivated to achieve goals: Knowing what is desired and motivated to make that happen.
- Willing to take initiative: Comfortable being the one initiating change and

## Low Self-Management

- Struggle to control emotions: People with lower self-management struggle to keep their own feelings, and therefore their own actions, under control. They typically respond emotionally rather than rationally.
- Struggle to take criticisms: Anything negative said toward those with low self-management struggle to keep their disappointment or other negative emotions in control after feeling criticized.
- Cannot cope with change or the unexpected: Those with lower self-management struggle when things do not go according to plans. Coping with the change is difficult, as change or the unexpected typically come with stronger negative emotions.
- Impulsive: Those with lower self-management struggle to keep their impulses under control. When given the chance, they will take something that they like better, even if it has a worse consequence. The consequence does not matter nearly as much as the happiness from going along with the impulse.
- Need instant gratification: Oftentimes, people with lower self-management tend to go with gratification sooner rather than

waiting for a better result. For example, they are likely to go through with buying something they cannot afford with cash and put it on a credit card where they will pay significant amounts of interest if the alternative is waiting for months to be able to afford to pay cash. They'd rather have the item sooner, even if the consequence is worse.

**Social Awareness**

Social awareness focuses on understanding what other people want and need. It is the ability to look at someone else and understand how they feel or what they need in that particular moment. Those who are socially aware can tell at a glance how they should approach another person and how to keep situations calm. They oftentimes go out of their way to meet the needs of other people just because they feel as though they can, so they should. Oftentimes, they exhibit some of these traits:

- Empathetic: A deep understanding of how someone else feels and what is needed in the moment.
- An understanding of group structures: They recognize how society works and the idea of give-and-take communities in which everyone contributes something.
- Service-oriented: They prioritize other people's needs and wants in order to ensure that they are met as much as possible.

When you have a high level of social awareness, you are able to consider other people's wants and needs effectively and meet those needs quickly. These people frequently excel at being leaders or public speakers: They excel at speaking in the way that the people want to hear and use that skill to gain the support they need at their jobs. These people are typically quite charismatic, but also selfless in the sense that they are doing their best to ensure that others' needs are being considered. Social awareness requires a developed sense of self-awareness to really be effective.

## Low Social Awareness

- Untrusting: Those who lack social awareness typically do not trust those around them, nor do they earn the trust of those around them. By never meeting other people's needs, they never establish themselves as trustworthy.
- Lack of empathy: When lacking social awareness, it is quite difficult to understand what other people are feeling. They struggle to relate to other people meaningfully because they cannot deeply understand the other people's needs.
- Selfish: When social awareness and empathy do not play a role in life, people do not feel the pressure to ensure that other people's needs are met.
- Manipulative: Those without much social awareness do not feel bad about using other people in order to get what they want. Their lack of empathy means they do not care as much about hurting other people.
- Closed-minded: Social awareness allows for thoughts of diversity and understanding how every person, no matter how different, can contribute in some way. Those lacking in social awareness may not see the use of some people's skills or understand how nonessential jobs or skills may still contribute to the overall well-being of society.
- Isolated: Because those lacking social awareness do not trust others and lack sophisticated empathy, they typically retreat to be by themselves rather than associating with other people. They do not build up social support groups and instead live on their own.

## Relationship Management

Relationship management is the most complex of the four quadrants of emotional intelligence. It involves the ability to influence other people through your own words and actions, allowing for inspiration, and the ability to mediate and solve conflicts that may arise within the groups you are inspiring. This is the ultimate trait for leaders: It is what enables you to lead effectively and kindly, earning that position as opposed to having to take it through domination. Those with high relationship management skills make conscious decisions about their interactions with others so they can get the desired outcome that best suits the needs at that moment.

1. **Make a decision** about the best way to proceed in the current situation. You have taken the time to analyze how those around you are feeling, as well as identifying the reasons for those feelings. From there, you will decide what the most effective ways to interact with those around you are, as well as considering the potential reactions you may get based on how you approach them. You will also consider how their reactions will affect you and have plans and skills in place to manage those potentially negative feelings effectively and appropriately.

2. **Interact with others** in the way that you have determined is the best possible course of actions. These interactions can vary in form. For example, it could be written or verbal, and with a single person or the entire group.

3. **Identify an outcome** you desire and tailor your interactions to that outcome. You will interact with the people in ways that you know will influence them to create the outcome you desire, adding an intentional element to the act of relationship management.

4. **Identify the needs** you are trying to meet in order to be sure that the outcome is the right one for the situation. You want your outcome to meet the needs of yourself, the people around you, or whatever the needs your decision is addressing are at that particular moment.

People with high skills in relationship management typically exhibit the following traits:

- Influential
- Inspirational
- Invested in the development of other people
- Willing to be the catalyst for changes
- Acting as the conflict mediator
- Cultivating and encouraging bonds between the people within the group
- Create teams that work well together and encourage teamwork or collaboration

## Low Relationship Management

- Ineffective leader: Those who struggle with relationship management fail at being in leadership roles. They are typically too self-absorbed or socially blind to understand the nuances behind leading a group effectively
- Untrusted and disliked: Typically, those with low relationship management struggle to prove themselves trustworthy or likeable. People prefer to avoid them.
- Act selfishly: They may fail to acknowledge other people's needs, or simply do not care about others' needs for other reasons. Regardless, they do not inspire much loyalty when they refuse to help others.
- Are uninspiring: No matter how much they may ask other people to help them or do something, people do not feel motivated, obligated, or a desire to do as they were asked.
- Likely see a constant revolving door of new employees or relationships: Because these people struggle with relationships, they are frequently seeing new ones, either at work or in their personal lives. This constant refresh of people in the person's life mean he or she never really learns to develop meaningful relationships.

**Interrelationship of Emotional Intelligence Components.**

Within emotional intelligence, all four quadrants are interrelated. They build upon each other to create a well-rounded, emotionally intelligent individual. The basic foundation is formed by self-awareness; having a certain degree of self-awareness provides you with the ability to begin thinking about both self-management and social awareness. If you struggle with self-awareness, you are likely to struggle to move to the next step of self-management or social awareness. Oftentimes, self-awareness is one of the best places to begin practicing and strengthening your emotional intelligence, as the others require the skills developed through self-awareness to be effective at the others.

After self-awareness is developed, self-management and social awareness become possible. You cannot manage yourself and your emotions if you lack a basic understanding of what your emotions are or how they work, and likewise, if you are unaware of your own feelings, you cannot hope to understand how someone else is feeling or what they may need. Developing both self-management and social awareness leads to an ability to begin developing relationship management. Without self-awareness, the entire process of developing emotional intelligence becomes increasingly more difficult. It takes a mastery of self-awareness, self-management, and social awareness to begin to learn relationship management.

## CHAPTER 14

# What is an Emotional Intelligence Test?

Imagine that you have just been fired from yet another job. You had always done your best at work but tried to keep to yourself. You did not care when people around you were struggling to complete their work, and even when you were free at that particular moment, you rarely extended an offer for work. Because you never developed many trusting relationships at work or went above and beyond, people were not particularly interested in helping you, either. One day, you were struggling to catch up on your work, and despite your best efforts, you could just not keep up. No one around you offered to help you, as you had never offered to help any of them, and eventually, you blew up at work. You could not take another moment of listening to two of your coworkers chattering right outside your cubicle, and in a moment of rage, you yelled at them to either make themselves useful and help you or get away from your desk. You may have even sprinkled in a few swears during your rant. Ultimately, you were fired and left wondering why, after all that time of you being a good employee who did the job and never caused trouble before, you were let go. Sure, you had one blow up, but everyone has a bad day sometimes, and that should have been excused considering your track record. This seemed to happen everywhere you went: You would go, do your job, keep to yourself, and ultimately be let go when you were doing your job regularly, and you could not understand why. Through some web searching, you found your answer: A lack of emotional intelligence.

You may be doing your job on a regular basis, but you have proven that you are not a team player in that particular situation. Workplaces want to build teams of people who work well together and will help each other when the need arises, not people who do the bare minimum to get their own work done while letting other people suffer the consequences of not having their work finished. With your newfound understanding of the value of emotional intelligence, you begin searching for how to improve it.

Ultimately, you feel lost. You may know that you struggle with anxiety sometimes, or that your ability to meet others' needs could use some work. Despite knowing this, you may have no idea where to begin or how to decide where to continue working on yourself. You know that you would like to be an emotionally intelligent person because emotionally intelligent people seem to do better in a wider range of situations, but are unsure of how to attain it or where you may need to improve yourself. Luckily for you, this is exactly why emotional intelligence tests exist!

Whether you want a general idea just for fun, or you are serious about understanding where you fall on the scale of emotional intelligence, taking a test can be a fantastic way to get that picture. While these may not always be accurate due to the way they are executed and because they rely on self-reporting of situations and moods, they still provide great general information that can point you in the right direction on your journey toward emotional intelligence.

Just as how IQ tests exist, there are also tests designed to quantify levels of emotional intelligence. These tests typically consist of several questions designed to assess your strengths and skills in emotional intelligence to create a hard number to represent your EQ. The tests can be crucial tools to understanding where your emotional strengths and weaknesses are, and can provide a more thorough understanding of yourself as an individual. These tests can come in a variety of forms, ranging from true or false questions, questions that ask you to quantify how much something describes you or the frequency of a behavior or can be verbal questions at an interview designed to gauge your emotional intelligence.

### How EQ Is Tested

Typically, EQ is tested through a series of questions. You will be given a sort of quiz with a series of situations and circumstances, and you must identify how you would react or whether it describes you. The goal is for you to identify as honestly as possible to create the most accurate assessment that can be created. Each question created to test an individual's EQ creates a situation in which there are several reactions possible and assigns each possible reaction a score in relation to a specific quadrant of emotional intelligence. For example, a question testing self-awareness would likely question one's own reactions in certain situations regarding being stressed, overwhelmed, or otherwise negatively influenced by emotion, often in a way that can assign a value. For example, you may see a question that asks if you do not let your emotions get the best of you, with the choices you are provided being "always," "sometimes," "rarely," and "never." Always would score 4 points while never scored a 0. This allows for a quantifiable assessment of your ability to control your emotions.

The tests frequently ask a series of questions for each quadrant of emotional intelligence, and at the end, they add them up and divide the scores into several categories to use to provide your results. If you score in the top percentile, you are said to have high intelligence in that category, while average scores mean it could use some work, and low scores implying that you need serious effort in that particular category.

Together, you are able to add your questions together and see where you score.

Sometimes, workplaces will perform EQ tests during interviews when seeking to hire or promote people. In those cases, the test is most frequently done verbally, with an emphasis on understanding your own personal reactions to certain scenarios, or with you providing a time that you had a conflict at work and asking how you may have resolved it. You will often be given a question, and then allowed a few moments to consider it before being expected to answer it.

These questions typically relate to empathy or conflict resolution, and they are some of the most important questions at your interview. If your interviewer is asking you questions to judge emotional intelligence, then they are oftentimes specifically seeking out someone with emotional intelligence, even if that person is not the most qualified academically or experientially.

### Why Test for EQ?

As discussed, emotional intelligence has a strong impact in virtually every aspect of your life. Understanding your EQ allows you to identify your strengths and weaknesses, which can be incredibly useful when it comes to recognizing your behaviors for what they are. You need to understand your weaknesses if you hope to compensate for them and begin to work on filling them in to prevent them from being problematic in the future. Your own relationships and general wellbeing will increase if you can raise your EQ, as you will become generally better at managing yourself and your emotional reactions. By bettering your control over yourself, you are able to avoid falling for the traps that many people do in communicating with others: Giving in to anger. You will be able to recognize your anger and use it to fuel your desire to fix the situation without lashing out or making the situation worse for yourself or others. You may find that your problem was a simple miscommunication, and someone who is emotionally intelligent can take that information and learn from it to ensure it is not a problem again in the future.

Beyond testing EQ to understand yourself, it is sometimes tested in other situations as well. Sometimes, interviews for jobs involve questions that test for emotional intelligence. It has been found that some of the best performing people in many different careers have higher EQs, even if they are less intellectually intelligent than some of the lesser-performing individuals. Ultimately, EQ has proven more accurate in determining success in workplaces than IQ.

Because high EQ is a better predictor of a good employee, many managers have begun using those questions to weed out people who are less emotionally intelligent and more likely to cause issues in the workplace. They ask questions that provide the hiring managers a better understanding of the interviewee's ability to recognize and regulate their own and others' emotions and behaviors, especially when needed to adapt to various workplace environments and situations. Employers want empathetic employees that are team players, great at communication, and well-equipped to handle a wide range of challenges or roadblocks that may be encountered during the work week.

Higher levels of social and emotional intelligence are important in a workplace, as those who are more emotionally intelligent place more of an emphasis on empathy, which means they will be there in support of their coworkers. If they see a coworker struggling, they are more likely to go forward and offer to help solve the problem than someone who does not see empathy as a major motivator. Those with higher emotional intelligence are also more in tune with their own strengths and weaknesses and are more receptive to feedback and constructive criticism than someone who struggles with their confidence.

### What to Expect in an EQ Test

When taking an EQ test, you should expect to see a wide range of questions on various subjects. Some may be quite sensitive, such as asking about your own personal confidence levels, whereas others may seek to identify whether you are able to resolve conflicts or put other people's needs in front of your own. The tests are typically rather boring, and provide a series of similar questions, though they do have slightly different purposes for your score. You may see questions about your own emotions, as well as your interpretation of others emotions in similar circumstances, or you may seek questions that seek to measure how well you cope with the unexpected. Regardless of what the questions are, they all serve one purpose: To identify your weaknesses when it comes to emotional intelligence.

When you take a test, you must be honest. It is often helpful for people to go with their gut reactions when reading a question, as that gut reaction is typically the most accurate. Do not answer the test based on what you think may be the right or wrong answer, as all that will do is skew your data. If you want your test to be as accurate as possible and give you the most straightforward information about yourself, you must answer truthfully, even if you know it is an answer that would be attributed to a lower level of emotional intelligence. EQ is flexible and can be strengthened, so you should want the most accurate picture painted when taking the test. That accurate picture will be your roadmap to becoming more emotionally intelligent.

While the questions do not necessarily have to be taken in any specific amount of time, it helps to do them in one sitting if you can. You should be free of distractions when you begin your test, and you should make sure you have an ample amount of time free to tend to it. Some of the tests available can take up to an hour, though the one you will be provided in this book will be much shorter. You want to be able to focus on your questions within the same mindset and without other things distracting you that could potentially make you misunderstand the question or your own answer to it.

You should expect the questions to be easy enough to understand, though they may be about situations or traits about yourself that you have never considered. Give yourself a quick moment to consider them, and then write down the answer. Again, make sure that you provide your own honest answers to the questions rather than how someone else would answer for you. The important part is your own opinions and interpretations of yourself, especially because two of the quadrants are about yourself, and the basis of the entire emotional intelligence structure requires your own self-awareness.

Lastly, you should expect that this test will not be 100% accurate! As it relies wholly on self-reporting and involves questions on emotions, which are widely variable between people, you should take this as a general guide rather than as a diagnosis for what kind of person you are. It can absolutely point out your strengths and weaknesses, but you should make sure you take you understanding of the results as general assessments as opposed to being official assessments of your own emotional intelligence.

### Sample Questions and Answers

The following questions and answers will be considered from the same hypothetical scenario introduced at the beginning of this chapter in which you imagine that you have been fired from your job after doing the bare minimum to meet your own job description without helping others at work and eventually having an outburst. Each question that will be provided will have an explanation of what it is testing for as well as the answer that the hypothetical you would provide, and what it would score if it were a part of this test.

### Sample 1:

*I am able to control myself when angry and keep myself from saying things I will later regret.*

1. *Never*
2. *Rarely*
3. *Sometimes*
4. *Often*
5. *Always*

You may have circled often here, with the reason being that oftentimes, you are able to control your anger. It is when you are already stressed out prior to being set off that you really struggle to control it and frequently say things in anger that you do not mean.

This question seeks to quantify self-management. It is asking you a question about your own feelings and your own behaviors to identify whether you are able to control yourself. One of the key facets of self-management is the ability to regulate your emotionally charged reactions, even when faced with the temptation to allow your emotions to rule you.

The answer never earns you 0 points, rarely earns 1, sometimes earns 2, often earns 3, and always earns 4 points toward emotional quotients. By answering that you can often control your anger, you earned 3 points toward your EQ.

**Sample 2:**

*I understand what makes me angry most of the time.*

1. *Never*
2. *Rarely*
3. *Sometimes*
4. *Often*
5. *Always*

You may have looked at this question and circled 3. You know some of the things that make you angry, such as when you feel the pressure to perform at work, but sometimes, you do find yourself angry without knowing why, and you have noticed that it can cause issues in your relationships.

This question seeks to quantify self-awareness. It wants to identify whether you are aware of your emotions and if you understand what is causing them. Since self-awareness is all about understanding your emotions and what influences them in order to be able to develop the self-management necessary to control them, this is an easy way to get straight to the point.

Just as the previous question scored answers, an answer of never warranted 0 points, rarely earned 1, sometimes earned 2 points, often earned 3 points, and always earned 4 points. Your answer of sometimes earned you 2 points toward your EQ.

**Sample 3:**
*People often look to me to lead group projects at work or school.*

1. *Never*
2. *Rarely*
3. *Sometimes*
4. *Often*
5. *Always*

Your answer here likely would have been 1. You never went out of your way to work with other people, nor did you ever try to assert yourself as a leader. You always did the bare minimum, and nobody in your workplace really trusted you since you never gave them a reason to do so. This question sought to understand and quantify your relationship management skills. It wanted to identify whether you were often seen as a natural leader or if people naturally wanted to do as you said and follow your lead. Those with high relationship management skills are frequently seen as natural leaders in groups, and when they work in groups, people naturally want to do as the leader says because they do trust that person's judgment and know that he or she will do what is best for the team.

This question also uses the same scale of 4 points for always, 3 points for often, 2 points for sometimes, 1 point for rarely, and 0 for never. Your answer warranted a score of 0 in relationship management.

**Sample 4:**
*I never concern myself with the welfare of others if it will be even a minor inconvenience to me to do so.*

1. *Always*
2. *Often*
3. *Sometimes*
4. *Rarely*
5. *Never*

After reading this question, you circled that you agreed with the statement. If helping others took away from your time at work or any free time you may have earned by finishing your work quickly, you would disregard the possibility of helping other people. You did not see a reason to do so, especially if it meant extra work for you that you would not be paid for.

This question sought to quantify your social awareness skills. This particular question was concerned with empathy and how much you showed for other people. Those with higher social awareness skills act empathetically, wanting to help other people, even if it is somewhat of an inconvenience. They do not mind helping out, so long as it is not directly harmful to them, and sometimes even when it is. Empathetic individuals will act selflessly for no reason other than they feel as though they should do so because they can understand and feel the other person's pain or stress.

This question changed the scoring pattern. In this instance answering always warranted a score of 0 often would earn a score of 1, sometimes earned a score of 2, rarely got a score of 3, and never earned a score of 4. Your answer assigned you a score of 0 for social awareness.

Ultimately, after taking your four scores from the four questions, you scored 5/16 in emotional intelligence. This is quite low and requires work in all quadrants based on the four questions answered.

## CHAPTER 15

# Measuring Emotional Intelligence

Understanding that you can quantify your EQ is fantastic, but you need to understand more thoroughly how to judge what those scores mean. Why are certain scores important? How do they tell you what you need to know? Whenever you are testing something as abstract as emotional intelligence, it can be hard to really accurately quantify results. After all, the numbers used are going to be arbitrary based on whoever is executing the test. Some tests will have you answer out of 10 and provide you a score of 0-10 to decide how emotionally intelligent you are. Others will provide it out of 160. This book will have you ultimately calculate your score with a max of 40 points per quadrant, totaling 160 when your individual quadrants are added together.

### How Emotional Intelligence Is Measured

As mentioned, your score will be measured out of 160 points. Each question you will answer in the next section can provide a minimum of 0 and a maximum of 4 points toward your quotient, just like in the sample questions that were discussed in the previous chapter. The questions that will be provided are carefully considered to analyze each of your four emotional intelligence domains. Each domain will involve 10 questions, providing a minimum score of 0 to a maximum score of 40. You will ultimately add up your scores after completing the questionnaire, and that is what you will use in order to identify what your EQ is.

When you have tallied up your score, you will want to compare it to the key that will be provided at the end. It will divide the possible scores into three different results that will tell you whether your score is low and requires attention to correct and develop it, effective, meaning that it is average, but could be strengthened, or enhanced, meaning you should utilize it to work on developing other quadrants that may be weaker or need work.

Remember, unless you somehow manage to score a perfect 160 on the test, there is always room for improvement. If you do not like the score you see in front of you after completing the assessment, you should use that displeasure as motivation to begin working on other aspects of yourself in order to better your emotional intelligence and strive toward a happier, more emotionally intelligent lifestyle.

At the end of the appraisal, you will be guided toward identifying your own personal weaknesses, as well as encouraged to work on the particular areas that are giving you a difficult time. You will learn where your weaknesses are through seeing your scores, and you will be given a baseline to work off of. Think of this first appraisal of your EQ as your pre-diet and workout weight and photos. This is where you are before you begin working to better yourself, and you should save it to look back on in the future after you have had time to dedicate toward growing your emotional intelligence. You may be surprised to see more growth than you initially expected, even after just a short time of working toward your goal of gaining a higher EQ.

### How to Use Your Emotional Quotient to Understand Your Needs

Your EQ will be scaled into one of three categories: needing enrichment, proficient and functioning, or enhanced and strong. Understanding where each individual domain's EQ is will help you see where you are doing well and where you are struggling. If you know that you are struggling with self-awareness because you scored a 15/40, for example, you can use that knowledge to begin studying self-awareness. The last third of this book is dedicated to provide tips to improve emotional intelligence for each domain, and that is a fantastic first place to start improving yourself.

On the other hand, if you score 35/40 in self-awareness, but you have scored 12/40 in social awareness, you can use your skills in self-awareness to apply strengthening to social awareness. You already know plenty about your own emotions, needs, and how the world impacts them, so you can begin working to develop empathy skills instead. Your own self-awareness skills will be the foundation to bettering your social awareness.

When you learn where your domain skills fall, you are able to further understand your own behaviors as well. If you know that you have always struggled with managing your anger, for example, seeing that your self-management quotient score lowly may help you understand why and point you in the right direction to bettering yourself. You can meet that need to manage your own anger so it will no longer be overwhelming by following some of the practical tips toward bettering self-management. You will also be able to create concrete goals toward bettering your self-management and find guides to help you, step by step.

Ultimately, the most important way that knowing where your EQ sits on the scale is knowing your own weaknesses. One of the fundamental parts of emotional intelligence is having an understanding of your own weaknesses and developing them over time in order to compensate for that natural weakness. Because an EQ is not concrete or fixed, no matter which aspect is your weakest, you could theoretically work with it enough to make that weakness into your strongest domain. If you have always struggled with leadership but want to learn, that is a possibility, no matter what your temperament or current EQ. If your goal is to be highly emotionally intelligent with a strong relationship management quadrant, you can do that with the help of understanding where you are at now.

## The Emotional Intelligence Scale

With many different methods to calculating emotional intelligence available throughout the world, it should come as no surprise that there are a multitude of scales available to judge that emotional intelligence as well. Each test is going to have a different scale that is used based on what is being measured.

The scale that this book will use is 40 points per quadrant with a max score of 160 for total EQ. Within this, scoring in the bottom 60% of any given category is seen as a weakness. Scoring between 60% and 85% is seen as being effective or proficient, but it could still be strengthened. Scoring in the top 15%, from 85% to 100% is seen as having enhanced or advanced levels of emotional intelligence. This higher level is incredibly tough to achieve naturally, but it can be consciously attained. See the following table for a basic breakdown of the results that will be used in this book's assessment.

| Score | Individual Quadrant EQ | Combined EQ |
|---|---|---|
| Area for Enrichment: Needs work | 0-24 | 0-96 |
| Effective Functioning: Proficient, but could be strengthened | 25-34 | 97-136 |
| Enhanced: High EQ | 35-40 | 137-160 |

Within this chart, you can identify the area for enrichment as a low EQ, effective function as average EQ, and enhanced as high EQ. People within these different scores may behave vastly differently due to the many different possible combinations of EQ. It is entirely possible to have someone that excels at both self-awareness and self-management but is poor at social awareness and relationship management. That person's score could potentially report as effective, or average, depending on how they scored. For example, assume you scored a 35/40 on both self-awareness and self-management, but only 22/40 on social awareness and 18/40 in relationship management. This person's social skills are quite low and needing improvement while self-centered skills are enhanced. This person's total EQ comes out to 110/160, which puts him firmly in the center of effective, or average EQ, though he cannot navigate a social situation for his life. While his total EQ may be acceptable, he is going to struggle with those low social scores. Despite these sort of outliers, EQ is still a generally effective way to look at emotional and social skills.

With an idea of what the scale looks like, it is time to look at some of the most common traits of people with both low and high EQ.

### Low EQ Traits

People with lower EQ typically are much more volatile and less stable than those with average or high EQ. They oftentimes are very emotional and unpredictable, and while they may come across as passionate and spontaneous to some people, it is actually a sign of lacking the emotional intelligence necessary to be successful socially.

- *Lacking control over their emotions:* People who struggle with their EQ frequently are controlled by their emotions rather than being in control. This can lead to situations that are emotionally charged quickly, becoming worse as fuel is thrown on the proverbial fire.
- *Does not understand the feelings of others:* Because those with lower EQs typically struggle with empathy, they frequently come across as clueless about other people's thoughts, feelings, or needs, even if their feelings are clearly displayed on their expressions.
- *Lacking friendships, or failing to maintain them:* Those who struggle with EQ frequently also lack meaningful relationships with friends due to not having the emotional intelligence necessary to maintain those relationships. Due to the volatile tempers

of those with lower EQ and a lack of good problem-solving and conflict resolution skills, friendships rarely last.

- *Keeps a straight face:* Those who keep their faces blank at all time typically struggle to express their own emotions. This is often due to a lack of understanding how to express their own emotions, a crucial component of emotional intelligence, rather than a need or desire to keep their emotions shielded away.

- *May be emotionally inappropriate at times:* Because people with lower EQ tend to struggle with reading other people's emotions, they may behave inappropriately, such as making a joke at a funeral or talking about sexually explicit topics at a family-friendly party with children present.

- *Cannot identify emotion from tone of voice:* People who struggle with EQ frequently struggle to identify emotion from voice alone. While people with average or higher EQ are able to identify the emotion being conveyed by tone alone, people with lower EQ typically fail to do so.

- *Lacks sympathetic behaviors:* Both empathy and sympathy require sophisticated emotional intelligence skills that those without much EQ typically lack. Because both empathy and sympathy require the emotional states of another person to be understood, it can be a big struggle for those with lower EQ.

- *Emotional reactions are typically intense:* Along the lines of being unable to control their emotions, those with lower EQs typically react incredibly strongly or intensely, even when it is not necessarily warranted. If something is annoying, they become irate, or if they are happy about something small happening, they may be absolutely ecstatic. These extremes are felt due to a lack of emotional control to keep reactions at an appropriate level.

- *Does not respond emotionally to movies:* Oftentimes, we feel emotional attachments to characters we see on TV. In a love scene, our feel-good hormones are pumping. In a tense horror scene, our own heartbeats quicken in response. These are empathetic responses with the characters in the movie or show, and someone lacking emotional intelligence is not likely to feel emotionally moved the same way as someone with a higher EQ.

- *Downplays the importance of emotions:* Almost as though they are in denial, oftentimes those who struggle with emotional intelligence typically try to downplay the importance of emotions and being able to communicate with them. They say that logic is more important, and lacking emotion is not nearly as much of an issue as lacking rationality. This is not true; however, as emotions and emotional intelligence are crucial to virtually every aspect of society.
- *Struggles with communication:* While the emotionally intelligent person is able to communicate tactfully, someone lacking a high EQ often resorts to name-calling, misdirection, and pushing the blame for situations onto the other person. This only serves to escalate the situation, rather than helping to deescalate it.

**High EQ Traits**

People with high EQ are typically much more adept at social situations than those with lower EQs. They are skilled at reading other people and juggling the needs of everyone, making sure that everybody is as satisfied as possible because of their own empathy. They are happiest when everyone else is content. These are some of the most common traits someone high on the EQ scale may exhibit:

- *Able to accurately name and describe a wide range of emotions:* Someone with high EQ is able to describe complex emotions beyond bad or good. They can say that they are feeling despondent or explain that they feel optimistically hopeful. Experts in the field have found that only about 1/3 of people are capable of this.
- *Balances rationality with emotionality:* Emotions do not run the show, though they may influence it. People with high EQ are able to think rationally during emotional times, and they are able to

use this skill to make good decisions, even during tough or distracting times or events.

- *Curious about others:* The curiosity of other people developed, regardless of whether you are actively interacting with that other person, is a byproduct of empathy. Because you are able to feel the emotional energy of other people, you become more curious about how others are doing.

- *Can regulate negative emotions:* While people with high EQ do not seek to avoid or quash any emotions they are feeling, they are able to regulate their reactions to them. Even when angry or scared, they are able to allow the rational part of their minds to control the situation. They never allow the negative emotions to overpower their rational thoughts.

- *Aware of strengths and weaknesses:* Because they are aware of themselves, they are able to recognize their strengths and weaknesses effectively and use that knowledge to prevent weaknesses from upsetting them or keeping them from succeeding. They are able to compensate for their weaknesses by using their strengths to their full advantage.

- *Good at judging other people's characters:* Because emotional intelligence is comprised mostly of social awareness, reading other people is a necessity. Those with high EQ have mastered this skill, and are able to make snap judgments about other people that are typically quite accurate.

- *Can manage toxic situations:* Because people with high EQs are able to control their own emotions and reactions, they are not fazed by the antics of toxic people. They are able to remain rational, which allows them to look at the situation empathetically to look for some sort of compromise that allows for the toxic situation to be deescalated.

- *Understand that perfection is unattainable:* People with high EQs know that perfection is impossible and do not seek it out. They understand that they will fail sometimes, and understand that they will have negative emotions related to failing. They do not feel as though failure has to be avoided at all costs because they recognize that everyone fails sometimes.

- *Take personal time:* People with high EQ are masters at managing their own emotions and stress levels. They frequently take personal time to allow them to do so.
- *Has power over negative thoughts:* While everyone is bound to feel negatively and have negative thoughts sometimes, those with high EQ are able to shut that negative narrative down. They look at the situation rationally, disconnecting their thoughts from their feelings through mindfulness in order to keep from spiraling into a cycle of negativity.
- *Can communicate and resolve conflicts skillfully and tactfully:* Those with high EQ are capable of looking at other people's perspectives, even in arguments, and use that skill to resolve conflicts without allowing resentment to fester in relationships. Their communication skills are much more tactful than those with lower EQ, designed to keep the other person's perspective in mind while still conveying the message.
- *Resilient:* Those with high EQ are capable of rolling with the punches. Even in times of stress, they are able to react in emotionally intelligent ways. Someone who is afraid may be able to overcome their fear to protect their family or to save the life of somebody in danger because, even when emotions are running high, they are able to think about things rationally and separate their rational thoughts from the emotions that they are feeling.

Remember, most people do not fall solely into one category or the other. It is entirely possible to see a mixture of these traits or behaviors, though they tend to trend one way or the other. Someone with generally high emotional intelligence may have some of the low EQ traits and vice versa. People with average EQ are typically somewhere between the two extremes listed above. They may be generally decent at communicating and solving conflicts but may become a victim of their emotions, which could make it difficult to see clearly or rationally. Someone could be great at reading and meeting other people's needs but struggles to meet their own, instead choosing to sacrifice himself to meet the needs of other people. Someone incredibly emotionally intelligent may be great at communication and empathy but never responds emotionally to movies.

When trying to decide where on the spectrum someone falls, remember that almost everyone will have some low and high EQ traits. Very few people fall solely into the high EQ categories, and if they do, it is because of years of effort to strengthen their skills.

Now that you have made it through this chapter, try to identify where you think you might fall on the spectrum. Which of the high and low EQ traits do you notice that you exhibit? Do you think that your EQ is generally high, low, or average? Try to do this before moving on to the next section. The next chapter will be an assessment of your EQ, and it can be quite telling to predict where you may fall and see where you actually do. It can help you identify disconnects in your thoughts and behaviors and help you identify how accurate your self-awareness actually is.

## CHAPTER 16

# Emotional Intelligence Self-Assessment

With your predictions for how you believe your own emotional intelligence levels will look, it is time to prepare to take the Emotional Intelligence Self-Assessment. You have learned all about emotional intelligence at this point and are ready to see where your own EQ stands so you can begin to work on strengthening it. You probably have a pretty good idea of your own strengths and weaknesses within the concept of emotional intelligence, but it is always helpful to see those strengths and weaknesses quantified in some sort of way to remove the abstractness from the concepts.

### Instructions for this Assessment

Set aside some time where you can sit down uninterrupted for at least 20 minutes. You want to go somewhere relatively quiet and free of distractions. Turn off or mute any cell phones and make sure you are somewhere without television or music playing in order to actually focus on the questions given to you. Gather up a piece of paper or a word document on your computer and label it with numbers 1-10 for each category.

You will record your answer to each question as the number of the answer for future scoring. For example, if you choose answer 3. Sometimes as the answer to that particular question, you would record 3 on your scoresheet for future reference.

Remember, each question should be given proper consideration, and you should answer each question as honestly as possible. In order to ensure the most accuracy, you must consider each question and choose the answer that best suits you. You have a choice of 5 answers per question, and you should be able to identify one of them that works for you.

When you are answering questions, make sure you pay close attention to the order and scale of the answers. Sometimes, they ask for your agreement or disagreement, while other times, they ask how frequently you do something.

They sometimes flip with answer 1 being always some of the time while answer 1 can be never other times. You must answer the questions according to the scale provided in each individual question in order to ensure your results are accurate.

Now, without further ado, it is time to begin your assessment!

**Self-Awareness**

- I frequently feel nervous or anxious about situations I am in, and I am frequently unsure why I am feeling the way I do.

  1. Always
  2. Often
  3. Sometimes
  4. Rarely
  5. Never

- I typically try to avoid negative or troubling topics because they make me feel bad.

  1. Always
  2. Often
  3. Sometimes
  4. Rarely
  5. Never

- My negative thoughts typically spiral out of control, and I struggle to reign them in. As soon as they start, they seem to have a mind of their own.

  1. Always
  2. Often
  3. Sometimes
  4. Rarely
  5. Never

- I am very stubborn or hard-headed and have a difficult time admitting to being wrong or taking fault.

1. Always
2. Often
3. Sometimes
4. Rarely
5. Never

- I am able to motivate myself to complete difficult or unpleasant tasks, even if I do not want to do them.

1. Never
2. Rarely
3. Sometimes
4. Often
5. Always

- I can be civil and polite to someone that I dislike if there is a situation that requires me to do so, such as at a business meeting or during a family event.

1. Never
2. Rarely
3. Sometimes
4. Often
5. Always

- I frequently hide my true emotions or feelings from others because ultimately, emotions are unimportant when trying to act in a rational manner.

1. Always
2. Often
3. Sometimes
4. Rarely
5. Never

• I am comfortable handling unexpected roadblocks that I encounter in life, such as a minor car accident, or being laid off from a job.

  1. Never
  2. Rarely
  3. Sometimes
  4. Often
  5. Always

• I am able to point out the good things in life that balance out the negative, even in bleak situations or times that are dark.

  1. Never
  2. Rarely
  3. Sometimes
  4. Often
  5. Always

• I am able to identify my emotions and accurately label and convey those feelings with words in ways that other people can easily understand (for example, telling someone that you feel anxious and agitated instead of saying that you feel bad).

  1. Never
  2. Rarely
  3. Sometimes
  4. Often
  5. Always

## Self-Management

- I make sure I adjust my behavior to reflect who I am interacting with (for example, speaking professionally and politely with my coworkers while speaking much more casually and joking around with my friends).

  1. Never
  2. Rarely
  3. Sometimes
  4. Often
  5. Always

- If I can tell that someone I am interacting with is feeling uncomfortable or intimated by me, I attempt to change my own behavior in order to make him/her feel more relaxed (for example, making a few jokes, lightening the tone, or adjusting body language).

  1. Never
  2. Rarely
  3. Sometimes
  4. Often
  5. Always

- When I am feeling anxious or afraid, I am able to calm myself down and regulate my feelings rather than falling victim to negative thoughts.

  1. Never
  2. Rarely
  3. Sometimes
  4. Often
  5. Always

• I struggle to make decisions in periods of emotional turmoil and freeze up in emergencies or other tense situations.

1. Always
2. Often
3. Sometimes
4. Rarely
5. Never

• I know exactly what role I can play on a team and how my own strengths can be valuable assets, and I can convey that message clearly and efficiently.

1. Never
2. Rarely
3. Sometimes
4. Often
5. Always

• I am always looking for ways to improve myself and strengthen my skills. Self-improvement is never finished, and there are always different ways to improve, even when you may not feel like it.

1. Disagree completely
2. Disagree somewhat
3. Neither agree nor disagree
4. Agree somewhat
5. Agree completely

• When I notice my emotions that I am feeling, I am able to accurately convey why I am feeling the way that I am, even if the cause of the emotion is somewhat obscure (for example, feeling sad on an anniversary of a bad event, or being reminded of grief because you saw something that reminded you of someone you lost).

1. Never
2. Rarely
3. Sometimes
4. Often
5. Always

• I feel the need to consult other people before making emotional decisions.

1. Always
2. Often
3. Sometimes
4. Rarely
5. Never

• I struggle with expressing myself when things get emotional and tend to shut down as opposed to open up in times of need or in stressful situations.

1. Always
2. Often
3. Sometimes
4. Rarely
5. Never

• When I feel as though I am stressed out, and life is overwhelming, I feel as though I should give up.

1. Agree completely
2. Agree somewhat
3. Neither agree nor disagree
4. Disagree somewhat
5. Disagree completely

**Social Awareness**

- When arguing with someone, I typically seek to compromise in order to end the conflict without either of us feeling as though we are the loser.
  1. Never
  2. Rarely
  3. Somewhat
  4. Often
  5. Always

- I find it difficult to take a look at someone else and understand how they are feeling by body language alone.

  1. Agree completely
  2. Agree somewhat
  3. Neither agree nor disagree
  4. Disagree somewhat
  5. Disagree completely

- Listening to people discuss their opinions that differ from my own is upsetting for me, and I struggle to see why they would think the way they do (For example, on topics surrounding politics or religion).

  1. Agree completely
  2. Agree somewhat
  3. Neither agree nor disagree
  4. Disagree somewhat
  5. Disagree completely

- When discussing something with someone else who seems to have a more basic vocabulary, I often try to adjust my own speech without commenting on the other person's capabilities to match the other person's level for optimal communication. I want the other person to understand me, even if that means simplifying my own speech beyond what I normally would do.

  1. Disagree completely
  2. Disagree somewhat
  3. Neither agree nor disagree
  4. Agree somewhat
  5. Agree completely

- I have no problems upselling someone a product that I know they do not need if it will better suit my own production or earn me a better commission, even though it will cost them money.

  1. Agree completely
  2. Agree somewhat
  3. Neither agree nor disagree
  4. Disagree somewhat
  5. Disagree completely

- I am careful to word things in ways that I know are the least offensive in order to get my point across effectively and tactfully. I care about how other people are feeling and do not want to offend them.

  1. Never
  2. Rarely
  3. Somewhat
  4. Often
  5. Always

• I am adept at handling toxic or high-conflict situations without letting emotions get the best of me. By making it a point to understand the toxic person's position, I am often able to find an answer that does not leave one person walking away entirely dissatisfied.

1. Disagree completely
2. Disagree somewhat
3. Neither agree nor disagree
4. Agree somewhat
5. Agree completely

• I am frequently the voice of reason within my group of friends, and they frequently come to me during emotional periods for support.

1. Never
2. Rarely
3. Somewhat
4. Often
5. Always

• Seeing other people unhappy or hurt genuinely upsets me and motivates me to try to help them in any way that I can.

1. Disagree completely
2. Disagree somewhat
3. Neither agree nor disagree
4. Agree somewhat
5. Agree completely

- I always consider how my own behaviors influence those around me when deciding the best course of action.

  1. Disagree completely
  2. Disagree somewhat
  3. Neither agree nor disagree
  4. Agree somewhat
  5. Agree completely

## Relationship Management

- I am able to motivate change in other people, both good and bad. People often look to me as inspiration and seek me out for advice on how to proceed in difficult or emotional situations because I have established myself as capable of being able to navigate through those difficult situations without allowing emotions to cloud my judgment.
  1. Disagree completely
  2. Disagree somewhat
  3. Neither agree nor disagree
  4. Agree somewhat
  5. Agree completely

- I can handle emotionally stressful or volatile situations calmly and can function rationally during emergencies, even when feeling intense emotions at the same time.

  1. Disagree completely
  2. Disagree somewhat
  3. Neither agree nor disagree
  4. Agree somewhat
  5. Agree completely

- I naturally fall into leadership roles during group projects at work and school due to my ability to recognize and juggle all of the members' unique needs, strengths, and struggles while balancing them with the need to complete the project.

1. Never
2. Rarely
3. Sometimes
4. Often
5. Always

- I can recognize that sometimes, the best course of action is to change, and I am not afraid to be the person that triggers or initiates the change, especially if those around me are hesitant to do so.

1. Never
2. Rarely
3. Sometimes
4. Often
5. Always

- I can identify the strengths and weaknesses of people around me, as well as the ways that the other people can build upon their strengths and work to strengthening their weaknesses in order to better themselves, and I can tactfully provide the feedback and criticism necessary to inspire the betterment of those around me without offending them.

1. Disagree completely
2. Disagree somewhat
3. Neither agree nor disagree
4. Agree somewhat
5. Agree completely

- People often feel inspired to do what I want them to do and frequently agree to do whatever I ask of them because of the way I go about asking for it. I am generally described as influential and charismatic.

1. Disagree completely
2. Disagree somewhat
3. Neither agree nor disagree
4. Agree somewhat
5. Agree completely

- I am considered trustworthy by most people I meet, and because of that trustworthiness, I am often able to foster a sense of teamwork within other people if I encourage it.

    1. Disagree completely
    2. Disagree somewhat
    3. Neither agree nor disagree
    4. Agree somewhat
    5. Agree completely

- I can listen to a disagreement between two people and carefully consider both positions before explaining each view in a tactful manner that allows the other person to better understand the opposing viewpoint, enabling me to quickly and efficiently solve disagreements between other people and calm the situation.

    1. Disagree completely
    2. Disagree somewhat
    3. Neither agree nor disagree
    4. Agree somewhat
    5. Agree completely

- People often describe me as inspirational and say that my charisma and social skills frequently encourage those working with me to do their best work. My own eagerness to complete the task and create a positive workplace environment triggers others to want to do the same.

1. Disagree completely
2. Disagree somewhat
3. Neither agree nor disagree
4. Agree somewhat
5. Agree completely

- Because I am an excellent judge of character, I can typically iden-tify people's strengths and weaknesses and use that information to create teams of people that work well together and bring out the best in each other.

1. Disagree completely
2. Disagree somewhat
3. Neither agree nor disagree
4. Agree somewhat
5. Agree completely

**Calculating Your Scores**

Congratulations! You have completed the questionnaire. That was the hardest part of this process. From here, your next step is to begin cal-culating your EQ, both in individual quadrants and as a whole.

The simplest way to do this is to add up the answers you got in each quadrant and subtract 10. The answers were designed, so every 1 was worth 0 points while every 5 was worth 4. The EQ score is calculated by taking the number of the answer you chose (let's say x for ease of un-derstanding) and subtracting 1. So the equation on an individual level is x-1= total EQ points per question with x being the number of the an-swer you chose. You can calculate it out by doing that for each individ-ual score and then adding it all up at the end, or you can shortcut by simply subtracting 10 from the entire sum.

This means that your quadrant score is calculated by adding up all of the answers within that quadrant and subtracting 10. When you have your four quadrant scores, you can add them together to get a total EQ score as well to get an idea of how well-rounded you are.

Remember to record both your quadrant and total EQs so you can begin to understand your score. Now that you have your scores recorded, it is time to begin interpreting each individual score!

### Your Results

Remember the table provided for you in the previous chapter that told you what to expect in terms of the scale this test will use? It is time to refer to that again. For ease of access, the table will be repeated here. This is the same table that was shown before with no changes made. It shows you how your score should be interpreted. In any given individual quadrant, a score of less than 24 means that area needs work to bring it up to functional. A score above 35 means that that particular skill is quite developed and you should consider it a strength, with anything between 24 and 35 being effective. It does the job, but is not necessarily strong and has room for improvement.

| Score | Individual Quadrant EQ | Combined EQ |
|---|---|---|
| Area for Enrichment: Needs work | 0-24 | 0-96 |
| Effective Functioning: Proficient, but could be strengthened | 25-34 | 97-136 |
| Enhanced: High EQ | 35-40 | 137-160 |

With this table, identify which ranges your EQ falls into and see the following categories for understanding what this means for you.

### Low EQ (0-24 individual quadrant or 0-96 total points)

With lower EQ, you often struggle with emotions and social situations in general. You are not in control of yourself or your life, and your emotions rule you. This frequently pushes other people away and makes understanding other people's communications with you quite difficult. You are easily offended and easily triggered into negative emotions.

You do not feel very good about yourself, and you may be very aware of how you never seem to quite mesh with people in social settings. You struggle with relationships of all kinds, and no matter how often you may try, you fail to better the relationships. You cannot help the urge to yell during arguments or disagreements, and because you cannot work through your emotions, people tend to avoid you.

You are ultimately likely incredibly unhappy in your life. You are frequently, or sometimes always, frustrated, feeling as though no one is understanding you without realizing that no one is understanding you because you are not communicating effectively. This only exacerbates your negative emotions as you are not only feeling upset or angry, but you are also further angered or upset because no one seems to understand the base feelings and you are unable to communicate them.

If you scored in this category, you have plenty of work to do to get yourself up to par emotionally. Scores in the low EQ range *require* further attention, or they will continue to be a detriment to you.

### Average EQ (25-34 individual quadrant or 97-136 total points)

People with an average EQ are fully functional members of society. If you scored within an average range, you typically get along with others well enough, though there may be some conflicts here and there that can create bumps in your relationships. While you like yourself more than someone with low EQ, you still recognize that you sometimes struggle with your emotions. You are able to control them when they are not particularly strong, but when you begin to get overwhelmed, you may lose that control you have. You may hurt your relationships sometimes, but you are also able to recognize when you do so and work to repair them.

You are willing to take responsibility for your actions if they cause problems in other areas in your life, but it typically happens after you have had the time to cool down and recognize that you said or did something that you wish you may not have. You may struggle to let go of mistakes that you or others make, and you may hold grudges.

While you are able to navigate social relationships well enough, they are frequently bumpy, and you still find yourself struggling from time to time. You wish that you were better at your relationships and that you could change who you are. You wish that you were better at managing your own emotions, especially during times of stress when you *know* that those are the most important times to have control of your emotions. Despite knowing that, you struggle.

If you have scored in this category, you are emotionally intelligent enough to get by and not fail at every social situation you have, but you still feel the struggle of acknowledging and managing both your own and other people's emotions, and that struggle can lead to feelings of unease and unhappiness, while also contributing to feelings of anxiety and stress. You should consider strengthening the quadrants that scored within this range, building upon the skills you already have, in order to feel more secure and established. The better your emotional intelligence, the more secure and successful you will feel, and the more successful your relationships will be.

### High EQ (35-40 individual quadrant or 137-160 total points)

Congratulations! You scored as having high EQ in one or several categories! This means that you are quite emotionally intelligent. You are in tune with your own emotions and understand how they influence yourself and those around you, and you have also developed the ability to control and regulate your emotions, so they do not dictate your actions. You are true to who you are and have a solid idea of your identity, values, and beliefs, and you will act in ways that line up with them.

While you are also aware of your own emotions, you are able to recognize the emotions in other people as well. You are skilled identifying the emotions and needs of those around you and are able to juggle both their and your emotions. You are likely extremely empathetic, enabling you to navigate through complex relationships while also influencing and managing other people's emotions and actions. You are likely a natural leader, charismatic and charming, and people frequently seek you out or choose to follow you.

You are enjoyable to be around in a wide range of emotional contexts, and people want to continue relationships with you. You are good at managing conflicts and defusing tense situations, which makes you effective in leadership roles. You are mature and willing to take jokes flung your way, even if they are deprecating.

You are likely flexible and go with the flow. It takes a lot to shake you or break your confidence, and most of the time, you are able to work with even the most difficult of unforeseen circumstances.

If you have scored highly in any of your emotional intelligence quadrants, you should use the skills you have in order to strengthen weaker quadrants in order to bring your total EQ up to this category. If all of your scores fall within this category, there is still work you can do to further develop and maintain your skills! Do not feel as though just entering this category is enough to warrant giving up on developing your skills. Seek to identify your weakest quadrant and start trying to bring it up to the same level as the highest.

### What Now?

With your understanding of your scores, you are ready to move on to the next step: Strengthening your EQ! You now know what your strengths and weaknesses are, and with that in mind, you can focus on the relevant sections in the next part of this book. Part III will provide 50 practical tips for each realm of emotional intelligence to help you begin to better your own EQ.

Remember, no one is ever done working on their EQ. Even if you score highly, you can still learn from the tips provided in the next section of the book. Practical advice can teach you new ways you may not have considered before to practice and maintain your EQ. Even those with high EQ levels will begin to lose those skills if they do not maintain them, and even those with high EQ levels are not perfect. Everyone has weaknesses that they should strive to reinforce to better themselves.

## CHAPTER 17

# 50 Practical Tips to Improve Self-Awareness

1. **Take time to reflect on emotions:** Every day, you should sit down and reflect on how you felt during the day. Think about how you responded to various situations, and name the emotion that was felt during that response, with particular focus on negative emotions. For example, if you feel as though your spouse is holding you to unfair expectations, how do you respond? How do you respond when a friend confronts you on something that you did that hurt his feelings? You need to be able to identify how you react in the moment to eventually begin to build up self-management.

2. **Keep an emotions journal:** Every day, write down the strongest emotions you felt throughout the day and reflect upon them. What made you feel that way? What was happening when you felt the way you did? Do you see any patterns?

3. **Be observant about your own current emotions:** Always be aware of how you are feeling in the moment. If you are stressed, acknowledge that. If you are sad, acknowledge that as well. You need to get in the habit of checking in with yourself to see how

you are feeling if you hope to recognize your emotions in a meaningful way.

4. **Ask others about how you act:** Sometimes, getting feedback from other people is crucial to understanding how you are portraying yourself. This can offer you valuable feedback about whether you are communicating your own emotions and needs effectively, or whether you need to continue working on conveying how you are feeling in the moment.

5. **Practice pausing before reacting:** It is easy to react in the moment when emotions run high. You need to get in the habit of pausing, taking a deep breath, and deciding on what you will say or do next. By giving yourself that moment, you can identify when something you wanted to say would not be conducive to bettering the situation.

6. **Ask yourself why you feel the way you do in the moment:** A large part of self-awareness involves understanding your feelings, including why you are feeling the way you are. You must be able to stop and analyze your feelings, including identifying why you feel the way you do if you hope to be in control of your emotions when you move on to self-management.

7. **Ask yourself what you can learn from criticism:** Criticism can be tough to hear if you already have low self-esteem. If you are not very emotionally intelligent, you may struggle regulating your disappointment when someone voices their criticism of you, but asking yourself whether that criticism could be beneficial to you allows you to make that criticism constructive instead of destructive.

8. **Ask yourself what you can learn from failure:** Like criticism, understanding what you can learn from failure to avoid repeating it in the future is important. If you learn from your mistakes, you will grow, whereas if you simply avoid trying again, you have stunted yourself.

9. **Practice using more descriptive vocabulary about emotions in general:** When you feel sad, are you despondent? Disappointed?

Ashamed? Fragile? Lonely? Learn to be more specific than sad, happy, angry, or other blanket emotions. This could be the perfect time to open up a thesaurus and widen your vocabulary.

10. **Always name every emotion to yourself as you feel the strong ones:** When you are feeling particularly emotional, make it a point to identify it. Putting a name to the emotion helps you understand what you are feeling, and also may help you regain control of the situation.

11. **Vocalize your emotions when talking to people you are close with and pay attention to how your voice changes based on your feelings:** People's voices change based on their emotions. You can hear the emotional crack in someone full of despair, or the harshness of the tongue when enraged. Listen to how your own voice changes when you are feeling a range of emotions.

12. **Practice pushing yourself out of your comfort zone:** No one likes being uncomfortable, but sometimes, you need to push yourself to get it over with. Just as sometimes, it is better to rip off the bandage, it can be better to force yourself into uncomfortable situations so you can learn to manage them. Be realistic with this step and slowly work yourself into uncomfortable situations as opposed to throwing yourself deep into your emotional triggers.

13. **Identify your emotional triggers:** Speaking of emotional triggers, learn to identify yours. You need to understand the things that are most likely to set you off so you can be prepared when you notice one of your triggers nearby and begin to rein in your reactions.

14. **Do not discourage or judge your feelings as they occur:** Good or bad, and you should allow you to feel your entire range of emotions. Just because you acknowledge them and feel them does not mean that you are a slave to them.

15. **Avoid making important decisions when in a bad mood:** Making decisions in a bad mood can lead to impulsive choices that you regret later. Reserve decision making for when you are calm.

16. **Avoid making important decisions in a good mood:** Similar to making choices when in a bad mood, making them in a good mood can also sway you to take risks you would otherwise be uncomfortable with.

17. **Check in with yourself during stressful situations and identify your emotions in that moment:** Especially when you notice that you are stressed out, you should check in with yourself. Identify how you feel in the moment and use that feedback to adjust your behaviors accordingly.

18. **Attempt to identify emotions of characters in the media:** Since a big part of being emotionally intelligent involves identifying emotions, try to practice identifying the emotions of other people as well. This is beginning to bridge your self-awareness skills to social awareness.

19. **Practice identifying expressions either online or with a trusted friend:** Make expressions related to various feelings and see if your friend can identify yours. This can give you an idea of whether you are communicating your emotions clearly or not.

20. **Pay attention to what happens in your body during emotional events:** When you are feeling high levels of emotion, pay attention to how your body feels and the body language you exhibit. If you are happy, are you smiling with a relaxed body? If angry, are you tense with your fists clenched or your arms crossed?

21. **Recognize that negative emotions are important and useful:** Negative emotions should not be avoided. They need to be embraced and understood if you hope to be an emotionally intelligent individual. You must be able to read a wide range of emotions, including the negative ones. They serve their purposes just as much as the positive emotions and deserve that recognition.

22. **Look for patterns in your emotional reactions:** Similar to the act of identifying triggers, and you should also identify patterns in all forms of emotional reactions. Identify what makes you a certain way by making a mental or physical note of what preceded

the emotional reaction. Eventually, you may begin seeing patterns in which feeling supported leads to you being happy and relaxed, or being busy tends to flare up your stress and anger responses.

23. **Practice mindfulness:** Mindfulness is the act of separating your actions from your emotions and allowing the emotions to occur while you observe them. Take a back seat and let your emotions free while you attempt to analyze them from a detached perspective. This may provide valuable insight to what is causing your reactions.

24. **Stop treating your emotions as good or bad and start acknowledging them for what they are:** Emotions all serve important purposes, and assigning them a normative value devalues them. You need to recognize that you are feeling your emotion for a reason, regardless of whether it is good or bad. You should not seek to avoid negative emotions, but rather to understand and utilize the negative emotions felt to respond appropriately to the situation.

25. **Become comfortable in your discomfort:** You need to learn to not shy away from your discomfort. As much as you may want to avoid it, learning to acknowledge and accept your discomfort is a surefire way to being able to control your own emotions. You must be okay with being in discomfort if you hope to be able to strengthen your self-motivation later on in the process of strengthening your emotional intelligence.

26. **Identify your values:** Understanding what you value is the first step in understanding what is motivating your behaviors. Take the time to acknowledge and identify the things you value most. This could be family, relationships, money, success, fame, reputation, or anything else.

27. **Identify how your values influence your behaviors:** Once you understand what your values are, take the time to notice how those values affect your behaviors. Do you act in ways that are conducive to your values? If not, how can you fix your behaviors to ensure that your values and behaviors line up? You will be

much happier without that sort of cognitive dissonance in your life.

28. **Create life visions based around your values and decide where you would like to be in the next five years:** With your understanding of your behaviors and your values, identify where you would like to be in five years. This should line up with your values, so if what you value beyond everything else is family, it may be related to your own marital and parental status. If you value success, you may decide that you want to achieve a promotion or two during that period.

29. **Learn your stress cues:** What do you do when you are stressed? Do you withdraw or become aggressive and agitated? How do you respond physically to stress? Does it make you nauseous or leave you itching for a fight? Do you lash out or shut down?

30. **Observe how your emotions seem to spread through your entire body and the effects they have:** Emotions are contagious, and while they may start in the mind, they quickly impact the rest of your body as well. Happiness may leave you relaxed and refreshed while anger leaves you feeling physically stressed.

31. **Constantly pay close attention to your own reactions and emotional states, even when they are primarily positive:** You need to learn to identify your emotions, both positive and negative and identify how they make your body feel. Pay attention to your breathing, heart rate, and body language and begin to label the physical reactions with the emotions felt.

32. **Create a regret letter:** Addressing this to yourself at a younger age, write down what you regret doing so far. Apologize to yourself for making the mistakes you feel are particularly pressing, such as skipping out on an opportunity to attend a school you really wanted to for a lackluster reason. This acknowledges your own failures without making excuses for them. You are able to practice addressing your own shortcomings to yourself, which is a low-risk situation.

33. **The funeral test:** In this activity, you should sit down and write your own eulogy. You should answer questions about yourself, such as how you would like to be spoken of at your funeral, what you want to be remembered for, and how people will think of you when you are gone, compared to how you think people would currently answer. This allows you to see, more or less, where you are now compared to where you want to be and allows you to further understand where you may need to make changes in life to make up for past mistakes.

34. **Write your most important tasks down daily:** Start each day asking yourself what you must accomplish during the day to reach your long-term goals. If your long-term goal is to strengthen your ability to read your own emotions, perhaps you write down three activities you will do for the day to reach that goal. This helps you identify your values and goals while giving you a clear-cut list that will guide your behaviors, even when your emotions may be trying to lead you astray.

35. **Practice apologizing:** No matter how painful you may find it, make it a point to apologize for any mistakes you have made, or if someone comes up to tell you that you did something to hurt them. Make your apologies meaningful as well: Identify what you did in the apology and promise to try to avoid doing it in the future. Even if you may not have felt like it was a big deal, you need to recognize how your own emotions or behaviors influenced other people.

36. **Practice grounding techniques when feeling stressed or overwhelmed:** Grounding techniques can help you stop and identify how you are feeling in that moment. It brings back your awareness of your current state and allows you to act wisely.

37. **Question assumptions:** If you find yourself reacting to assumptions you have made about other people or their behavior, ask yourself why you made the assumption in the first place and analyze its validity.

38. **Trust your intuition:** We make snap judgments for a reason. Trusting your intuition is different from responding emotionally. Trust your intuitive judgments without allowing your emotions to rule the situation.

39. **Listen to your inner monologue:** When learning to track your emotions, allow your inner monologue to go uninterrupted while paying special attention to your train of thought. It can provide valuable information about why you feel the way you do.

40. **Tell yourself 'no':** Teaching yourself to refuse some instant gratification can teach you to control your impulses. Make it a point to tell yourself no to at least five different small temptations a day, whether they are a beer; time wasted watching cat videos or other junk food.

41. **Hold yourself accountable:** Acknowledge when you make mistakes and make it a point to tell yourself what you can do differently next time to avoid repeating them.

42. **Stop the excuses:** If you have made a mistake, do not make any excuses. Similar to holding yourself accountable, you should make it a point to own your mistakes and do not try to minimize or downplay them in any way, no matter how badly you think it will reflect on you.

43. **Stop gut reactions:** When lacking self-awareness, you run on auto-pilot and allow emotions to rule, responding with gut reactions. You need to stop those gut reactions in the act, or preferably before they happen.

44. **Avoid negative self-talk:** Do not talk down to yourself. This can lead to stress and anxiety and should be avoided. There is enough negativity in the world without you adding more toward yourself.

45. **Learn about body language and use it to fix your own:** Use biology to your benefit and take poses that naturally encourage hormones and confidence, such as standing straight up. Learn to mimic people that can communicate charismatically and effectively, such as hand gestures.

46. **Understand your personality type:** Take a personality test and identify whether you are an introvert or extrovert. It will explain an awful lot about your behavior if you understand what kind of person you are.

47. **Meditation:** Practicing meditation teaches you to get better at relaxing your body and focusing on your breathing. You will also learn how to keep your mind on track when it begins to wander.

48. **Identify strengths and weaknesses:** Consider what your greatest strengths and weaknesses are. Understanding these will make you more self-aware and allow you to utilize them where they can be beneficial.

49. **Acknowledge you are not perfect:** By accepting and acknowledging that you are not perfect, you alleviate the fear of failing. Failure is inherently human, and when you acknowledge that, failing becomes infinitely less frightening.

50. **Monitor progress:** Track where you are before you start trying to strengthen your self-awareness. Look at your EQ score and compare it to where you are a month or even a year from starting. See how it has changed.

## CHAPTER 18

# 50 Practical Tips to Improve Self-Management

1. **Breathing practice:** In moments of stress or high emotions, remember to regulate your own breathing. Be aware of how your breathing changes when you are stressed or angry and make it a point to regulate your breathing to control your mood. After a few deep breaths, you may find yourself feeling calmer and more in control of the situation.

2. **Weighing emotion vs. rationality:** Consider the pros and cons of responding to a high-risk situation with emotion and rationality. Is it something that requires passion and emotion, such as deciding whether to propose to someone? Or is it a situation that requires logic, such as deciding how much house you can afford with your current income? By being able to step back and weigh the benefits of responding emotionally and rationally, you will begin to see a clearer picture of the situation at hand.

3. **Make goals known to those around you:** By making your goals publically known, you force yourself to be accountable for those goals. People will have expectations that you will meet them, and may even help you in the process of achieving your goals, which also asking as deadlines loom closer. What better way to kick

yourself in gear than to make your goal known to others, especially when it is a goal that directly affects them?

4. **Take a moment to count to 10 before responding:** When you are feeling emotional in a situation, take a few seconds to take in a deep breath and count to ten in your head. This allows the moment of emotion to pass and keeps you from reacting with negative emotions. You can instead respond with something that will benefit everyone.

5. **Take a night before you decide on important choices:** It can be easy to want to respond with emotion when facing a big decision. Rather than making those decisions based on emotional gut reactions, give yourself a night to mull over the decision and allow the most intense emotions to pass.

6. **Talk to people who are skilled at self-management:** Get advice from people around you that are good at managing their own emotions. Those people may be able to provide you with their own tips and tricks to managing their emotions!

7. **Take the time to smile more:** Our bodies often respond with emotion to physical stimuli, and if you smile, you can improve your emotional outlook. Make it a point to smile and feel your entire emotional state begin to slowly shift to a positive one.

8. **Make time daily for problem-solving:** Schedule in a time that allows you to address the day's problems tactfully. This way, if you run into a complication during the day, you know there will be time to address it later if it can wait, and it becomes less stressful.

9. **Control your inner monologue:** It is hard to be outwardly positive and in control of your negative emotions when they are running rampant in your mind. Make sure that you control your thoughts and keep them away from negativity. Use the skills developed in self-awareness, such as meditation, to keep your mind on track.

10. **Drown out negative thoughts with positive ones to keep yourself motivated:** Challenge yourself to come up with two

positive thoughts every time you have a negative one. This drowns out the negativity and allows you to see positives that you may not have considered otherwise.

11. **Visualize what success looks like for you:** Create a picture in your mind that you are working toward. Decide exactly what you want it to look. This is what you will seek to create with yourself and provides motivation. You know what success looks like and will be able to clearly identify your goal.

12. **Plan the steps necessary to achieve that success and act toward them:** Begin to plan out the steps that you will need to take to achieve your goal. If you want to be a more reliable friend, make it a point to plan out what a reliable friend will look like and what steps you need to take to make that happen, such as always following through with what you promise.

13. **Engage in self-care:** Make sure you maintain yourself. Take the time to exercise, eat healthily, and do something for yourself to alleviate stress levels. When your stress levels are lower, it is generally easier to control your negative reactions.

14. **Focus on your skills and abilities rather than on what you cannot do:** If you focus on the negative, your entire mindset will remain negative. Rather than dwelling on what you cannot do in a situation, instead focus your attention on what you can do instead.

15. **Make it a point to take away something valuable from every encounter:** There is something valuable to learn within every single encounter, whether it is how your own body language or tone affected another person or how you responded in a certain situation. Make it a point to find something valuable in encounters, especially if you feel as though the encounter was pointless.

16. **Schedule in time for yourself to relax:** You need to keep your stress at a manageable level if you hope to be effective at managing your emotions.

17. **Recognize that you can strengthen these skills, and your current abilities are not your permanent limitations:** Your self-

management skills are not inherent or fixed. Remind yourself that you can influence them, for better or for worse.

18. **Make a plan for handling your negative emotions when they occur:** If you struggle to react well in certain situations, try to make yourself contingency plans that will help you mitigate negative behaviors or thoughts. By having a plan, you will have something to fall back on if the stress is too much.

19. **Work on rewarding patience and discouraging instant gratification:** You want to avoid being impulsive or making decisions solely based on emotion. Try to reward yourself when you were patient and rational about a situation.

20. **Make it a point to control your emotions using body language:** Use your body language to influence your emotions. If you are keeping your body in a relaxed pose, your mind is more likely to follow through than if you are actively preparing for a fight.

21. **Show people around you that you are listening and attentive with positive body language:** Practice using your body language to convey that you are attentive to other people. You can communicate an awful lot just through facial expression.

22. **Make plans to manage your stress levels:** When stress begins to get to be overwhelming, create plans to bring it back to a manageable level. Perhaps you could break down whatever task you are working on into smaller steps, or take a break from the work altogether if that is an option.

23. **Create a good work-life balance that is tolerable:** You need an appropriate amount of time to yourself to enjoy with your friends and family, and if you want to keep your stress levels down, you will find a balance between the work you have to do and being there for your loved ones.

24. **Eliminate toxicity and negativity wherever appropriate:** Just because you can deal with the toxicity and negativity does not mean that it is not draining. Remove things that bring you noth-

ing but negativity. Without the constant negativity, you may be blown away by how much easier it is to manage your emotions.

25. **Imagine a wide variety of different circumstances and predict how you will react within each:** This is similar to planning out how you will handle negative emotions, but with a twist. You are to play out how the variety of scenarios will go and predict your own reactions and results, as well as how changing your reactions may impact the results. This is more of a thought experiment than planning out your actions.

26. **Break your routine to get yourself out of an emotional funk:** If you feel as though you are stuck in an emotional rut, you can kick yourself out of it by changing your routine. By doing something new and unpredictable, your body does not have a natural, habitual response, and you will be able to do a sort of emotional reset.

27. **Create a schedule that you adhere to** While this may seem counterintuitive after the previous suggestion, remember that schedules keep things manageable. If you are juggling a lot, setting a schedule with strict times at which you rest, work, problem solve, take time to yourself, and fit in anything else you need to, you will be able to better manage your needs. Having needs met means your emotions are easier to control.

28. **Remind yourself that you are in control of your actions:** No one makes you do anything. Only you can choose to do what you are doing. Keep this in mind the next time you are slipping into negative actions.

29. **Remind yourself that emotions are fleeting:** Remind yourself that your emotion is temporary and fickle. They are impacted by everything, and just because you feel one way at that moment does not mean it is appropriate to act upon it.

30. **Remind yourself that emotions are nothing more than your brain trying to process data:** By reminding yourself that emotions are simply data and not actions or orders, you remove the

control over yourself from them. You recognize that the emotions are only as powerful as you let them be.

31. **Treat others fairly and with respect:** Remember to treat those around you kindly and fairly. You should treat them the way you would like to be treated. Yes, the kindergarten golden rule still applies in adulthood, even for people you dislike.

32. **Always keep your word in order to develop trust with other people:** In order to establish yourself as trustworthy, make it a point to always follow through with what you say you will do. Not only is this an excellent exercise in self-control, it also sets the stage for social awareness and relationship management.

33. **Always look for learning experiences, even in mistakes or mishaps:** Even if you mess something up, seek to learn from the mistake. Understand what you did wrong and learn from that to ensure you do not repeat it in the future. Sometimes, the best way to learn is to fail and face the consequences.

34. **Challenge yourself regularly:** Do not allow yourself to fall into complacency and comfort. You should always be seeking to better yourself and hone your social skills, especially if you want to have good leadership or relationship skills.

35. **Always ask yourself how the other people feel in various situations:** Practicing empathy in real time can be particularly useful in helping you manage your own behaviors. If you can see that your behaviors are hurting other people, you are more likely to rein in those behaviors in order to avoid inflicting that pain.

36. **Encourage adaptability or flexibility through spontaneity:** While routine is important, you do not want to become too rigid. Sometimes, spontaneity is the perfect way to practice your flexibility skills. You can challenge a friend to come up with an entire day's worth of activities with no input from you to see how you respond to the surprises and lack of a plan.

37. **Continue to work with self-awareness techniques:** Do not forget your prior skills that you practiced in self-awareness just because you have begun focusing on self-management. Remember

to continue practicing labeling your own emotions in real time, while also applying them with empathy and seeing how other people are responding to your emotions.

38. **Recognize the separation between yourself and your emotions:** Remember, just because you feel emotions does not mean that you *are* your emotions. You can feel angry, sad, or even foolish or weak, without defining yourself. Do not allow your emotions to define you. Instead see them for what they are: Your current emotional state and nothing more.

39. **Pick your battles:** Even when something is bothering you, only push the point or challenge it if you feel like it is worthwhile. Sometimes, it is not worth the trouble to correct something or be bothered by something someone said. Only pick battles that you feel strongly about.

40. **Let the little things go:** Along with picking your battles carefully, know when it is okay to let things go. Sometimes, you have to agree to disagree and walk away from an argument for everyone's sake, and that is okay. Knowing when it is that time is a fantastic example of self-management skills.

41. **Choose how you want to respond to a situation and stick to it:** Is this a situation in which you want to be defensive? Offensive to protect your beliefs? Should you be doubtful of your actions? Or is this a situation in which you need empathy or self-awareness? Choose which of the responses you need and try to stick to it.

42. **Ask for feedback from others around you:** After handling an emotionally volatile situation, try asking someone who was nearby, but not involved in the situation actively, how they felt it was handled, particularly in regards to your own feelings. Make sure that you are open to hearing the potential criticism that you will receive in return.

43. **Ask yourself how you would feel toward someone else behaving the way you are:** Take a moment to reverse the roles in your mind. How would you feel if the other person were treating you

the way you are treating them? If you feel as though you would be comfortable with it, then you are probably handling the situation well, whereas if you would be bothered, you may want to correct some of your behaviors.

44. **Practice communicating clearly in ways that are not offensive and are tactful:** Even when you may feel tempted to say something that you know is rude, and even if you feel as though that rudeness might be justified, try to find better ways to convey your point that are not offensive. This shows self-restraint, which is important when you are trying to manage your emotions.

45. **Celebrate your successes:** While you have learned that you should make sure you treat failures and mistakes as learning experiences, you should also recognize successes as worthy of celebration.

46. **Listen to what others are saying and do not interrupt:** Especially in situations in which someone else is complaining to you, make it a point not to interrupt. Even if you feel as though the problem is that person's fault in the first place if accusing them of failing is going to worsen the situation, simply provide an attentive ear. Pay attention to the other person's cues before providing your own feedback, and if you will be calling them out, make sure it is done in a tactful manner.

47. **Remember that positive attracts positive:** Just as ruminating on negative thoughts can continue to spiral your mood down, your own positive thoughts can become infectious as well. If you are generally behaving positively, you own emotions will better the moods of yourself and those around you.

48. **Choose productive actions:** If you choose to behave productively, you will find yourself feeling positively in general. It may be easy to slip into old habits or to choose gratification over productivity, but remember, you will be happier and less stressed if you ensure that your work is done before your time that you use for yourself.

49. **Seek advice from someone who is not currently emotionally invested in your situation:** This allows you to see someone else's perspective on a problem that you may have tried to solve but found that your methods were not very effective. You also may get feedback you never considered, such as one of your actions coming across as inflammatory.

50. **Remember that this is a process:** Recognize that there is never an end to learning how to self-manage. No matter how good you are at it, you are never going to be perfect. There will always be room to improve.

## CHAPTER 19

# 50 Practical Tips to Improve Social Awareness

1. **Make it a point to learn the name of everyone you regularly interact with:** This small step means that you have taken the time to acknowledge other people and you are willing to show them that they are important. This shows them that you acknowledge their existence and recognize them as individuals.

2. **Be mindful of your body language as you go through your day:** By presenting yourself as open and relaxed, people around you will feel more at ease, especially if they have to come up to you to speak or interact for any reason.

3. **Understand the importance of timing when delivering unpleasant news:** Knowing when to mention problems is almost as important as knowing how to break bad news. If you time what you are saying just right, you minimize the risk of upsetting the other person.

4. **Have icebreaker questions planned to break the awkward silence:** Have some sort of conversation topic you can use during those awkward silences that tend to happen at the most inopportune moments. The other person will likely appreciate having the

silence filled, and you may even manage to make a friend with a new person.

5. **Be attentive during meetings or interviews:** Especially during meetings and interviews, you should be focused on the other people in your group. Make sure that you are always showing signs of attentiveness, such as making eye contact and nodding your head.

6. **Always prepare for social gatherings:** When you know, you will be at a social event, make sure you have a few basic conversation topics to fall back on and that you have considered the setting, mood, and type of event. You would not wear a suit to a football game, and likewise, you should not go to a causal birthday party expecting to speak about the most recent problem at work.

7. **Be in the moment with people you interact with:** Really give people you are talking to your undivided attention. Show them that they are valued and important to you when you are speaking to them. This strengthens relationships and also encourages more empathy and understanding.

8. **Identify the feelings of people out and about, even if they are strangers:** Take a day to people walk and identify how people may be feeling based solely on their body language. You can tell a lot based on how someone is behaving and holding themselves, and this is an excellent exercise in practicing being able to read someone else.

9. **Practice how to listen effectively:** Make sure that you are really hearing the other person, rather than pretending to listen while really thinking about other things or doing something else. Giving undivided attention to someone shows respect and acknowledgement.

10. **Understand and accept differences and diversity:** Welcome that some people have different opinions, and that is okay. Even if you and your coworker do not agree, recognize that diversity allows for broader opinions.

11. **Practice empathy:** Make it a point to understand how those around you are feeling. Really feel what they feel, relating to them on a more personal level and use that to strengthen relationships.

12. **Try to see the bigger picture in your interactions:** What is the context of your interaction? Why are you having the conversation that you are? Is this important or conducive to the atmosphere of the group? Consider all of this.

13. **Identify the mood in the social setting:** What is the general mood of the group at this moment? Is it somber? Why? Is it more lighthearted? How are people behaving? These types of questions will help you develop a deeper understanding of those around you.

14. **Observe how your words impact other people and learn from the reactions of others:** This is important to understanding how to communicate. You should be able to tell at a glance how other people are understanding your words. If they seem to be shying away from your words or tone, it may be time to reconsider your methods.

15. **Ask follow-up questions to develop a deeper understanding of what the other person is saying:** When you are listening to another person, make sure you ask questions about what is being said to not only show that you are listening but also to develop a deeper understanding.

16. **Change your tone to match the setting or audience:** Some people require different tones. You should speak to children differently than your coworkers, and people at a party differently than people grieving at a funeral. Knowing how to adjust your behavior based on situation shows that you understand emotional intelligence.

17. **Remind yourself that not everyone has the same experiences or worldview as you:** Just because you have a deeply held belief does not mean that other people share that belief. Other people may have had the opposite experience or may have developed different worldviews that directly contradict yours. Recognize that

they have every right to their opinion in the same way that you do.

18. **Pay attention to small details and quirks of those around you:** If you notice that people have routines that they follow, you will be able to notice when they do not follow that routine, which can cue you to double check that everything is okay.

19. **Especially in workplaces, do not interrupt people:** When you are listening, do not cut other people off to change the subject or argue. Your job is to listen well until it is your turn to talk.

20. **Maintain gentle eye contact while talking with other people:** By maintaining eye contact, you are cuing the other person that you are actively listening, and by making sure that eye contact is gentle and friendly, you are conveying that you are not a threat.

21. **Always apologize when it is warranted, and even if you have unintentionally insulted someone:** Being able to put aside your pride and apologize to someone else shows that you value and respect the other person's opinion and feelings. Even if what you are apologizing was not intended to be hurtful, you are acknowledging the other person's feelings as valid.

22. **Keep your cell phone or computer off or closed during social interactions, barring actual emergencies:** When you are interacting with someone else, make it a point to give them undivided attention. Do not make them compete with your phone or your computer. You should ideally have both put away out of sight when interacting with other people.

23. **Ask guiding questions:** When you are trying to understand a dynamic, situation, or another person's emotional state, especially relating to a conflict, asking guiding questions can get you the information that has not been provided that you need to proceed. By guiding the conversation, you may be able to fix the conflict.

24. **Repeat back what was said to you worded slightly differently to confirm you understand:** Yet another skill related to good listening, by repeating back what you heard, you not only cue that

you listened to the other person, but also that you understood them as well.

25. **Do not take notes during meetings or interviews:** Note-taking is important in college when there are vast amounts of information to absorb, but in meetings, you are expected to contribute. Instead of focusing on taking notes, you should focus on developing a working understanding of the material through interactions.

26. **Help people when they seem stressed or overwhelmed:** Going back to empathy, you should seek to help other people just because they are stressed out. By doing so, you help ensure their needs are met and strengthen your relationship with them.

27. **Take a genuine interest in other people:** Be interested in what the people around you are doing, even if it something you personally do not care for. While you may not enjoy writing, you can still be interested in your coworker working on a novel and cheer for her when it is completed.

28. **Take a genuine interest in the welfare of the people around you and be willing to intervene if you can help:** Related to the prior step, taking an interest in the welfare of others can build rapport with other people. People are more inclined to like you and trust you if you help them.

29. **Do not be afraid to suggest something new in a situation that is not working:** Social awareness involves being aware of how you can influence others, and that sometimes includes triggering change. Suggest a new perspective when you have a situation that is failing. It might be a perspective that has gone unconsidered until the.

30. **Always put the needs of the group ahead of the needs of yourself:** Because social awareness involves empathy and taking care of the group, there is no room for selfishness. You need to put the group ahead of yourself sometimes for the betterment of the entire group, and you need to know when to do that.

31. **Be honest in how you respond when asked, even if the honest response may be unwanted:** When someone asks you for feedback, you need to ensure that you provide it honestly and thoughtfully. Even though sometimes, you may have to share an unpopular opinion, you should be free to share your thoughts.

32. **Communicate with tactful language:** By keeping your language tactful and neutral, you will be able to explain difficult or unwanted topics in a way that minimizes hurt or emotional harm. This is what doctors call bedside manner, and it is helpful in far more situations than just medical settings.

33. **Acknowledge the skills of other people:** Being able to look at other people and recognize their own skills and strengths takes empathy and social awareness. By acknowledging the other person's skills, you may be able to find ways that those skills can benefit everyone.

34. **Provide other people feedback to help them develop who they are:** Being able to see people's weaknesses is also important, as is being able to point out ways that those weaknesses could be patched up to keep them from becoming too detrimental in the future.

35. **Limit or eliminate social media for a week or two:** We often spend far too much time obsessing over our social media, and it comes at a cost of empathy and isolation. By forcing yourself to step back, you will further foster actual human interaction instead of staring at a screen.

36. **Begin networking and meeting new people:** One of the easiest ways of developing social awareness is to go out and meet new people from all sorts of backgrounds. Meet people with new or different worldviews or people who are in different professions. You never know when you might meet someone who can help you in the future.

37. **Avoid voicing complaints:** If you want to bolster your social awareness, you need to avoid voicing too many complaints. Those complaints can bring the general atmosphere of the social interac-

tion down as well as paint yourself as a victim that cannot fix the situation you are complaining about.

38. **Avoid causing drama, or allowing other people to cause you drama:** Along with avoiding complaints, you should seek to avoid drama. People, by and large, do not enjoy dealing with drama, and they will go out of their way to avoid it. Likewise, you should not allow other people the ability to influence you so strongly that they create drama for you.

39. **Try to keep your speech and general demeanor positive:** Positivity is infectious, and if you are able to keep your own speech and demeanor positive, you will see the positivity of the entire social setting increase.

40. **Avoid giving in to peer pressure, especially if whatever others are pressuring you into is something you do not agree with:** When you are in social settings, you may feel pressure to do things that you are not comfortable with. You should not feel as though you have to sacrifice your own values for other people, especially if you disagree with them.

41. **Toe the line between helpful and overly critical:** It is important to be able to provide constructive criticism, but that criticism can quickly become negative and overbearing if you are not careful. You must be mindful to keep your criticism helpful without sugar coating it while making sure that what you are saying is still constructive.

42. **Do not dwell on the past, especially regarding what other people may have done to you:** Being able to recognize that the past is in the past and forgive others for mistakes, especially when those mistakes where truly mistakes and not intentional, you are recognizing the humanity in other people. You are recognizing and accepting that people are not perfect and sometimes make mistakes. This keeps you out of the negative grudge trap.

43. **Join social groups with people who share similar interests as you:** Further extrapolating on the importance of social interaction in order to develop social awareness, try to find groups out-

side of your comfort zone who share similar interests. You may be pleasantly surprised at the new kinds of people you can meet by joining clubs or groups in your area, and your social skills will thank you for it.

44. **Compromise when there are conflicts:** Recognize that there is no way for everyone to walk away from a conflict entirely happy. The best you can do is offer up compromises where each person gets some of what they need. Identifying conflicts and the compromises that can solve the conflict requires higher levels of emotional intelligence.

45. **Find some sort of common ground between yourself and the other person:** When you find yourself interacting with someone who seems entirely foreign to you, seeking out some sort of common ground is the perfect way to relate to each other. This can be anything from a common hobby or taste in music, or even as simple as having a sibling that is the same age. By connecting to someone when you first feel that connection is impossible, you are using your social awareness.

46. **Pay attention to how closely people orient themselves to other people:** Be aware of the physical distances between people. Those who are uncomfortable with one another typically keep a larger physical distance between them than people who are comfortable. This can be an important part of body language.

47. **Volunteer and get involved in your community:** This suggestion sees you getting involved in your community while also helping meet needs that would otherwise go unmet. This is the perfect way to practice your empathy and skills involving understanding diversity.

48. **Observe how people naturally respond to you and respond to those reactions:** You can tailor your own body language and communication skills to situations by watching how other people seem to react to you. This empathy makes you appear to be very emotionally intelligent.

49. **Use mindfulness to look past emotions and get a better understanding of the situations at hand:** When you are in an emotionally charged situation, remembering to step back with mindfulness to reevaluate the situation can help you see where a disconnect may be. Perhaps something you have said is insensitive. Knowing where you went wrong will enable you to correct for it.

50. **Continue to practice self-awareness and self-management to better your social awareness:** Remember, all of your emotional intelligence skills build upon each other. You need to maintain all of them to be a well-rounded individual.

## CHAPTER 20

# 50 Practical Tips to Improve Relationship Management

1. **Be open-minded:** You should be willing to consider anything anyone suggests to you without feeling strong emotions either way toward the suggestion. By being open-minded, people will not feel judged when they come to you with problems, suggestions, or other conversation topics. They will feel as though they can trust you, and that trust will go a long way.

2. **Enhance and deepen your communication:** Find your way of communicating and enhance it to make it as effective as possible. If you know that you like to make compliment sandwiches to deliver criticism, for example, master the art of tactfully explaining parts that need work.

3. **Communicate clearly:** Always be as clear as possible when communicating. Seek to use specific language that is difficult to mix up or misunderstand. Words that lack ambiguity will be your best friend when trying to communicate clearly and effectively.

4. **Ask if others have any questions for you:** Always encourage those you are working with to ask questions after you finish ex-

plaining something. This enables them to mull over the material you have provided while also showing that you value them and their understanding.

5. **Remember to pay attention to details:** Small details in relationships and communication matter! Recognize even the smallest and most insignificant of strengths and weaknesses, as you never know when they will be relevant to your projects.

6. **Be welcoming to feedback:** Always welcome criticism, no matter how harsh, and make sure those you work closely with understand this. When you are provided with feedback, make sure you thank the other person for it and make it clear that you mean it. If you are gracious about receiving feedback, even when it is negative, you are more likely to get honest feedback in the future.

7. **Be trusted:** Do everything you can to establish yourself as a trustworthy individual within your social and workplace groups. By being trustworthy, people are more likely to be swayed by your words because you have never steered them wrong before.

8. **Be the person anyone can talk to about anything:** An open door policy harbors further trust and makes people feel as though they can approach you without fear of judgment.

9. **Don't try to avoid what will happen anyway:** If the inevitable is something you would rather not deal with, it is better to get it over with quickly. This shows your social circles that you are not afraid to approach uncomfortable or undesirable situations quickly and with tact.

10. **Acknowledge the feelings of those within your groups:** This leaves all members of your group feeling validated, which in turn lends itself to creating a group of people more inclined to help you or follow your lead.

11. **Be a complementary person:** Always seek to insert yourself into situations that you know your own skills complement. If you are good at organization while another person is good at research, the two of you have skills that complement each other, and you could be valuable assets to each other.

12. **Be a complimentary person:** Yes, this is different from #11! Compliment people on a job well done. This acknowledgment of their skills and success will make those around you feel recognized and valued.

13. **Show that you care:** Little tokens of appreciation, such as a hand-written thank you note or a birthday card, let those around you know that you value them as individuals and strengthens your relationship with them.

14. **Be decisive:** Do not be afraid to make a decision, especially when others seem to be struggling with the task of doing so.

15. **Explain why you make decisions:** Along with being willing to make the decision, you should have the tact and communication skills to explain to those around you why you made the decision you did.

16. **Be able to provide direct, constructive feedback:** You should be able to quickly and tactfully identify and suggest areas that those around you need to improve, with those suggestions developed after time spent getting to know the individual.

17. **Make sure your intention and impact are in sync:** Saying the wrong thing with the right intentions is just as harmful as saying the wrong thing with the wrong intentions. Make sure that when you are wording something, especially if it is negative or a criticism, that you word it in a way that is constructive and cannot be misconstrued negatively.

18. **When addressing a challenge, offer a solution to it:** The solution should be something that you see as a potential fix to the problem! This points the other person in the right direction.

19. **Be able to handle tough or uncomfortable conversations with tact:** Do not shy away from difficult subjects. People will appreciate you more if you discuss things tactfully and directly.

20. **Set boundaries:** You should develop your own boundaries and enforce them. This lets other people know just how far they can go with certain things before you have a problem.

21. **Respect boundaries other people set:** Complementary to your own boundaries, you should try to recognize the boundaries that other people set and enforce.

22. **Assume people mean the best, even when things don't work out:** Try not to be offended if someone struggles to communicate and bungles the message. Instead, assume they meant the best and move on with life. There's no use to clinging to negativity.

23. **Volunteer for uncomfortable leadership roles:** There is no better way to start practicing your relationship management skills than taking a leadership role. Even if you feel out of your element, give it a shot.

24. **Be willing to question status quo:** Do not be afraid to challenge how things are being done and suggest new ways to try things out.

25. **Offer advice and opportunities to help other people grow:** Whenever you are working with other people, offer ways that they could further enhance their skills, or even suggest that they try something new.

26. **Earn the loyalty of other people through your own actions:** Those with high relationship management quotas win the backing of people through their behaviors. You should make it clear that you are worthy of that loyalty by always seeking to help other people.

27. **Prove yourself trustworthy:** Always follow through with what you say you will do so people around you know they can count on you to help them when they need it.

28. **Be able to identify ways that other people can work together:** Especially if you are a leader in a group, try to pair up people who seem to work well with each other, whose skills balance out the weaknesses of the other person and vice versa.

29. **Learn to to quickly identify and deescalate conflict within groups:** Try to watch for rising tensions so you can deescalate them before they blow up. This will further earn trust as you manage to stop conflicts in their tracks

30. **Give every member of your group a task that allows each to be productive in their own ways:** Being able to identify the different strengths people bring to the table celebrates diversity and develops trust that you are seeing a bigger picture.

31. **Be able to talk someone down from high emotions quickly and efficiently:** Learning this skill means that you have mastered the art of influencing other people's emotions. Other people may feel like you always have the right words for every situation.

32. **Develop the ability to relate to other people easily:** If you can relate to anyone quickly and easily, you are able to better empathize with them quickly, and they will be more inclined to listen to an empathetic person.

33. **Be grateful when someone shows an act of kindness toward you:** You should always show that you appreciate those around you, especially if they show an act of kindness. Send them a note thanking them or tell them in person.

34. **Ask yourself what you can do for the people you believe can help you too:** Before asking yourself what other people can do for you, you should first ask how you can benefit each other. Relationships should be mutually beneficial.

35. **Always ask for what you want:** The worst that can happen is someone says no. By always asking for what you want, you are clearly stating your desires, and those who agree or align their desires with you will be able to do so.

36. **Always try to create win-win situations:** Situations should create the best possible solution for as many people as possible. A situation in which one person is on top while everyone else suffers is not conducive to a team environment and should be avoided.

37. **Find ways to create a team identity:** Your team should be more concerned with a group identity and success than individual success. If you want to have higher relationship management skills, you should foster this through team-building exercises and rewarding them for group successes.

38. **Foster bonds within the team:** Along with a team identity, creating bonds within the teams encourages people to work with each other and genuinely enjoy doing so rather than seeing each other as inconveniences.

39. **Always show up a few minutes early:** To be on time is to be late, and is incredibly disrespectful. Instead, you should always aim to be at least 5 minutes early. This shows that you value the other person's time.

40. **Treat everyone you meet, no matter what they look like or how they act, as incredibly important:** Basic human decency says we all deserve the same basic consideration, and you should remember to acknowledge this.

41. **Under-promise so you can over-deliver:** This is a sort of workaround to managing expectations. If you promise to have something done by Friday to give yourself extra time, you can return the project by Tuesday and win brownie points for having it done three days early.

42. **Work with your peers' strengths and weaknesses:** When working with others, make sure you insert yourself in areas that you believe you will be the most effective and useful at complementing everyone else. This shows them that you are seriously considering their abilities and recognizing them on individual levels.

43. **Accommodate other people whenever you can:** Empathy allows for compassion, and by accommodating others, you are showing that you are empathetic to the struggles of juggling both workplace and outer stressors.

44. **Understand that those you work with have lives outside of the office and that those lives should be the workers' priorities:** This may be one of the most important keys to remember to strengthen relationship management: Ultimately, people's loyalty will default to their families first and foremost, and if you can remember that, you will quickly become a close 2nd in their list of loyalty.

45. **Inspire others to try to succeed, even when the odds are stacked against them:** Be the reason that people try things that they will most likely fail. Encourage them to try and inspire them by trying to achieve the nearly impossible yourself as well.

46. **Seek to persuade other people without manipulation:** Learn how to ask and receive what you want or need without having to rely on manipulation to get it. If you develop a good enough rapport with those around you, this should be a no-brainer.

47. **Create a productive work environment for yourself and others:** You want to make an environment that people are happy to enter. Happy people are more productive and more loyal people who will be more willing to try to help you if you ask for it.

48. **Always opt for personal interaction as opposed to digital when it is realistic and convenient:** To truly strengthen the bond between yourself and those around you, you should aim to make your communication as personal as possible. If you can do it face-to-face, that is preferred to digital or texting.

49. **Lead by being actively involved in the work rather than by dictating what other people do:** The easiest way to inspire others is to be involved yourself. If they see you in the trenches, they see a leader who is not afraid to help them and get dirty, who is far more trustworthy than a leader who would rather sit back and order people around.

50. **Remember to use your self-awareness, self-management, and social awareness skills in all of your interactions!** As mentioned before, remember that all of your other emotional intelligence skills should be used toward strengthening your relationship management! Do not forget to utilize the most important skills within those quadrants.

# CHAPTER 21

# Conclusion

Hopefully, the information contained in these pages has been beneficial to your understanding of how emotional intelligence works, as well as toward your own current EQ. Throughout this part, you were provided with the knowledge you would need to begin taking control of your EQ and becoming a more emotionally intelligent individual, something that could have lifelong positive benefits to you.

As you make your way through your journey to higher emotional intelligence, be sure to remember some of the key features: You must understand how the four domains of emotional intelligence play off of each other and how each domain is important for social interaction. If you want to be a well-rounded individual, capable of empathy and emotional intelligence, you must have a fundamental understanding and control of your own emotions, as well as the empathy necessary to see how your actions and emotions impact other people. Without that fundamental understanding, your empathy will be meaningless, as you will be unable to relate to those around you.

Remember, you are not trapped at your current emotional intelligence level. Your EQ can grow or shrink based on your own personal behaviors, choices, and development. You can become as charismatic as some of the greatest leaders if you care to put in the effort, or you can retreat as much as you would like and avoid interacting with others.

Ultimately, the choice is yours, but research has found that those with higher emotional intelligence levels tend to be happier and healthier.

If you do decide to move forward with bettering your EQ, do not forget the tips provided within these pages! Each tip and challenge requires you to work toward bettering each EQ domain, and if you are able to accomplish all of the challenges and suggestions, you will find your social skills increasing immensely.

Now that you have reached the end of this practical guide, it is time for you to begin! Go out and put your newfound skills to good use in the real world and see where they will take you! Work on strengthening your emotional weaknesses while relying on your strengths that were identified during the assessment. With your newfound knowledge, you are armed with what you will need to begin the process. Good luck, and please feel free to come back to this part as much as is necessary or beneficial to you!

# PART 3

# Emotional Intelligence for Kids

## CHAPTER 22

# Introduction:

Nearly every parent has been there. Walking through the grocery store with your child who has been on perfect behavior, everything seems perfectly fine. You are thrilled with your child's good behavior. Then *it* appears. You know what it is.

*The dreaded candy aisle.*

The child sees the aisle filled with brightly colored candy and asks for a piece, as children tend to do. You tell your child no, that is not a healthy choice, but you are more than happy to allow the child to pick out a piece of fruit or a healthy snack of some sort. You can see it in your child's face; a switch was flipped, and the tantrum is coming.

Suddenly, your child is screaming and flailing in the middle of the candy aisle begging for candy, and you can feel the humiliation burning as brightly as your cheeks. What do you do next?

Some parents may respond with their own emotions, snapping at the child to knock it off, or there will be punishments. Threats to spank, return other food, leave, ground, or otherwise punish the child are voiced, but those only serve to further enrage the child, who may or may not be flailing on the ground and shrieking about you being the worst parent in the world at this point. Emotions continue to rise, and neither side seems willing to listen, and the entire situation escalates.

Other parents prefer to face their children's tantrums with an entirely different tactic altogether. They prefer to teach their children to be emotionally intelligent, and instead, try to solve conflicts with emotion coaching. Through the art of emotion coaching, parents guide their children through five steps: They are aware of their children's emotions, acknowledge emotions as learning opportunities, listen and validate their children's feelings, label emotions, and offer advice on problem-solving. Through these five steps, parents teach children to handle their emotions, good and bad, rather than punishing them for having them. This parent will see the disappointment and frustration in the child and put names to them. Calmly justifying the child's emotions, the emotionally intelligent parent will acknowledge the feelings, saying that he or she can see that the child is very upset and disappointed, as well as relating it to a time that the parent was also disappointed by not getting something desired. The parent would listen as the child confirms that yes, he or she does feel disappointed and upset, and would then offer up a solution to the problem, suggesting that they pick out something healthier but still yummy. Quickly, the tantrum has settled, and the child has learned to identify another feeling and has seen the parent settle the conflict quickly and calmly without letting emotions rule the scenario.

This part teaches you how to approach your children's large feelings from the standpoint of understanding that children cannot inherently control themselves. It recognizes that children, especially younger children, are easily swayed by their emotions and acknowledges that the best way to handle tantrums, anger, frustration, and other negative emotions or behaviors, is to teach children how to think about things in an emotionally intelligent way. This includes being able to identify their own emotions, control their own emotions, and recognize the ways their emotions can impact other people.

Through this part, you will learn the ins and outs of parenting in an emotionally intelligent way and given a step-by-step guide to begin emotion coaching. You will learn the importance of raising a child with a high emotional intelligence quotient (EQ), and you will see just how vastly different your child's behaviors could become if you teach him or her how to act in emotionally intelligent ways. These are lifelong skills that will provide your children with the best chances of success in their futures. Delve into this part now to learn all you need to know about raising emotionally intelligent children.

## CHAPTER 23

# What is Emotional Intelligence?

Emotional intelligence: We all have it. It is the skill with which we manage our emotions. It is our ability to be aware of and clearly express our emotions and the way we handle our interpersonal relationships. Each person's individual emotional intelligence quotient is different from the next, but we all have it to some degree. Emotional intelligence is believed to be one of the key predictors of success, with those having higher levels of emotional intelligence more likely to be successful than those with lower EQs, even if those with the lower EQ have higher IQs. In order to truly understand emotional intelligence, you must begin to understand the foundations that build it.

### Understanding Emotions

Emotions are fleeting and fickle. They come and go, based on everything around you, your thoughts, your current mental state, what you are doing at the moment, who you are with, or even what you have eaten for the day. Everything around you is sorted into one of four categories: happiness, sadness, anger, or fear. Virtually everything around you has some sort of impact on your emotional state. Despite how widely emotions can swing and how easily influenced they are, they serve very important parts in our lives.

### Cause of Emotions

Emotions are our first defense against the world. They provide us with snap-judgments and prepare our bodies for reacting in ways conducive to survival. Several theories attempt to explain the cause of emotions, but they are typically reduced down to emotions being a combination of external stimuli meeting internal thought processes. The three most common theories are the James-Lange theory, the Cannon-Bard theory, and the Schacter-Singer model.

The James-Lange theory says that emotion is how people understand the changes to their body in response to certain stimuli. For example, if someone is confronted by a person with an angry face who charges at them aggressively, their body first goes into fight-or-flight mode. The rush of adrenaline, which triggers a racing pulse, tingling, and hyperawareness of the situation, is interpreted by the mind as fear.

With the Cannon-Bard theory, it is believed that when we sense things around us, the information is sent to two separate parts of the brain. The cortex makes an emotional reaction while the hypothalamus creates the physiological changes associated with that emotion. Following the example previously introduced, the person confronted in anger feels the emotion of fear while simultaneously feeling the physiological effects of the emotion at the same time. Both physical and emotional sensations are concurrent.

Lastly, the Schacter-Singer model recognizes that emotions are the result of a combination of physical responses plus thoughts on whatever stimulus triggered the physical thought. For example, if your experience with someone charging toward you with an angry face is that you will be hit, when you see that person angrily approaching you, your physical reaction of arousal to being approached will pair up with the apprehension or fear at the idea of being hit, which leads to an overarching sensation of fear. The thoughts on the matter skewed the emotion to fear.

**James-Lange Theory**
- Emotion is the person's understanding of changes to the body

**Cannon-Bard Theory**
- Emotional and physical changes occur together and combine to create the sensations we know as emotions

**Schacter-Singer Model**
- Emotion is a combination of physical changes and conscious thoughts about the stimulus

### Reason for Emotions

Emotions are important. Their sole purpose is to process the world into a language the body and mind can understand. They are easily swayed and happen in snap judgments based on what is happening around us. They are instinctual, leading us to behave in ways that are conducive to our own survival. Emotions allow us to communicate with those around us to ensure that we are taken care of and to ensure that we are taking care of those around us. Each particular emotion comes with its own expressions and body language, which other people are able to use as cues to your current mental state.

Because we are a social animal that lives in groups, we need the ability to communicate quickly, efficiently, and wordlessly to allow for seamless cooperation. By knowing at a glance whether your tribe afraid of something, you are able to immediately begin meeting needs without the need for a drawn-out conversation. Likewise, if you see your tribe members looking happy, you are able to relax, knowing that all needs have been met.

**Happiness**
- Needs are currently met; encourages keeping status quo

**Sadness**
- In need of support; conveys that something has ben lost or harmed

**Anger**
- In need of boundaries; conveys a sense of being wronged or betrayed

**Fear**
- In need of safety; conveys that there is an imminent or current threat

Of course, these emotions also bring with them the ability to empathize with others. Empathizing is to understand and feel another's emotions as if you, yourself, were going through them at the moment. For the most efficient communication between people, you must be able to feel how they feel. This motivates you to alleviate the pain and suffering of those you hold dear.

### Understanding Emotional Intelligence

Emotional intelligence is your ability to understand emotions, both your own and those of other people, as well as the ability to sway those emotions. By understanding and being in tune with your own emotions, you are able to practice empathy, which grants you an understanding of other people's emotions. Between knowing your own and the emotions of those around you, you are able to better understand how your own behaviors influence other people. When you understand how your behavior influences other people, you are able to start influencing others' behaviors in ways that are beneficial. You are able to change your own reactions to deescalate situations or to sway people into doing what you would like for them to do.

### Emotional Intelligence Framework

Emotional intelligence is typically divided into four distinct domains or quadrants. When the four quadrants come together, an emotionally intelligent person is created. This provides four distinctive traits that comprise emotional intelligence and provides for distinctive skills that can be strengthened in order to raise EQ. These four skills are:

- *Self-Awareness*
- *Self-Management*
- *Social Awareness*
- *Relationship Management*

These four skills build upon each other, starting with self-awareness.

- **Self-awareness** involves understanding your own emotions at their cores. Those who are strong in self-awareness are self-confident, recognize their own weaknesses, can accurately label and understand their current emotional states, and can recognize how other people or outside stimuli influence their current emotional states. It also creates a foundation for emotional intelligence. If you cannot do the most basic of tasks, understanding your own emotions, you have little hope of being able to manage your own emotions or understand the emotions of others. Self-awareness affects both self-management and social awareness. If your self-awareness is low, there is a good chance that self-management and social awareness skills will also be stunted.
- **Self-management** involves controlling your thoughts, feelings, and behaviors. Those with stronger self-management skills show considerable restraint and are able to feel their emotions without acting upon them. They understand the difference between their feelings and themselves, and because of that, they know that acting on such unpredictable whims would be detrimental to themselves and their relationships. Instead, they override their emotional impulses with rationality. They are frequently flexible and trustworthy and are willing to take the initiative to change things if they think that is in their best interest. People with high levels of self-management are able to use those skills, along with

social awareness in order to develop better levels of social management.

- **Social awareness** involves understanding other people's wants and needs. It involves a great degree of self-awareness along with empathy in order to develop a high social awareness. People with high levels of social awareness can tell at a glance how those around them are doing, especially people they know quite well, and they can recognize how their own behaviors influence other people's emotional states. They typically are quite service-oriented, meaning they put a priority on the emotional needs of other people whenever possible. They are often charismatic and well-liked because of their skills, and people naturally gravitate toward them. High levels of social awareness create a foundation for relationship management.

- **Relationship management** involves being able to influence other people. Those with high relationship management skills are the ultimate leaders. They are charismatic, inspiring, and influential. They are skilled at dissolving conflicts and are frequently the catalysts for change in the world around them. They typically prioritize the needs of the group and can influence those around them to do so as well. These people can recognize how to best assemble teams in ways that bring out the best of everyone and encourage and strengthen bonds between those around them.

**Self-Awareness**
•Ability to understand one's own emotional states

**Self-Management**
•Ability to control one's own emotional states and behaviors related to those states

**Social Awareness**
•Ability to understand and influence the emotional states of others

**Relationship Management**
•Ability to influence and inspire others and effectively lead and mitigate conflict within teams

## Emotional Intelligence Quotient

Ultimately, emotional intelligence is quantified with an emotional intelligence quotient or EQ. Think of this as the IQ of emotional intelligence: It allows for a numerical representation of something that would otherwise be unmeasurable. There are no natural ways to identify or test for EQ the way you can test blood counts or other physical values, so one was developed. Through a series of tests and questions meant to identify and rate the domains of emotional intelligence, the ability to quantify EQ was born. Those who want to see what their EQ is must take a self-reported test, of which there is no shortage. There are plenty of places you can take these tests, both online, and in other books on the subject.

Through scoring the various domains of emotional intelligence, individuals are able to see where their scores fall in relation to other people. They are able to better understand their weaknesses and strengths in social situations, which can prove to be invaluable. Luckily for those who score poorly on these sorts of tests, EQ is something that can be strengthened and raised over time. Through effort and dedication, you can bring your score up by working on your weakest domains in your EQ and using your strongest domains to help bring the weaker ones.

### Why Emotional Intelligence Matters

Now, you may be asking yourself why any of this matters. Who cares what your emotional intelligence score is? Why is it important, and how is it relevant to parenting a child or to be successful? Is it really that relevant to your job? After all, isn't rationality the most important part of navigating through life? Who cares what the emotional states are. Emotions and emotional intelligence are, in fact, incredibly important, both to yourself and to any children you are raising.

Considering emotions play a significant part in everyone's lives, it should come as no surprise that emotional intelligence is also incredibly important. Understanding your own emotions is crucial to controlling them and keeping that delicate balance between emotional and rational that will maximize your chances for success. Those who are emotional are more impulsive and easily swayed. Those who swing the other direction and are too firmly rooted in rationality begin to lose their capacity for empathy or caring what other people want, need, or think. They begin to believe that the ends justify the means, though when it comes to humanity, people should not be seen as simply a means.

Furthermore, people with high EQs tend to be more successful and happier than their lower EQ peers. People around them prefer their tact and grace, whereas those with lower EQ, unable to control their own emotions, are typically not a choice company. Higher EQ people, more able to solve conflicts, control their own emotions, and recognize the emotional needs of those around them, are typically much happier in all kinds of relationships, professional, and personal. People love those who are empathetic and self-aware, and the higher the EQ, typically the more empathetic and self-aware you become.

Workplaces even typically ask questions to determine EQ when interviewing prospective employees. Questions about handling conflicts, defusing tense situations, and strengths and weaknesses are commonplace today at interviews, as it has been found that those with higher EQs are typically better employees. They are more interested in working as teams than those with lower EQs, which leads to better team morale and productivity.

In terms of parenting, ask yourself how you can possibly raise a child to be emotionally intelligent if you, yourself lack the EQ necessary to do so? If you cannot identify and control your own emotions, can you really guide your child to do so? If you lack the empathy needed to recognize when your child is having a hard time and help him or her worth through problems, can you really expect your child to learn to regulate emotional states? If you cannot solve your own conflicts with your child, can you teach your child to solve conflicts or problems on his or her own?

The answer to all of the above is no.

If you, your child's biggest teacher in life, cannot properly manage to live in an emotionally intelligent way, then you cannot realistically expect your children to. Your children look to you to guide them and develop your methods for handling conflict, stress, and their own emotions. In order to be the teacher that your children need to be successful, you must have a great deal of your own EQ. If you need to see this exemplified again, refer back to the introduction in this book. The lower EQ parent struggled to deal with the unruly child, whereas the higher EQ parent was able to quickly and efficiently stop the tantrum while turning it into a learning opportunity for the child.

Children need to have high EQ behaviors modeled around them to develop them. They need to see their parents using problem-solving skills and acknowledging their emotions if they hope to do the same. They will almost always emulate what they see around them, and for that reason, you should seek to develop your own high EQ to better your children's lives and chances of success. Both you and your children will be happier if you do.

## CHAPTER 24

# How is Emotional Intelligence Developed?

With an understanding of what emotional intelligence is, you may be wondering how it is developed over time. It all starts in early childhood. The development of EQ begins with the earliest interactions with your child and continues throughout life, constantly changing as you grow and develop as a person. Ultimately, it can also be strengthened and developed like a muscle, rather than being a fixed value.

### Natural Development of EQ

Throughout your life, your EQ is being impacted. It is developing as you grow and your brain develops, and ultimately, the EQ you develop by the time you finish adolescence becomes the habitual EQ you utilize throughout adulthood, where it is more or less stable unless you make conscious efforts to alter your behavior. In each of the stages of development, the early years, childhood, adolescence, and adulthood, more is modeled and learned.

### The Early Years

Developing EQ begins when the baby is fresh out of the womb. In the earliest days, starting in infancy, your talk of emotions to your child helps him grasp the concepts of what he is feeling and enables him to put a name to them. Your attention to your child when your child is in need models empathy, teaching him to consider other people's needs. Nurturing your child in the early days, and ensuring that your child has an environment that is secure and consistent is crucial to creating that foundation for emotional intelligence.

The first year of a child's life involves learning self-soothing. Children begin recognizing that they have emotions as they approach one year old, and they begin experimenting with those emotions and how they communicate, such as fake crying to get attention.

Between ages 1 and 2.5, children become more self-aware in general. They recognize that they have emotional responses. Children in this age range are happy and proud when praised, or seem guilty when shamed or feeling as though they have disappointed their parents. They are beginning to learn the words associated with emotions, and begin to show signs of developing empathy, as noted through mimicking faces, or seeming concerned when someone else is crying.

During the preschool years, ages 2-5, children begin to attempt to regulate their emotions, beginning their journey into developing self-management. They may cover their eyes or ears in the response of a stimulus they do not want to see, and they begin to communicate their emotional states more regularly, paying attention to the feelings of others as well. They also begin to develop pretend-play, toying with how emotions and words can have an impact on other people, and they begin to show sympathetic behavior. A child with a sandwich may share half with a child without any food or will offer a hug and a kind word to a peer that is upset, showing the beginnings of developing social awareness and relationship management.

### Childhood

Within early elementary school, ranging from ages 5-7, children become more motivated to regulate emotions they would consider self-conscious, such as embarrassment. They are beginning to work on developing problem-solving and coping mechanisms, though they still frequently turn to their parents for help. They are interested in being seen as calm or in control around their peers and work hard to avoid crying or showing other strong displays of anger, sadness, or fear. They are also beginning to get better at investing in other peoples' emotions more and practice further relationship management and social awareness.

Middle childhood, ranging from ages 7-10, marks the time when children begin distancing themselves. They avoid things they dislike or that are troubling, while still working on coping with strong emotions and developing problem-solving skills that will be necessary for relationship management. At this age, children will begin to try to manage relationships, such as smiling at a friend while voicing disapproval or something that they are upset about in order to make sure their friend does not think they no longer like them. They also begin to recognize that they can feel more than one emotion at a time, especially in context with other people, such as being happy to see a friend, but annoyed that the friend did something that bothered him, and they seek to use information they know about other people to help in developing friendships or relationships, furthering social awareness and relationship management skills.

Preadolescence, ranging from ages 10-13, involves a large shift in emotional awareness. They begin to see the world more realistic than the naïve innocent eyes of a young child, and they use their understanding of the world to aid in coping with stress or conflict. They are typically able to develop multiple solutions to problems, which encourages flexibility. They also begin to understand the difference between expressing themselves genuinely with their friends and how they manage their emotions around other people. They may approach their friend to vent their anger and frustration, but to those around them, they may appear as though nothing is wrong. They are able to recognize social roles, such as recognizing various interpersonal relationships, and they begin to develop an idea of how those roles work, which is another crucial aspect of relationship management.

### Adolescence

In adolescence, ranging from 13 to adulthood, children become much more aware of the cyclical nature of their emotions. They see how they may feel angry with a friend, but then later feel guilty about feeling angry, and that sort of insight is a motivator to managing relationships and problem-solving tactfully. Teens also begin to understand their own personal values and put more of an importance on them, especially when dealing with stress. People with an emphasis on loyalty may be willing to tolerate more from a friend than someone else, whereas someone who genuinely wants to see the best in people may be quick to forgive, but not forget. Teens also begin to master the art of presenting themselves in ways that are beneficial to them, furthering their self-management skill. They also recognize the mutual nature of relationships. They see how communication has an impact on both people, and effective communication of emotions is crucial to strengthen and maintain good relationships with their friends. They see how their own emotions can hurt their friends, and seek to manage their impact on those around them. By the end of adulthood, all four of the key EQ skills have been developed at about the level they will remain in adulthood without proper intervention.

### Strengthening EQ

At any point, EQ can be strengthened. You can strengthen the EQ of your children with age-appropriate methods, or you can strengthen your own through a series of challenges and life changes meant to habituate the behaviors that come together to create your EQ. These six simple practices can help in developing EQ in people that feel the need to further their own development.

### Practice identifying all emotions and their accompanying sensations

Self-awareness is the basis of emotional intelligence, and you cannot have highly developed self-awareness if you are unable to identify your emotions. If you find that you struggle to identify your emotions, you should practice doing so. Elevate yourself beyond feeling good or bad—instead, seek to use the most vivid words you can think of. It may be helpful to locate a feelings chart that authors commonly use to elevate their own writing. If you are feeling bad, try to put a more specific name to it. Are you angry? Scared? Sad? If you are angry, is it frustration? Irritation? Jealous? Likewise, if you are feeling good, is it happiness? Contentment? Are you feeling excited? If you make your emotions as specific as possible, you will begin to develop your capacity for identifying them as they are felt in real-time.

Along with naming your emotions you feel, you should make it a point to identify every sensation in your body as it occurs. Feel the quickening of your pulse along with the flash of adrenaline running cold in your veins when you are scared and put a name to the feeling. If you feel the rage burning in your gut, paired with tenseness and a quickened heart rate, name that for what it is. If you are shaking uncontrollably while sobbing, name that feeling. By putting names to the physical sensations as well, you are doubly solidifying your ability to be able to identify and understand your own emotions. This is a good first step! You are well on your way to being able to manage your emotions once you are able to recognize them.

### Manage negative emotions

It is easy to get carried away by emotions in general, though the negative ones seem to be far more powerful at swaying our behavior. By learning to manage your emotions, you no longer allow them to have that sway over you. While this is much easier said than done, you will feel far better if you keep those negative emotions from ruling over your reactions.

One of the easiest ways to manage negative emotions is to create a pause between your feelings and behaviors. Whether you take a deep breath or take a few seconds to count to four, you need to create that gap. By creating a delay between emotion and behavior, you are able to let the most intense moment of emotion pass, allowing you to better regulate your behaviors. If your child refuses to do something you have asked, for example, and you immediately feel the anger building up within you, stop, force yourself to take a deep breath, hold it as you count to four, and then exhale and act in a way that is productive instead of a way that will only serve to further exacerbate the situation. Over time, this concept of pausing before acting becomes a habit, enabling you to further control your emotions as you develop self-management.

### Choose your words carefully

Vocabulary is everything when communicating with other people. People who have higher EQs typically are able to communicate more efficiently than those who have lower EQs. They are able to choose words in ways that can aid in preventing and correcting miscommunications, and that allows for more immediate action toward conflicts. Word choice is the most basic building block of verbal communication, and if you cannot communicate effectively or tactfully, you are going to struggle in relationships with other people. Whenever you have an interaction that does not quite go the way you were hoping it would take a moment afterward to reflect on the interaction and identify ways you could have communicated better or more clearly. You may be surprised to see that even just tweaking your wording can change the entire mood of the interaction, especially in the context of conflict resolution.

For example, think of how you would react if someone came up to you and shouted, "Wow, why are you so stupid?! You couldn't even clean up that smoothie you spilled on the counter! It's all dried on now! I can't believe you did that; look at the giant mess I'm going to have to clean up because of your carelessness!" Compare that reaction to the one you would have if someone calmly approached you and said, "Hey, I feel really disrespected when you don't clean up after yourself. It makes me feel like my own time is not valued, especially when it takes me so long to clean up after it has sat for a while. Can you please be more mindful of your messes and ensure you clean them up as soon as they happen?"

Look at the key differences in these interactions—one is all about the angry individual blaming you while the other focuses on the individual's own feelings. The one who yelled would likely immediately put you on the defensive, as you suddenly feel attacked and challenged. On the other hand, the calmer response focused on how your actions impacted the other person and how it made them feel, along with a simple request to ensure that it does not happen again. While still awkward to be directly challenged, you are not being attacked in any way. The exchange is quiet, factual, and directed toward the other individual instead of toward you, meaning you do not feel the desperate need to defend yourself.

Now, imagine if you took that concept and projected it elsewhere. You would be focusing on positive language, carefully choosing your words to get the results you would like without conflict. Think about how much happier you and those around you would be if you could solve the conflict by communicating efficiently. You would be able to immediately defuse difficult situations without them blowing up in everyone's faces, and that skill alone is invaluable.

### Practice empathetic responses

Empathy is the ability to feel and understand the emotions of those around you. When you empathize with someone, you feel their emotions so deeply and profoundly that it is as if you, yourself, are going through the same situation. It is your ability to intimately relate to another's experiences and provides the feedback necessary to have seamless nonverbal communication of emotions. By being able to look at someone and feel what they are feeling due to being able to relate to them, you will be able to help meet their needs and take care of them. This is also an important cue to let you know when you are overstepping or doing something that is harmful or upsetting to the other person, allowing you to identify that you should take a step back and lighten up on the situation at hand.

You can practice empathy by identifying the feelings of those around you and also imagining yourself in their shoes. If you have a coworker you have been working with who has suddenly become quite difficult to be around, you may ask yourself what is happening in her life to cause so many issues as of late, and you may realize that your coworker's dog had to be put to sleep not too long ago. Imagining what would happen if you had to put your beloved pet down allows you to see further into your coworker's position, and you begin to feel what your coworker is feeling. You understand how deeply having your dog put down would impact you, and you begin to understand why your coworker is short-tempered. Acknowledging the situation enables you to calmly and rationally respond compassionately to the situation. You may be a bit more patient with her, understanding to a degree what she is going through.

### Know your triggers

Emotional triggers are the things that have a tendency to set us off. Typically, these stimuli are related to something upsetting and sometimes are connected to something reminiscent of a traumatic event. Whatever the trigger may be, they are often followed by intense, disproportionate responses to stimuli that are considered unwarranted. Someone who is easily triggered by feeling criticized may scream and yell when someone voices that he did something wrong while kindly suggesting a way to fix the mistake. The person who has been triggered is unable to control his reaction and lashes out in his emotional volatility.

Learning to identify your triggers will allow you to recognize when you may be facing an outburst soon, or allow you to avoid the situation altogether. If you know that being criticized is an emotional trigger for you, you can take steps to keep yourself calm when you know that criticism is coming, such as when you go into an annual review for work. Likewise, in parenting, if you know that your toddler screeching the word "NO!" at you tend to send your blood pressure spiking, and you know that it is a common trigger for you, you are able to recognize what is happening once you have identified the word or defiance as your trigger. When you are aware that it is occurring, you are better able to keep it in check, reminding yourself that exploding will not be conducive to parenting and will not better the situation.

**Do not give in to adversity**

Remember, everyone faces challenges or adversity at some point. It can be tough to deal with these challenges, but despite that, you should persevere. Your reactions to these challenges are a valuable learning experience, even if you react poorly. Remember that even when you make a mistake, or you fall victim to your emotional triggers, or you blow up a conflict, you can fix that mistake. Do not complain and allow yourself to become a victim; instead, look at ways you can learn to avoid that mistake in the future.

After making a mistake, ask yourself questions about what happened to further understand the situation. Keep yourself thinking positively, reminding yourself that every experience has value, no matter how poorly it went, and you are able to set yourself up for success in the future. Remember that failure is not permanent. You can continue to build upon it to strive toward success.

Consider if your child screaming no has triggered your own negative emotions, and in the heat of the moment, you yelled at your child to listen to you. Immediately after yelling, you see the look of panic in your child, followed by your child running away and crying hysterically. Overall, this situation seems like a giant failure, but keep in mind that you can take away knowledge from anything. Remind yourself that you messed up, but it can be turned into a learning experience, for both you and your child. You can go and apologize to your child, telling her that sometimes, even mommy or daddy does something they regret in anger, but it is not okay, and it is important to apologize after hurting someone. You also now have that image of your child afraid of you at that moment to remind you to keep your temper in the future.

## CHAPTER 25

# Raising Emotionally Intelligent Children

Emotional intelligence is important in all aspects of life, and while children do develop some degree of EQ on their own, frequently, the biggest influencers of their EQ is their parents. They learn the foundations for emotional intelligence from their parents, while the rest is formulated by interactions with their peers. Children and teens with higher EQs are typically happier and well-adjusted than their lower EQ peers. They are more skilled at handling intricate social situations and solving conflict without escalating it, and they are typically much better at handling and maintaining their friendships.

### Raising an Emotionally Intelligent Child

In the context of this section, the child will refer to any minor child from infancy to preadolescence, differentiating them from teenagers, or adolescence. This age range is where the vast majority of the foundations of emotional intelligence are developed, and they are among the most crucial ages. It is important to understand what you can do in order to help your child develop a healthy amount of emotional intelligence.

How to Encourage Emotional Intelligence in a Child

- **Smile often:** You should smile at your child regularly. This is the beginning of teaching your child to read body language, and also acts to teach empathy.
- **Nurture your child:** By tending to your child's needs, you are teaching your child to put others' needs in front of his or her own, especially when the other person cannot take care of their needs on their own. Your child learns that you are supportive and that you can be trusted. These are behaviors he will seek to emulate later in life.
- **Explain why you say no:** Offer age-appropriate explanations when correcting behavior, with an emphasis on how your child's behavior impacts others. While your child is still quite young and unable to fully comprehend what you are saying, it builds a foundation. The lessons are beginning to be learned, and the vocabulary necessary to be emotionally intelligent is being developed. For example, if your toddler hits you, very gently but firmly tell your child, "No, we do not hit other people. It hurts and makes them sad. Hands are for hugs or high fives instead." In that short dialogue, you set a boundary, explained the reason for the boundary, explained how your child's behavior would hurt other people, and offered an acceptable alternative to the behavior.
- **Listen closely and carefully:** Your child should always feel like communication is open between the two of you. You need to be able to listen and really hear your child when your child approaches you, no matter what the subject is. This teaches the importance of efficient communication, and your child will need those skills in adulthood.
- **Name feelings as they arise:** Starting at an early age, name specific feelings as they are felt. This teaches your child to identify the feelings as language is developing, especially in infancy and the early toddler years. This foundation is one of the most important building blocks for raising an emotionally intelligent child.

- **Work on problem-solving:** When your child feels stuck on something, instead of swooping in to help, try guiding your child through what she may think she needs to do to solve her problem herself. Ask questions that will point her in the right direction while leaving her free to identify the solution on her own without your input.

- **Model empathy:** Remember, your child is not likely to develop much empathy if your child is never shown empathy. By guiding your child through the steps of empathy and always approaching situations involving your child empathetically, you teach your child to consider emotional states of others as well. Your child will watch you acknowledging his or her feelings and emulate that behavior with others.

- **Model coping with negative feelings:** It is also important to model negative feelings for your child as well. If you are sad and crying in front of your child, that is okay! Turn it into a learning experience and explain that people cry when they are sad. If you are angry, take a deep breath and calm yourself down before explaining that you are angry and why you feel that way. By modeling these negative emotions, you are showing your child that even strong; negative emotions can be managed and worked through. This is a lesson your child will learn and internalize, and it will serve him well

### Signs Your Child Needs Extra Support Learning Emotional Intelligence

- **Your child is easily frustrated:** Children struggling with emotional intelligence typically are easily frustrated. If your child seems to blow up at the slightest provocation, such as not having her sandwich sliced just right for lunch, or screaming because you accidentally bumped into her, she may be struggling with emotional regulation.

- **Your child frequently gives up when confronted with a problem:** Oftentimes, children who cannot self-manage feel frustrated when a problem arises. They do not have the flexibility to think about the problem and figure out the best way to solve it, and instead, they give up. They see no reason to try when they are sure they will fail anyway, even though, learning is done in part through failing to succeed.

- **Your child is prone to yelling:** If your child often resorts to yelling when angered or upset, he may be showing signs of low emotional intelligence. Children who yell often do so because they cannot think of how to properly communicate with others, and it seems to be the only option for them to be heard.

- **Your child thinks and speaks negatively:** Children with low EQs are typically hyper-focused on the negative. They may dejectedly talk about how the Lego set they struggled with is stupid, or that they don't like pizza anyway when told they cannot have it for dinner. Instead of being able to cope with their negative feelings, they instead allow the negativity to color everything.

- **Your child struggles to ask for help:** Children struggling with EQ often do not ask for help, or when they do, they do not do it in the best way they could. They struggle with communication, and because of that, they cannot quite clearly convey that they need extra help or support, whether emotional or with schoolwork or chores.

- **Your child struggles to make friends and maintain relationships:** Children who struggle with emotional intelligence typically also struggle to maintain relationships with other children. If you notice that your child is struggling to make friends, or is frequently cast aside by others, especially if there are other signs of low emotional intelligence present as well, your child may need extra help and support navigating social situations.

### Raising an Emotionally Intelligent Teen

Teens are a little tougher to influence than children just due to the nature of adolescence. Teens are seeking to put as much distance between themselves and their parents as possible as they prepare to leave the nest and make their debuts into adulthood. Their bodies are going through an intense hormonal shift from a child into adults capable of reproduction, and those hormones create intense feelings that can be difficult to navigate. Further, teens also feel the pull of peer pressure and self-consciousness as they struggle to find their places in society. With a few tips in mind, you can help encourage emotional intelligence before your child leaves the nest for good. Remember, all of the tips for raising emotionally intelligent children also apply to teens.

### How to Encourage Emotional Intelligence in a Teen

- **Ask Guiding Questions:** Remember, teens are all about rebellion and doing the exact opposite of what their parents say. Teens want to do things their own way, and that is okay! It is a normal part of growing up and separating from parents. This means, however, that you cannot just tell the teen how to do something, especially when it comes to conflicts or relationships with those around her. Instead, try to ask guiding questions to gently lead the teen to the answer on her own. If your child is upset about an interaction with a friend, you can try asking, "What would you feel if your friend treated you like that?" or "What would you like the other person to do if roles were reversed?"
Sometimes, teens are thinking about things in a self-centered manner and need that little extra push to start thinking about how other people might see how their behavior. Teens, by and large, do not want to feel embarrassed or self-conscious at all, and once you have them thinking about how they would respond to someone else doing the same thing, they may see the error in their ways without needing you to overtly point them out.

- **The "Maybe" Game:** The "Maybe" game involves understanding why others do what they do. If you see someone out and about who is in a bad mood, each person in the family should suggest a potential reason for the bad mood. For example, if you see someone ranting and raving to a manager about how his meal was not quite right and he demands a refund when your family goes out to dinner, have each person take a moment to suggest why he is in such a bad mood. "Maybe he's getting a divorce." "Maybe he just lost someone close to him." "Maybe he just got fired." "Maybe it's his birthday, and he has no one to spend it with." "Maybe he got into a fender bender."
  This begins to solidify to your teen the habits of trying to understand the context of emotions rather than just seeing the emotions themselves. When you are able to understand the what and the why behind emotions in other people, you are developing empathy skills, and this is a fantastic opportunity for teens. As it is habituated, the teen is more likely to bring those skills to interpersonal conflicts with friends, and instead of being annoyed or angry when a friend is upset or irritable, your teen will be able to stop and start figuring out why emotions are running as high as they are.

- **Praise behavior that shows high emotional intelligence:** Just as with younger children, teens love to be praised. They may act embarrassed about it at the moment, but acknowledging when your child is doing well reinforces the good behavior. If your teen acknowledges your feelings when you confront him about not doing the dishes, you should praise the act of acknowledging your feelings. If your teen solves a conflict with siblings in a constructive manner, praise that. Let your teen know you are watching and that you see how much effort he is putting into behaving thoughtfully. He will appreciate it.

- **Be empathetic:** Modeling good emotional intelligence does not end when your child hits the teen years. Showing empathy to your teen, and especially with your teen around, teaches her to cue into other people's emotions. If she sees you putting in the effort to understand how other people are really feeling, she will learn that that is an important part of social interactions.

If your teen is upset about a breakup, for example, you could make it a point to go to your teen and tell her about the first time you broke up with someone and how much that hurt. Label her feelings, let her know that you can see how upset she is, and show her that you are there for her if she wants to talk, or if what she needs is a pint of ice cream and some movies to binge-watch on her own.

- **Pay attention for signs your teen is struggling:** You know your teen better than anyone, though it may not always feel that way. You should pay attention to behavioral changes or signs that your teen is struggling to cope in an emotionally healthy manner. If you see signs that your teen is struggling, do not try to explain it as a one-time issue, and instead make it a point to address the problem. For example, if you notice that your teen is putting an extra emphasis on social media, obsessing over it and trying to look Instagram ready at all time, you may want to intervene. Putting in all of his energy to one thing can become a problem if unaddressed, and while teens revel in the attention, they may get on social media, putting their entire sense of self-worth on how many likes or shares or followers they get is unhealthy.

    If your child's teacher approaches you with concerns about behavior as well, it is important that you pay attention and follow up. If your child is struggling in school, where you are not likely to see, your child may need more support than you can offer, and it may be time to consider getting a professional involved.

- **Avoid trivializing your teen's feelings:** As an adult that is removed from most situations within your teen's social life, you can quickly identify when you feel as though your teen is being melodramatic or over-exaggerating a problem. While the solution may be clear-cut to you, remember that it is not necessarily that clear to your teen. Do not disregard your teen's feelings as illegitimate or irrational. Remember, emotions are the opposite of rationality, and they do not have to make sense; they only have to be acknowledged. Make sure that you do not invalidate your teen's feelings. Trivializing your teen's feelings is not empathetic and does not help your teen learn to acknowledge and manage her own feelings. Instead, it teaches her that her emotions should be ignored or disregarded, which only serves to make situations worse. Emotions are important and should be acknowledged and legitimized, no matter how much you, as a third party, can see that they are not necessarily warranted to the extent that they are felt. Struggling to regulate the intensity of emotions is a sign of lower emotional intelligence, and learning to regulate them is a skill that takes practice. That can only be practiced through living through the stronger emotions and learning coping skills that work for the individual.

- **Seek therapy if necessary:** If all else fails, and you feel as though your teen is struggling to cope or develop appropriate levels of emotional intelligence, seeking a professional trained in guiding teens through the process is an acceptable option. Therapy is beneficial to nearly everyone and can teach your child some very important coping mechanisms that will last a lifetime. If this step is necessary for your teen, start by speaking to his primary care physician to get a referral.

**Signs Your Teen Needs Extra Support Learning Emotional Intelligence**

- **Your teen does not perform well in school:** Teens with lower EQs struggle in school due to their struggles socially. They may withdraw and not put in the effort necessary to be successful, or they may be too afraid to ask for help when they need it, getting overwhelmed easily and instead choosing to give up.
- **Your teen is overly-critical:** If your teen has some sort of harsh criticism of everything, even when it is not constructive, he may struggle with EQ. He may not see how his words impact others, or he may struggle with communicating efficiently in ways that

would come across constructively. He also is prone to criticizing everything as a coping mechanism for struggling in the first place.

- **Your teen bullies others:** Teens who have lower EQs frequently have their own frustrations build up, feeling self-conscious and misunderstood. Because they struggle to identify or regulate their own feelings, as well as the struggle to really understand how their actions hurt others, they frequently lash out at other people and may even bully others in order to try to make themselves feel better, or as an impulsive reaction to feeling sensitive or self-conscious.

- **Your teen struggles to control anger:** Teens who have lower EQs tend to struggle with controlling their anger. As having self-management skills is a fundamental component of emotional intelligence, it is a common weakness of those struggling with their EQs.

- **Your teen constantly blames everyone else for problems:** While people with higher EQs tend to control their emotions in order to grant them clarity to see situations rationally and aid in problem-solving, those with lower EQs tend to struggle with that. Someone with lower EQ sees themselves as a victim much of the time, not acknowledging how his or her own negativity or lack of communication may have contributed to things blowing up. Your teen may struggle to see how he or she is involved in negative situations and instead seeks to push the blame of friendships failing or conflicts exploding on everyone but him or herself.

- **Your teen cannot cope when plans change:** Flexibility typically comes naturally to people with higher EQs. Since they have a better handle on their emotions, they are more able to cope when things go wrong, leading to a much more flexible person in general. When your teen struggles with her EQ, she may be unable to deal with changes in a healthy manner as a result. Your teen may have made plans with friends, and when a friend cancels, or the group decides to do something different, the disappointment and negative emotions may become overwhelming for her.

- **Your teen is negative and pessimistic:** Teens who struggle to self-regulate frequently find themselves stuck in a constant loop of negativity. Their negative feelings breed more negativity, keeping that mindset. Teens with lower EQs tend to look at things pessimistically instead of shifting their mindsets toward positivity, which is typically much more productive.

- **Your teen struggles to read body language:** Emotional intelligence is all about being able to understand other people. People with high EQs are adept at looking at a person and being able to see exactly what they are feeling based on body language alone. If your teen seems to be unable to read the body language of yourself or other people, it may be a sign of struggling with emotional intelligence.

- **Your teen gives up easily:** People who struggle with emotional intelligence frequently prefer to give up rather than keep trying when they face adversity. They feel as though they cannot cope with the negative feelings that come along with struggling, and instead prefer to give up. Giving up and playing the victim role is easier than struggling to proceed, even if giving up eliminates all chances of success. Your teen may struggle with a question on a homework assignment, and instead of persevering and trying to work past it, he instead decides not to do any of it, even though he likely would have still gotten a good grade on it, even missing the one question.

- **Your teen is more confrontational and argumentative than normal:** Teens who struggle with emotional intelligence typically fall victim to arguing. Even if the other person has disengaged, the teen with a lower EQ is likely to keep pushing the point. They cannot accept the possibility of them not being right, no matter how much the other person tells them they are done discussing this. If your teen feels like she has to win every argument, she gets into, no matter how inane, or how wrong she was, she may need to work on her EQ.

## CHAPTER 26

# Parenting Styles in Regards to Emotional Intelligence

Everyone parents differently. There are various different parenting styles for a wide range of situations, and those parenting styles can yield vastly different results. Every parent is going to have their own methods, but unfortunately, some are not as beneficial to children as others. Certain parenting styles are absolutely more conducive to raising healthy children. The four types of parents in terms of acknowledging and handling children's emotions are dismissing, disapproving, laissez-faire, and emotion coaching. Each of these types of parenting creates different types of children, and of the four, emotion coaching parents are the most likely to create happy, well-adjusted, emotionally intelligent children.

## The Dismissing Parent

Dismissing parents are typically prone to avoiding or dismissing their children's emotions whenever possible. They seek to stop emotions and distract from them, as opposed to recognizing that they should be worked through. Dismissing parents typically tell their children to get over it when they are faced with tough emotions, implying that the child's feelings are unimportant. They would soon ignore the emotions than help fix the problem. They see emotions as troublesome, instead of as an opportunity to connect with and support their children, and will oftentimes downplay the event leading to emotion as not being that bad.

Typically, the dismissing parent will say things like telling the child that there is no reason to be angry, sad, afraid, or whatever else she is feeling. The problem with this is that the child learns that emotions are not to be trusted, and may even lead to the child being unable to trust her own gut reactions. If the child grew up being told not to feel certain ways or that she has no reason to feel the way she does, she is likely to believe that her own feelings are untrustworthy and irrelevant. From a perspective of developing emotional intelligence, it is easy to see how feeling as though you cannot trust your own emotions would lead for you to struggle to accurately identify what you are feeling at any given time. This can have major negative repercussions on a child's emotional health.

Further, dismissing parents also typically dismiss their own emotions as well, while also discouraging the child from speaking emotionally with her parents. The dismissing parent may be uncomfortable with emotions in general, or may just not understand how to work through emotions. They see the passage of time as the perfect cure as opposed to developing real problem-solving abilities.

The dismissing parent results in a child who believes there is something inherently wrong with her. She feels inadequate, and as though her perception of reality is skewed if she is feeling inappropriate ways. She learns to dismiss her own emotions rather than seeing them as important. She does not see the benefit in attempting to talk about her emotions, as they have always been considered irrelevant or inaccurate. She is also likely to learn that problem solving is not necessary, as she believes that time will resolve any issues she encounters.

Consider a child who is feeling quite angry at that particular moment. You, a dismissive parent, see your child melting down, screaming because he really wanted that new toy at the store. Instead of talking your child through it, you tell your son, "Oh, come on. It's not that bad. You'll get over it. There's no reason to be that mad over this; you have three other toys at home that are really similar to this one. What's the problem?" This, of course, does nothing to help the child actually get over it. Just because it was suggested does not mean it will happen, and just because you may not see being denied the toy as a big deal, your child certainly did.

### The Disapproving Parent

The disapproving parent, like the dismissing parent, sees emotions as inconvenient or a problem that needs to be avoided at all costs. The disapproving parent, instead of saying that the feelings should be gotten over, says that the child should not feel the way he or she does, to begin with. Emotions are seen as a sign of weakness, and expressing them is seen as even worse. They disregard their own emotions while also encouraging their children to do the same, treating any emotions a child may express negatively. One of the most commonly heard phrases from the disapproving parent is, "You should not feel like that!" and is typically followed with threats if the child does not get his act together and stop the show of emotions.

Typically, the disapproving parent believes that emotions, particularly negative ones, are a waste of time. There is no point in wasting time or energy focusing on emotions when they are unimportant anyway, and for that reason, they are typically disregarded, or even punished. They also sometimes feel as though children use negative emotions as a manipulation tactic rather than seeing them as legitimate. Because of the perceived manipulative nature of the emotions felt, the disapproving parent sees emotions as something that needs to be quashed rather than encouraged or taught to control.

Typically, the disapproving parent is far more negative and judgmental of emotions and is typically authoritative. They are far harsher than the dismissive parent and seek to control and criticize all expressions of emotion. The repercussions of this are quite similar to what happened as a result of dismissing parents: Children grow up out of touch with their emotions. They learn to dismiss and ignore their emotions rather than learning to control or cope with them. They never learn how to properly name their emotions, and they certainly never learn good ways to deal with other people's emotions, typically defaulting to dismissing or disapproving of them.

Let's again revisit the child who felt angry about not getting the toy at the store. If you were a disapproving parent, you likely would have told your child, "Stop overreacting! You shouldn't feel like this over a toy! It's just a chunk of plastic. Stop your whining and stop acting like a crybaby, or I'll treat you like one. If you don't stop your whining right now, you will regret it. I'll take one of your toys at home and throw it away!" Instead of coaching your child through feeling emotions, you command and threaten to make the emotion disappear, though this is rarely effective. If the child does obey, it is out of fear of the consequences more so than out of being able to control emotions in a healthy manner. Despite the disapproving parent's stance on the matter, a child's emotions do not make him weak, nor does a child need to forego emotions in order to survive. In fact, it is quite the opposite: Children need to learn to manage their emotions in order to survive in a social setting. A child will never learn to interact in meaningful, emotionally intelligent manners if he is never granted the ability to explore emotions in a safe setting without worrying about threats or punishments.

### The Laissez-Faire Parent

Laissez-faire is derived from French, literally translating to "let it be." Parents who are deemed laissez-faire are typically permissive, to a fault. They allow all emotions to be felt and treat all emotions as acceptable, with no regard for the behavior that may follow them. The children are free to feel. However, they feel and are never taught the ways necessary to mitigate the control emotions may have over them.

This sort of permissive attitude means they are never able to develop important coping mechanisms that allow for them. These children are raised without structure or support they need, and while it is important to allow children to feel their emotions in order to develop thorough self-awareness, the children also need the guidance to help them through handling those emotions. The skill to handle those emotions is not learned solely through experiencing the emotions. They need to be taught coping methods and problem-solving skills that the laissez-faire parent disregards. Rather than teaching children to cope, the laissez-faire parent allows for the feelings to be felt until they run their course, much like how the dismissing parent considered the time the ultimate coping mechanism.

Unfortunately, this sort of permissive parenting brings a whole new slew of problems to the child. Children raised by laissez-faire parents typically struggle with self-control. They are typically quite disobedient and impulsive, while still being quite dependent at the same time. Because they were never encouraged to develop much past the early childhood ages emotionally and they never felt many consequences for their actions from their parents, they never developed the skills they would need to problem solve on their own. These children typically struggle to self-regulate or self-soothe when feeling intense negative emotions, and also likely struggle to make friends since they never learned to pick up on social cues necessary for social success. Most children do not want to play with the kid who does not realize how his own behaviors impact others.

Again, we will revisit the example of the child complaining at the store because he was not allowed to buy a toy. As a laissez-faire parent, you would look at your child throwing a tantrum for a moment, nod your head, and say, "Okay," while continuing to go about your business, offering no support for your child. You would not be discouraging the emotional expression, but you would also not be teaching your child to express himself. This teaches your child that emotions are acceptable, but also teaches your child that his tantrum is an acceptable way to deal with them. Since you did not correct the behavior, the child believes it is acceptable by default. In those early days where you are setting the stage, you never teach your child that sort of behavior is unacceptable, and those behaviors are repeated elsewhere, where people are far less tolerant. This, of course, then makes your child typically avoided or disliked, as he is incapable of dealing with his emotions appropriately and becomes an annoyance to those around him.

### The Emotion Coaching Parent

The last of the four styles of parenting is emotion coaching. This style of parenting puts an emphasis on practicing empathy and guiding the child through emotions. The emotion coaching parent seeks to teach the child how to identify his emotions and how those emotions affect him, as well as those around him. These parents value teaching and guiding rather than allowing the child to learn through trial and error. They seek to be involved, but not controlling of their children, and that balance enables them to be effective with their parenting approach.

Emotion coaching parents do value all emotions and teach their children that all emotions are important and acceptable to feel, but not all behaviors, especially those that are emotionally motivated, are acceptable. Behaviors that are harmful or not productive are typically discouraged, with the parent gently guiding the child through processes to better cope with the feelings and emphasize thinking critically to solve problems effectively. Through patience, empathy, and time, emotion coaching parents are able to create emotionally intelligent young children who develop higher EQs.

Children raised by emotion coaching parents are usually much more well-adjusted than children who were not. They typically do better in social settings, making friends more often, and maintaining those relationships better. They are usually able to control and regulate their own feelings and reactions, no matter how angry or upset they may be. They are much better at self-soothing, allowing them to regulate their behaviors and keep from doing things they will regret later due to impulse control issues. They are usually happier because their emotions are not a point of contention for them, and they are typically closer to their parents, seeing parents as valuable teachers and reliable support in times of need.

We once again return to the example of the child throwing a tantrum who is crying because he wants a toy you have declined to buy. As an emotion coaching parent, you would get down to his eye level and put a hand on his shoulder. You would calmly voice that he looks angry and disappointed that he is not getting the new toy and that you understand that. You would also remind him that just because he is angry does not mean that he can throw a tantrum in the store, and you would offer an alternative, such as taking a deep breath to calm down so he can use his words to communicate with you. The end result is a child who feels acknowledged, heard, and valued.

## CHAPTER 27

# Marriage, Divorce, and Your Child's Emotional Health

Your child is deeply impacted by every aspect of your romantic relationship with her other parent. If her parents share a happy, healthy relationship, your child learns to expect that. On the other hand, if your child sees an emotionally unhealthy relationship, that becomes what she learns to expect in her future. Your relationship impacts your child's emotional health, whether you want it to or not. No matter how hard you may try to keep some aspects away from your child, she will see it for what it is.

### Marriage and Your Child

Especially if your marriage is to the child's other parent, your child will see the two of you as one unit. You and your spouse are the child's natural family unit, and it is a given that the two of you will be together. They will develop an opinion on the nature of your relationship, and that will color their expectations for the future. For this reason, it is incredibly important for you to model a healthy marriage for your child to see. Ask yourself if your relationship with your spouse is one that you would like your child to live in as well, and if not, it may be time to make some serious changes to your relationship.

In a healthy marriage, your child will see you and your spouse modeling empathy, conflict resolution, and genuinely caring for each other. This modeling sets a serious example for your child and should be fostered and encouraged. They should see you and your spouse, both during good and bad times. Conflict is okay, so long as they also see the resolution of the conflict as well. You want to make sure you are modeling those conflict resolution skills and making it clear that marriage and love do not have to be perfect. Conflict is inevitable and does not mean a relationship is doomed. What is important is whether you and your spouse can resolve the conflict, especially with young eyes watching closely to see how you handle the situation.

When you stay in a toxic marriage, your child sees it all. No matter how hard you may try to hide it, your child is absorbing what is going on. Your child will feel helpless and frightened of the tension that hangs in the room whenever both parents are present. They may even begin to internalize that blame on themselves. They may even try to fix the problems they see, essentially becoming the adult in the house, so to speak, as they try to smooth over conflicts, instead of their parents being the ones to guide them through the process of developing healthy coping skills. This essentially forces the child to grow up far too early, which can cause many emotional issues for your child or teen.

Children growing up within a toxic marriage, depending on their personality, either internalize shame and guilt, feeling insecure most of the time and frightened by their parents' interactions, especially when there is plenty of yelling about hate from both sides. Your child, especially at a younger age, identifies closely with both parents, and to hear one parent say they hate the other is something young children internalize and take to mean the parent hates them too. They develop low self-esteem and often feel unworthy of loving themselves, considering they may have internalized the blame for the conflicts and disagreements. They learn to model unhealthy relationships, not knowing any different, and this sets them up for romantic failure later in life. If all they see is yelling to solve arguments, they will likely resort to yelling within their own romantic relationships as well.

If you have read this book this far, you may begin to recognize some of the effects of toxic marriages on children as signs of low EQ. The child is locked in a loop of negativity, accepting helplessness. This is a sign of low self-management. The child may act out regularly around other people, showing low self-awareness. They may struggle in relationships in the future, showing low social awareness and relationship management. Staying in a toxic marriage sets your child up for emotional failure later in life and is something that should be avoided. When the choices are - a child growing up either with parents in a toxic marriage or happily divorced parents, the happily divorced parents will always be the best option, even if it cuts the time the child sees parents in half.

### Divorce and Your Child

Sometimes, divorce is the best option within a marriage. Things may have escalated so far that neither spouse is willing or able to reconcile, and one or both partners feel as though they would be better off without the other. This does not necessarily have to mean that one of the parents was a bad person; sometimes, two people do not mesh well and simply bring out the worst in each other. Divorce will always be difficult for your child, but there are ways for you to minimize the damage. Children are resilient, and while they may struggle at first, they will bounce back with the proper support and guidance.

Children, especially at the younger ages, may see divorce as an impossibility or refuse to acknowledge or accept it. It is likely that your marriage is all your child has ever known if you are still married to their other parent, and that sudden dissolution of his family unit can be absolutely devastating. No matter how peaceful your divorce may be, it will have negative effects on your children. The negative effects of the child's parents divorcing can be seen in all aspects of life, especially if the child struggles to cope with the change. Those with a lower EQ are more likely to suffer to a greater extent, though even children with higher EQs are going to struggle to cope to some degree. Oftentimes, children who have gone through a divorce are likely to experience emotional instability, they may out, experience depression or anxiety, or struggle in school.

**Emotional Instability**
- Children may feel stuck in the middle of the conflict and struggle to manage their emotions.
- *They may be angry beyond belief, or sob uncontrollably.*

**Acting Out**
- Especially if they have seen toxic coping in the marriage, they may engage in bad behavior, both alone and socially.
- *They may begin to bully or pick on peers or siblings, or try to steal to get attention*

**Depression or Anxiety**
- Children may withdraw emotionally or become fearful of further loss of family
- *They may frequently be sad or frightened, and lose interest in the things they loved*

**Struggling in school**
- Children may be preoccupied with their feelings and unable to focus on schoolwork
- *They may give up on homework assignments because they did not pay attenton during the school day and do not understand it.*

Children with lower EQs will need much more guidance in coping with divorce than children with higher EQs, but they will be able to do so, given the right support. Understanding the ins and outs of emotion coaching will be essential in aiding your child to cope with the loss of a family unit, he may never have been able to even imagine would degrade. Remember to acknowledge your child's feelings to help him cope with such sudden changes, and to keep in mind that it may take your child some serious time to begin to comprehend such drastic changes. Further, children with lower EQs may struggle to ask for the support they need from you as they need it.

Children with higher EQs are likely to cope with their feelings better in general. They typically are better at handling their emotions, and while they may be devastated at such a drastic change, they can typically manage their reactions better. You still may face them acting out as they struggle, but you can typically speak with them and help them work through it. They are able to communicate their own feelings with you better, which enables you to give them the support that they need and ask for. Your child with a higher EQ is also likely to be more resilient in general than a child with a lower EQ. She will have the coping skills that will be beneficial for coming to terms with the divorce. While your child with higher EQ will still struggle in similar ways to the child with a lower EQ, overall, your child will be better equipped to cope.

### Divorce and Your Teen

Teenagers, despite their increased levels of maturity, are still inclined to struggle when their world is rocked in such a drastic manner. Like children, teens have come to identify their family unit and having that suddenly and irrevocably destroyed can be absolutely devastating. They have always known things to be a certain way, and maybe reluctant to see how things will change and evolve. Teens are likely to go through a stage of denial, in which they refuse to acknowledge the impending changes. While they may try to pretend to be mature about things, they are still likely to be deeply hurt at the idea of losing their family and will act out accordingly.

Like children, they tend to show similar signs of emotional distress. They may suddenly regress and become less able to control or regulate their own emotions, even if they were pros at it before. They may become angry or upset, and constantly resort to criticism to lash out at those around them, likely as a result of criticism being present in a degrading marriage. Oftentimes, when marriages fail, there was conflict in the home long before the divorce, and the teen will typically try to act accordingly. They may show signs of negativity. They feel as though their family, who has been the vast majority of their world for most of their lives, is shattering. They struggle to cope with the loss of that family unit.

Teens whose parents are divorcing are also more likely to rebel or act out than their peers, often engaging in antisocial behaviors. They may engage in risky acts, such as unsafe sex or experimenting with drugs and alcohol as a way of trying to cope with the loss of attention and affection from one parent. In a divorce, at least one parent loses out on their parent-child relationship, and more frequently, both parents lose out on it as custody is split. The teen, feeling the need to cope with it somehow, seeks the affection and attention elsewhere, even if their methods for attaining it are rather extreme. These rebellious acts, such as stealing or engaging in unsafe sex, can lead to lifelong consequences, especially if your teen is close to adulthood and gets caught committing crimes, gets an STI, gets pregnant, or impregnates someone else.

Teens whose parents are divorcing, especially if the divorce is particularly messy or painful, are at a higher risk for becoming entangled in addiction or drug abuse as they seek out alternative ways to cope with their painful, overwhelming feelings during such a difficult time. Despite the risks, they engage in these acts anyway if they find it lessens the pain at all. This can have lifelong implications, as not only can addiction ruin a person's life, it could potentially kill them. They may not think about the risks, or rather, they may choose not to care about the risks, and continue to engage anyway if they choose to go down this road.

Like children, teens also may struggle with academic performance in the event of a divorce. Due to the emotional turmoil, they may have been exposed to; they may find it difficult to focus on tasks at hand in school and instead eventually just accept the struggles and failures. Their grades begin to suffer, which can have lifelong implications on the teen, especially if prior to the divorce, she was interested in going to a university.

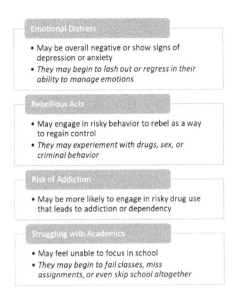

**Emotional Distress**

- May be overall negative or show signs of depression or anxiety
- *They may begin to lash out or regress in their ability to manage emotions*

**Rebellious Acts**

- May engage in risky behavior to rebel as a way to regain control
- *They may experiement with drugs, sex, or criminal behavior*

**Risk of Addiction**

- May be more likely to engage in risky drug use that leads to addiction or dependency

**Struggling with Academics**

- May feel unable to focus in school
- *They may begin to fail classes, miss assignments, or even skip school altogether*

As children, teens with higher EQs are a bit more equipped to deal with these situations as they arise. They may be devastated and upset, but they are still more resilient than their peers. They will still require support, but with their improved emotional intelligence skills, they will do far better in the long run. They will not be as impulsive, and while they may be moodier than usual, they are less likely to try to cope by resorting to dangerous and unhealthy habits. They are far more likely to look at the risks and decide they are not worth them and will be more likely to be able to find the good in situations, no matter how bad the situations may be. The higher the teen's EQ, the better they are likely to take the divorce, especially if they feel blindsided by it, to begin with.

# CHAPTER 28

# The Father's Crucial Role

No one will argue that fathers are not important in a child's development. After all, it takes two parents to make a child, so it makes sense that two parents are optimal for raising a child. As society has changed, the father's role in child-rearing has also changed. Nowadays, fathers are far more involved with parenting than they ever were before, and because of that, their roles in raising children are becoming further studied. Research on emotional intelligence has begun to discover that the father's role is maybe even more important than previously believed.

## The Relationship Between Father and Child's Emotional Intelligence

From birth, fathers have an impact on their children. Children who grow up with a father actively involved in their lives are more likely to grow up to be more emotionally secure. They are more confident and willing to explore and take chances. As they age, they develop to have better relationships of all kinds than peers who grew up without a father. Children who grow up with fathers are more likely to perform better in school and less likely to commit crimes. But why?

The answer is emotional intelligence.

Fathers with higher EQs are more interested in being involved with their children's upbringing, and their interactions with their children reflect emotional intelligence. They are more likely to be nurturing, empathetic, and supportive in the way that their children need because of their EQs, and in turn, their children grow up to become emotionally intelligent as well. Because children see their father's EQ modeled for them throughout their early development, they naturally tend to take the skills equivalent to their father's EQ.

A study testing for a relationship between children and fathers' emotional intelligence found that there was, in fact, a statistically significant relationship between a father and his children's emotional intelligence. The study, performed by Mojgan Mirza and Ma'rof Redzuan in Malaysia, found that the majority of children studied that tested with higher EQs had fathers that were also emotionally intelligent. The conclusion found that fathers are statistically significant to the development of their children's emotional intelligence.

This study was conducted studying Iranian students within Iranian primary schools in the city of Kuala Lumpur, Malaysia. They studied 107 father-child pairs, with the children ranging from 8-10 years old, and the fathers being a graduate or Ph.D. students at the universities throughout the country, ranging from ages 25 to over 40. They used the Bar-On EQ-i to test for the father's emotional intelligence while using the EQ-i Youth Version for the children, along with a short questionnaire about demographics. Within every category, the scientists tested (intrapersonal, interpersonal, stress management, adaptability, general mood, and total emotional intelligence), there was a statistically significant relationship. This means that the father's own emotional intelligence was statistically reflected in their children's own EQs.

## The Importance of the Father's EQ

If the father has a significant influence over his children's EQ, it should come as no surprise that the father's role in childrearing is important. Fathers play a crucial role in developing cognitive, behavior, and general health. Further, boys who have grown up with a positive male role model tend to develop better, more positive gender-role characteristics. They are more likely to be positive male role models themselves when they grow up. Girls who grow up with positive male role models tend to develop better opinions of men in general, as well as develop a better understanding of men.

Children with involved fathers tend to do better educationally and are associated with stronger communication skills, critical thinking, and academic achievement in adolescents. This may be due to the fact that compared to mothers, fathers spend a larger portion of their one-on-one interactions engaging in play than mothers do. These playful interactions become the basis for children learning to manage their emotions and behaviors.

Overall, the father's contribution to the child's emotional intelligence is just as significant as the mother's. Fathers with higher EQs tend to have some of the following traits:

- Engage emotionally with his children's own emotional states (empathetic)
- Avoids telling children how to feel
- Teaches problem-solving skills
- Guides children through challenges through adversity and everyday challenges
- Positively models management of negative, strong emotions
- Makes time to play with children

Each of those traits has significant impacts on a child's emotional development. The emotionally intelligent father is empathetic, focuses on problem-solving, and models positive coping mechanisms. Because children learn through play, they often emulate their fathers in play. They learn to develop their fathers' behaviors because those are what is modeled. If a father shows signs of low EQ, the children are likely to follow suit.

### Effect of Father's EQ for Children in Action

Now that it has been established that fathers are incredibly important to the development of EQ for children, let's take a few moments to see this in action. We will follow two different situations: A child who is afraid of the dark and cries at bedtime, and a teen who refused to do the dishes after dinner and has now lost electronics privileges and throwing a fit about it. We will look at each of these situations and how they would be likely to play out with both low and high EQ fathers, paying attention to both the father's actions and the child or teen's responses.

### Low EQ Father Interacting with Child

Ava, a 9-year-old, is terrified of the dark. She always has been, and she struggles to sleep without a night light, or without the hall light on. Every time the light is turned off, Ava cries and begs for it to be turned back on. If it gets turned off before Ava's father heads to bed and Ava wakes up in the middle of the night, she screams in terror and begs for help and for her light to be turned back on. When asked what her problem is, she never has a clear answer, instead just insisting that she is scared.

Her father, assuming he has a lower EQ, hears Ava screaming in her room in the middle of the night. He jumps out of bed, furious about the interruption, and storms to her bedroom, flinging the door open and further terrifying the child. Without stopping to see that his child is scared or in need of comfort, he immediately begins to yell. "What is wrong with you?! Just go to sleep! You shouldn't be afraid of the dark—you aren't a baby! There are no monsters in the dark! Just *stop crying and go to sleep!*"

Of course, this tirade does nothing to help Ava calm down. She hears her father yelling, and suddenly a monster in the dark seems far more real to her. She sees her father's face, but all she hears is the monster that is his rage, roaring at her to stop being afraid. She cries more uncontrollably at the situation, and her father responds in turn by shutting her door and leaving her in the dark to further cry to herself in fear.

He disregards her feelings, downplays and dismisses them, and acts in ways that do not exemplify problem-solving or teaching her to cope with her fear. Instead of helping her, he threw fuel on the fire, and she has learned that he cannot be trusted in critical moments when she is terrified. She learns that yelling at people that are annoying you is acceptable and that children do not need to be comforted or taken care of during periods of emotional turmoil. Her father's low EQ is learned by her as well, and she never is taught the proper way to manage her emotions.

### High EQ Father Interacting with Child

Now, imagine Ava's father within this scene with a higher EQ. He hears the sound of his daughter crying out for him in fear. Despite his initial annoyance at being woken up yet again, he takes a deep breath and gets up to tend to his daughter, reminding himself that she is having a hard time and needs the extra support.

He arrives at her room and sees his daughter sobbing in bed. "What's wrong?" he asks. He tries to encourage her to verbalize how she is feeling in hopes of being able to suggest actions to help with the situation. He reaches over to hug his daughter, recognizing that his child needs extra support during this emotional event. She shakes her head no in response, not answering. "Are you scared?" She nods. "Why?" She shrugs.

Seeing that this situation is not likely to be resolved by speaking alone and recognizing that getting frustrated is likely to only escalate the situation further, her father decides to offer solutions instead of fighting to tell her that she is wrong and being irrational. He understands that he cannot control her emotions and that she may be struggling to control them herself.

Instead of arguing, berating Ava, or lashing out angrily, her father instead offers up a few solutions. He asks if she wants her desk lamp on to sleep and she nods her head, tearfully looking up at her father. He obliges and turns it on. While he really only substituted one sleep crutch (sleeping with the hall light on) for another (sleeping with the lamp on), he has proven that he is supportive of his child. He offered her a solution that she accepted, and he is able to go off to sleep after another quick hug and reminding her that she is safe and to let him know if she needs anything else.

In this situation, despite the fact that Ava's father was frustrated, he acted with emotional intelligence. He did not take his frustration out on Ava, despite how much he may have been angry at being woken up yet again. He did not leave Ava to deal with her problem on her own. He did not belittle her feelings or demean her. He acted compassionately and approached the situation, knowing that his own interactions with her would set the stage for future interactions. If she felt as though she could not trust him, she would not be able to express her feelings, now or later. He offered a solution that was acceptable, helping her solve the problem and reminding her that she has the option to sleep with a lamp turned on if she needs it.

In this situation, Ava learned that her father approaches her with empathy and compassion, two skills that she is far more likely to internalize if she is typically on the receiving end of them. She learned to look for solutions for problems instead of staying the victim and being afraid to try to fix the problem. She learned that her emotions are allowed to be expressed and that she can trust her father to help her if she needs his support, no matter how inconvenient it may have been. She begins to pick up her father's higher EQ skills by watching them modeled for her.

### Low EQ Father of Teen

Now, let's imagine teenaged Brian. He hates doing chores more than anything and constantly seeks ways to avoid having to complete them. After dinner, his father asks him to take care of the dishes, as it is his week to do them. Brian says okay but never gets around to them. An hour and a half later, his father comes back and takes all electronics as a result. He removes Brian's tablet, phone, and game system from his room, and as a result, Brian flies into a rage about how those are his own belongings, and they cannot be taken away.

In response, the father with lower EQ skills likely gets just as angry as Brian has. The two of them feed into each other's anger, with it progressing further and further with neither of them being willing to admit fault or blame. Instead, both people refuse to back down, and Brian's father may even resort to doing something he will regret, such as breaking

Brian's phone in his rage to prove that he is in charge and can take, or destroy, anything he is paying for. This, of course, only serves to worsen the situation altogether. Brian is far less likely to listen when his own emotions are running high, and if his father cannot control himself, how can Brian really be expected to have the necessary skills to do so?

This entire situation ends with Brian learning that it is acceptable to smash things in his anger, solidifying lower EQ coping mechanisms as acceptable. He never learns how to communicate his own disdain or anger any better, and never learns to be held accountable for his own actions. He sees his father as an adversary rather than a support, and his father has irrevocably damaged his relationship with his son by destroying something belonging to him.

### High EQ Father of Teen

Now, imagine Brian's father has a higher EQ. Angry at seeing that his teen has not completed the dishes as expected to, he goes over to his son's room and walks in. Brian is texting someone on his phone instead of getting up. Instead of lashing out angrily, Brian's father calmly tells his son that it is time to do the dishes or there will be consequences. His son seems to shrug it off, not really caring. He once again reiterates the consequences of refusing to do the dishes.

Brian continues to resist doing his chore and instead goes back to his phone. His father nods and walks away to follow through with the consequence. He goes and locks down Wi-Fi and locks Brian's phone on the family plan. Within a minute of his consequence, Brian storms out, yelling about his electronics not working and generally raging.

Brian's father waits for him to finish speaking, and nods, acknowledging that he did disconnect the electronics. He gently reminded his son that nothing in life is free, and if he refuses to go to work, he will not have Wi-Fi or a cell phone to use. His father reiterates that chores must be done, and if Brian refuses to contribute to the household, he will not get the benefits of the household, such as having electronics paid for. He acknowledges how frustrating it is to have to do something that you do not want to do, but enforces the importance of responsibility. He relates to not wanting to go to work to pay for such a high phone bill but doing so out of responsibility and obligation. Adulthood is full of doing things you do not want to do, and it would be best if Brian learned that lesson sooner rather than later.

Brian seems surprised at first but seems to get the idea. He realizes that he has no choice but to contribute and take care of his chores if he wants to continue using his phone. While he may be furious at the results, he sees that there are no other options for him that he wants to go forward with. He begrudgingly does the dishes, learning the lesson of consequences for his actions. He sees that his father did not yell or scream at him, and instead spoke calmly and clearly. He sees the value in properly communicating with his father instead of shouting at him, and learns the valuable lesson of having to do things that you do not want to do, teaching self-management skills. With his high EQ father, he saw emotional intelligence modeled and will be more inclined to follow that example in future conflicts.

## CHAPTER 29

# Assessing the Effectiveness of Your Parenting Style

If you are reading this book, you are probably concerned with your own parenting skills to some degree. You are probably wondering just how effective you are with your parenting, and wondering what you could do to strengthen weaknesses. Luckily for you, this book has your back! This chapter will provide you with a simple questionnaire that you can use to analyze just how effective you are at parenting, as well as providing you with feedback based on how you score and what you can do with that information. The questionnaire is quite short, clocking in at just 50 multiple choice questions, which you will then score after completing them.

**What to Expect**

This questionnaire is filled with 50 multiple choice questions, each of which is tailored to be easily understood and answered. They will seek to assess just how effective you are at parenting, with a special emphasis on emotion coaching. There will be several questions relating to the five steps of emotion coaching, so you can see which steps you are already skilled at and which you need to work on. If you still feel a little lost about what emotion coaching is and what it entails, do not worry!

That is the focus of Part III, which comes right after completing this questionnaire. This assessment is presented first to enable you to comprehend where you stand in terms of effectiveness in the various steps so you can focus on the categories you need the most work on in the next section. Now, whenever you are ready, turn the page to begin the test!

### Emotion Coaching Parent Effectiveness Assessment

### Instructions

Welcome to the Emotion Coaching Parent Effectiveness Assessment! This test will analyze and evaluate your effectiveness in regards to the several steps and skills necessary to be an effective emotion coaching parent! Each of these questions will be presented in a multiple-choice format. Be sure to answer each question honestly and carefully to ensure the most accurate results. Remember, this test does not replace the opinion of a licensed professional who understands the ins and outs of your specific situation, and should instead be taken as a general suggestion for how to progress in your journey toward becoming an effective parent as opposed to an expert opinion. Pay special attention to the options of answers, as sometimes, they may change order, or shift from always-never to agree-disagree, or describes me-does not describe me.

When you are ready to begin, make sure you can set aside maybe 15-20 minutes that will be uninterrupted, and bring a piece of paper and a writing utensil, or prepare to record answers on your phone, computer, tablet, or other note-taking apparatus. Focus solely on this assessment without distractions and really consider your answers. Oftentimes, your gut answer will be the most accurate. When writing your answers to your question, record the section, the question number, and the number corresponding to your answer for the easiest grading.

## Section 1

- I frequently can tell what my child is thinking or feeling at a glance.

  1. Disagree completely
  2. Disagree somewhat
  3. Neither agree nor disagree
  4. Agree somewhat
  5. Agree completely

- My child often gets frustrated with me because I react differently than he or she wants or needs

  1. Agree completely
  2. Agree somewhat
  3. Neither agree nor disagree
  4. Disagree somewhat
  5. Disagree completely

- I know what typically triggers my child's negative emotions

  1. Disagree completely
  2. Disagree somewhat
  3. Neither agree nor disagree
  4. Agree somewhat
  5. Agree completely

- I can predict when my child is likely to meltdown

  1. Never
  2. Rarely
  3. Sometimes
  4. Often
  5. Always

- My child's emotions are difficult for me to understand or recognize. It's like my child is a blank slate and does not emote.

  1. Always
  2. Often
  3. Sometimes
  4. Rarely
  5. Never

- I always know exactly what to do to cheer up my child when he or she is feeling sad.

  1. Disagree completely
  2. Disagree somewhat
  3. Neither agree nor disagree
  4. Agree somewhat
  5. Agree completely

- My child's emotions seem to catch me by surprise

  1. Always
  2. Often
  3. Sometimes
  4. Rarely
  5. Never

- My child trusts that he or she can come to me with anything and know that I will do my best to support him or her.

  1. Disagree completely
  2. Disagree somewhat
  3. Neither agree nor disagree
  4. Agree somewhat
  5. Agree completely

- I can name how my child is feeling based on his or her body language.

  1. Never
  2. Rarely
  3. Sometimes
  4. Often
  5. Always

- I can often tell there is something wrong with my child, even if he or she says otherwise.

  1. Never
  2. Rarely
  3. Sometimes
  4. Often
  5. Always

## Section 2

- When my child is emotional, I try to walk him or her through what is being felt

  1. Never
  2. Rarely
  3. Sometimes
  4. Often
  5. Never

- When my child does something inappropriate in response to his or her emotions, I:

  1. Scold him or her for feeling that way. It was unnecessary and unwarranted, and all it did was cause trouble.
  2. Tell him or her to get over it and get his or her act together.
  3. Did nothing and allowed my child to feel how he or she wanted.
  4. Point out how my child's misbehavior is a problem and tell them not to continue the behaviors.
  5. Point out that it is okay to be upset, but those bad behaviors are unacceptable and offer an alternative behavior.

- I encourage my child to consider how his or her behaviors stemming from strong emotions impact other people as well.

  1. Never
  2. Rarely
  3. Sometimes
  4. Often
  5. Always

- I frequently try to vocalize how I am dealing with my own strong emotions when in the presence of my child.

  1. Disagree completely
  2. Disagree somewhat
  3. Neither agree nor disagree
  4. Agree somewhat
  5. Agree completely

- After my child has calmed down, I try to guide him or her through reflecting on the results of strong feelings and the behaviors that came with them to understand the consequences of what happened.

  1. Never
  2. Rarely
  3. Sometimes
  4. Often
  5. Always

- I always encourage my child to reflect upon what happens, good and bad, and identify how things could have been different with different actions.

  1. Disagree completely
  2. Disagree somewhat
  3. Neither agree nor disagree
  4. Agree somewhat
  5. Agree completely

- I want my child to learn from his or her actions and emotions.

  1. Disagree completely
  2. Disagree somewhat
  3. Neither agree nor disagree
  4. Agree somewhat
  5. Agree completely

- My child knows he or she can ask me any questions about feelings and get honest answers from me

  1. Disagree completely
  2. Disagree somewhat
  3. Neither agree nor disagree
  4. Agree somewhat
  5. Agree completely

- Inappropriate behaviors are a natural consequence of negative emotions and should be accepted and allowed as freedom of expression

  1. Agree completely
  2. Agree somewhat
  3. Neither agree nor disagree
  4. Disagree somewhat
  5. Disagree completely

- I make it a personal goal to guide my child through understanding how he or she feels, even if it can be tough at times.

    1. Disagree completely
    2. Disagree somewhat
    3. Neither agree nor disagree
    4. Agree somewhat
    5. Agree completely

## Section 3

- I stop what I am doing to hear my child out when he or she comes to me and is visibly upset.

  1. Disagree completely
  2. Disagree somewhat
  3. Neither agree nor disagree
  4. Agree somewhat
  5. Agree completely

- When my child is crying, I typically acknowledge that and try to relate to a time that I was also upset over something similar.

  1. Never
  2. Rarely
  3. Sometimes
  4. Often
  5. Always

- My child trusts me enough to come to me in times he or she needs extra emotional support or guidance

  1. Disagree completely
  2. Disagree somewhat
  3. Neither agree nor disagree
  4. Agree somewhat
  5. Agree completely

- I try to tell my child that getting upset over things is not important and is a waste of time

1. Always
2. Often
3. Sometimes
4. Rarely
5. Never

- When my child is upset or angry, I try to distract them from their emotions.

  1. Agree completely
  2. Agree somewhat
  3. Neither agree nor disagree
  4. Disagree somewhat
  5. Disagree completely

- I am trying to teach my child to disregard emotions as they are not conducive to rationality.

  1. Agree completely
  2. Agree somewhat
  3. Neither agree nor disagree
  4. Disagree somewhat
  5. Disagree completely

- I react negatively to my child's emotions.

  1. Always
  2. Often
  3. Sometimes
  4. Rarely
  5. Never

- My child's emotions are treated as an afterthought, especially if I am busy or if they interfere with what needs to get done.

  1. Always
  2. Often
  3. Sometimes
  4. Rarely
  5. Never

- I take the time really understand and acknowledge how my child is feeling, no matter how silly it may seem to me

  1. Never
  2. Rarely
  3. Sometimes
  4. Often
  5. Always

- My child's emotions are always a topic of discussion. I tend to ask how he or she felt about topics that are brought up or about things that happened during the day.

  1. Never
  2. Rarely
  3. Sometimes
  4. Often
  5. Always

## Section 4

- I have a wide range of vocabulary to cover various emotions.

    1. Disagree completely
    2. Disagree somewhat
    3. Neither agree nor disagree
    4. Agree somewhat
    5. Agree completely

- I use a wide range of vocabulary to voice my emotions in ways that other people can understand and try to explain those words to my children.

    1. Never
    2. Rarely
    3. Sometimes
    4. Often
    5. Always

- Specific words for emotions do not matter, so long as the basic idea is conveyed (e.g., bad or good).

    1. Agree completely
    2. Agree somewhat
    3. Neither agree nor disagree
    4. Disagree somewhat
    5. Disagree completely

- I seek to voice what my child is feeling in order to instill a better ability to communicate his or her own emotions. For example, if he is crying, I may say he seems so sad or disappointed, depending on the context.

1. Never
2. Rarely
3. Sometimes
4. Often
5. Always

- The more specific the word, the better when it comes to naming emotions

  1. Disagree completely
  2. Disagree somewhat
  3. Neither agree nor disagree
  4. Agree somewhat
  5. Agree completely

- When someone asks me how I'm feeling, I answer honestly

  1. Never
  2. Rarely
  3. Sometimes
  4. Often
  5. Always

- I have always struggled to identify and name other people's emotions

  1. Agree completely
  2. Agree somewhat
  3. Neither agree nor disagree
  4. Disagree somewhat
  5. Disagree completely

• I can clearly identify and differentiate between similar emotions, and am teaching my child to do so as well (e.g., guilt vs. shame or pride vs. happiness)

1. Disagree completely
2. Disagree somewhat
3. Neither agree nor disagree
4. Agree somewhat
5. Agree completely

• I understand what people mean when they list specific emotions (e.g., feeling ecstatic or despair).

1. Never
2. Rarely
3. Sometimes
4. Often
5. Always

• I struggle to communicate my emotions verbally.

1. Agree completely
2. Agree somewhat
3. Neither agree nor disagree
4. Disagree somewhat
5. Disagree completely

## Section 5

- I let my child flounder and fail when confronted with adversity, and do not intervene, no matter how bad the situation may get.

  1. Agree completely
  2. Agree somewhat
  3. Neither agree nor disagree
  4. Disagree somewhat
  5. Disagree completely

- When my child is facing a problem, I ask guiding questions to help lead him or her to potential solutions.

  1. Never
  2. Rarely
  3. Sometimes
  4. Often
  5. Always

- If my child is struggling, I will take over completely to ensure he or she does not fail.

  1. Always
  2. Often
  3. Sometimes
  4. Rarely
  5. Never

- My child should never experience failure. Failure is a sign of weakness and incompetence and should be looked down upon.

1. Agree completely
2. Agree somewhat
3. Neither agree nor disagree
4. Disagree somewhat
5. Disagree completely

- Adversity and problem-solving build character, even if failure happens, and I encourage and welcome that for my child.

1. Disagree completely
2. Disagree somewhat
3. Neither agree nor disagree
4. Agree somewhat
5. Agree completely

- I will tell my child exactly what to do to fix a problem without making him or her come up with the answer.

1. Agree completely
2. Agree somewhat
3. Neither agree nor disagree
4. Disagree somewhat
5. Disagree completely

- My child is learning the value in failing in controlled environments where I can intervene if necessary.

1. Disagree completely
2. Disagree somewhat
3. Neither agree nor disagree
4. Agree somewhat
5. Agree completely

- My child is encouraged to think of solutions to problems underneath my supervision and is welcome to ask for help if necessary.

  1. Disagree completely
  2. Disagree somewhat
  3. Neither agree nor disagree
  4. Agree somewhat
  5. Agree completely

- When I am faced with my own conflict around my child, I make it a point to talk out how I am solving it so my children can see what good problem-solving skills look like.

  1. Never
  2. Rarely
  3. Sometimes
  4. Often
  5. Always

- My child is encouraged to see failure as a learning experience and not something to be embarrassed or self-conscious about.

  1. Disagree completely
  2. Disagree somewhat
  3. Neither agree nor disagree
  4. Agree somewhat
  5. Agree completely

### Calculating Your Scores

Congratulations! You have finished the questionnaire! Now for the fun part—calculating your score. Luckily for you, this questionnaire had ease of scoring in mind. Each answer should be scored as the number of the answer subtracting 1. So if you chose answer 4, you would award 3 points for that question in that section.

| | |
|---|---|
| Answer 1 | 0 points |
| Answer 2 | 1 point |
| Answer 3 | 2 points |
| Answer 4 | 3 points |
| Answer 5 | 4 points |

For further ease, you could add up the sum of all answers within your section and subtract 10 (1 point per question) from the final result to get your score per section. When you have your category scores, you can begin to identify what your scores mean for you.

Each section of the assessment related to a different emotion coaching skill.

| | |
|---|---|
| Section 1 | Awareness of Child's Feelings |
| Section 2 | Seeing Emotions as Teaching Experiences |
| Section 3 | Listening and Validating Child's Emotions |
| Section 4 | Labeling Emotions |
| Section 5 | Encouraging Problem-Solving |

### Your results

This table shows how you should expect your results to be calculated. You can look at this table at a glance to see which category each of your skill levels fell into, as well as seeing how your general effectiveness holds up.

| Result | Individual Emotion Coaching Skill Effectiveness | Total Emotion Coaching Effectiveness |
|---|---|---|
| Area for Enrichment: Needs work | 0-24 | 0-120 |
| Effective Functioning: Proficient, but could be strengthened | 25-34 | 121-170 |
| Enhanced: Highly effective | 35-40 | 171-200 |

### Area for Enrichment (0-24 individual skill effectiveness, or 0-120 general effectiveness)

In this category, you show that you are struggling to parent in a way that is reminiscent of emotion coaching. You likely are not very in control of the situation when one arises, and you may struggle to help your child process emotions healthily. You, yourself, likely have some sort of impaired level of emotional intelligence, and likely find yourself losing your temper frequently when interacting with emotionally volatile children.

This can lead to a lot of tension with your child, as your child never gets the support needed to develop healthily. You struggle to emulate skills your child would learn through watching you, never giving your children the foundation that would make functioning throughout adulthood far easier. Your child is likely to pick up negative coping mechanisms or attitudes surrounding emotions, especially for negative emotions, and this can lead to many issues overall. Your child may struggle to

If you score in this category for either individual skills or as a whole, you need to work on your emotion coaching to become more effective. The most effective way to go about this would be seeking out books about strengthening your own emotional intelligence. There are two other books in this series: *Emotional Intelligence 2.0* and *Emotional Intelligence Practical Guide* that could work help you with that process. By raising your own emotional intelligence, you will find that the skills involved in emotion coaching come easier.

If you struggle with only one or two skills in emotion coaching, then you should seek to bolster it with your other skills. For example, if you are great at seeing emotions as learning experiences, but you struggle with encouraging problem-solving, you can work to use your skills at making things learning experiences to start looking at problems as more learning experiences. By shifting your expectation and mindset, you may be better able to encourage problem-solving, as problem-solving itself becomes a learning experience in your mind. Instead of seeing it as your child failing, you would see your child learning. Come up with ways that your stronger skills can strengthen and support your weaknesses, and you may find yourself performing better with emotion coaching.

## Effective Functioning (25-34 individual skill effectiveness, or 121-170 general effectiveness)

If you fall into this category, your skills are at the very least functional. You can emotion-coach well enough, but you likely still struggle sometimes, especially with some of your weaker skills. There is always room for improvement, and you should consider any skills that fall within this category as worthy of revisiting and attempting to better, but they will do in a pinch.

If you are effective at emotion coaching, you are likely pretty average in terms of your own EQ as well. You are content in your life, though you may run into roadblocks that you struggle to overcome sometimes.

You may run into bumps, especially with your children, as you try to guide them through the messiness that is their emotional state. Because you, yourself, do not have a mastery over your own emotional control, you may make mistakes frequently, though you likely admit to them and apologize to your child for them as well.

As a parent, you can probably navigate through day-to-day emotions just fine with your children, and you find coaching them during mild anger, sadness, or fear easy enough, you likely struggle as soon as emotions are heightened, as they often are with children. You may fail to communicate effectively enough to really prevent most arguments or backlash, and you likely also may fail at really defusing the tensest emotional situations effectively.

If you have scored within this range, your skills will suffice, but you should seek to strengthen them over time. Keep practicing those skills until you become more effective! Likewise, look into strengthening your EQ! You always have room to improve!

### Enhanced Skill (35-40 individual skill effectiveness, or 171-200 general effectiveness)

Congratulations! This is the best score category you could have achieved! If your scores have fallen within this range, you have a near-mastery of the skill you tested. You are effective and efficient in the skills that scored at this level, and you are likely extremely efficient at emotion coaching in general.

This has great connotations for your children—they are likely getting the best upbringing they could from you. You are preparing them for the real world and creating a foundation of emotional intelligence. You are giving them the skills that they will need to set themselves up for success in the future.

If you scored within this range for emotion coaching in general, you are likely within a high range for your own emotional intelligence. You probably manage to guide your children through difficult situations with relative ease, and frequently are able to settle conflicts quickly and maturely, something your child appreciates. You are likely quite empathetic with your children, and always consider their own emotions when approaching or parenting them. If you have scored within this range, keep up the good work and make sure you continue to practice such good emotion coaching skills!

## CHAPTER 30

# Emotion Coaching
# Elements

There are several various elements to emotion coaching that arise as recurring themes to the skill. Within the five steps, these elements should be present. These elements help keep both yourself and your child in line, as well as set the stage for the steps of emotion coaching to run its course in the most effective manner. The four most important elements underlying emotion coaching are:

### Unconditional Love

Every child needs love to grow and develop. It is so inherently important that many of the interactions with young children and their parents are designed to biologically create a deep bond between the two. It has literally been ingrained in our instincts to fiercely love and protect our children from anything that may threaten their survival or success. Unconditional love is love that will be there no matter what. It is the idea that nothing your child could do would ever diminish or mar the love you feel toward him or her.

This is an incredibly important foundation in emotion coaching; by providing your child with unconditional love, he or she learns that any communication and any expression of emotion is acceptable to you, so long as it is verbal. Your child knows that, even when acting out, or making mistakes, you will not love your child any less. This is an important foundation of trust.

Through trusting you, your child will be more willing to heed advice, and more inclined to go to you when she needs help, even if it is her own fault that she is in the mess she has gotten herself into, such as she decided to drink at a party and now is afraid to drive home. A teen with trust in her parents' unconditional love is likely to call and ask for a ride home, knowing just how dangerous driving home after drinking could be. This is a good thing—it means your child has developed coping skills and knows she can communicate with you.

### Providing Ample Space

Teaching your child how to manage problems is important. For this reason, you must give your child the space necessary to make mistakes in order to teach him how to solve them. If your child never makes mistakes, he is never in a position where he has to fix things, meaning he never develops crucial skills that he will need in adulthood. If you solve every problem for your child as they come up, all your child learns is that you will always be there to bail him out—but what happens when you are no longer there? Every person dies at some point, and if you were to have an untimely death late in your child's teen years or early into adulthood, he would not have the skills he would need to survive socially.

No parent enjoys seeing their child suffer; however, it is an important part of growing up. Instead of being afraid of your child failing, you should be recognizing that failing is a necessary step toward succeeding. There are plenty of things that are failed dozens of times, or even hundreds, or thousands, or countless times before someone succeeds. Think of landing on the moon; that was once an impossibility, but now it is commonly accepted as doable. You must be able to provide your child with the space necessary to explore and develop important skills.

By having the space necessary to develop individually, your child is working on foundations for problem-solving and communicating effectively with peers. These skills are invaluable and absolutely necessary to be a successful adult.

### Mentoring Relationships

Rather than seeing the parent-child relationship as the parent being in a position of power or authority over the child, or seeing the parent-child relationship as a friendship, you should aim to create a mentoring relationship between the two of you. Within a mentoring relationship, you acknowledge that you are teaching and guiding your child rather than controlling and asserting authority over her. She needs to be treated as her own individual rather than controlled. She is her own person and will have her own likes, dislikes, emotions, and preferences. Your job is to ensure she has the social skills and emotional intelligence to cope with whatever life throws at her while allowing her to flourish into whoever she was destined to be.

By keeping your relationship in terms of a mentorship rather than one built on the authority vested in you simply because you are the parent, you will be in a better mindset. Your job is to teach, not command. You will keep your interactions with your child tailored to inform how best to act rather than requiring it. Just as you can lead a horse to water, but can never force it to drink, you cannot force your child to follow through with what you have suggested. The best you can do is hope that your modeling and teaching has paid off and your child has heeded your suggested.

### Healthy Boundaries

Every relationship requires healthy boundaries, and the parent-child relationship is no exception. While your child should feel comfortable coming to talk to you in confidence about anything, that should not be reciprocal. You should not be burdening your child with your own heavy thoughts or feelings, especially if those things are relevant to your child's other parent. You should not try to make your child your own confidante. While it is true that you should be open and honest, you should stick to facts rather than giving the child details that he has no business knowing.

Likewise, there should be boundaries the other way as well. Your child needs to develop independence somewhere, and you need to make sure that you give your child all the privacy he or she requests, so long as it is safe to do so. Most teens will be fine with that sort of privacy, barring any other physical or mental health issues, and you need to give that to them. As your child will hopefully eventually enter the world on his or her own, you need to respect desires for boundaries or privacy, as well, which further gives your child the chance to begin mastering managing emotions and solving problems, two of the important parts of emotional intelligence. Children who are given the reins while still being guided by you are far more likely to be successful than children who are constantly directed, or children who do not receive any real guidance at all. Toeing that fine line between following, crossing, and not coming close enough to the boundary is difficult, but is worthwhile when it comes to your child's emotional intelligence.

### Common Emotion Coaching Mistakes

Within emotion coaching, several mistakes can happen pretty frequently. It should come as no surprise—emotion coaching is just as much of a series of skills as emotional intelligence is, and it requires practice to get right. No parent is magically fantastic at emotion coaching, and no parent ever gets it perfectly from the get-go without ever making mistakes at some point. Perfection and humans do not go hand in hand, and you should not feel bad about making any of these mistakes.

Instead, just as you teach your children, look at your mistakes as learning opportunities and aim to avoid making them in the future as well. With practice and perseverance, you will get it.

### Overly-permissive

If one of the important elements of emotion coaching is providing space for the child to develop and grow on his or her own, it should come as no surprise that people often overcorrect and grant their children too much freedom. Oftentimes, this can be done with good intentions, but they do say that the road to hell is paved with them. No matter how well-meaning you may have been, your child needs guidance somewhere. Yes, your child should be allowed to make mistakes and flounder now and again, but you do not leave your child to flounder alone. You need to be there to catch your child before he is seriously hurt. You are still there to guide your child, even if you are not micro-managing. Think of this as supervising your young child at the playground—you are there if your child needs you, but not constantly trying to tell him how to play or what to do or say. You would not allow your young child to try to climb on the outside of the slide that is 15 feet tall and would likely intervene if you saw your child trying to. You should take that same sort of stance with your child in other aspects of life as well, allowing him to experiment and explore, but drawing a line where lines must be drawn for safety's sake.

If you know that your child is engaging in unsafe sex, for example, you should not allow that to continue. While you cannot necessarily police a teen's sex life, nor can you control your teen at all hours of every day, you can step in, have the safe sex talk, and offer to take the teen to get birth control and provide condoms. This is not overly controlling—this is teaching your child life-long lessons and ensuring that she does not do something that could have permanent repercussions for her, such as having a child as a teen or catching an STI. Teaching your child about safe sexual practices, consent, and birth control is well within the normal realm for parenting responsibilities, and not having those conversations would border on neglectful.

### Solving the problem for the child

Remember how not helping the child at all was a problem and lead to the child struggling to solve problems at all? Well, doing all of the work is another common overcorrection. People may feel as though they are too permissive and overcorrect by not allowing the child any opportunities to attempt solving the problem at all. Parents may insert themselves where they are unwanted or unwarranted, rather than allowing their children room to grow. These children grow to be overly dependent on their parents and generally incapable of managing life on their own.

Frequently, their peers look down upon them due to their stunted nature, and no one wants to befriend the person with the emotional maturity of someone several years younger than them. Especially once your child goes off to college, if that is something he chooses to do, he is going to struggle greatly if you have spent his entire life working things out for him. He needs to have the chance to grow on his own without parental involvement since it is really only the first 20% or so of a person's life that they require such intensive involvement from another person. Especially as your teen gets through the middle-late teen years, he needs to experience the consequences of failure. If he needs his gym shorts clean for the next day but left them in the washer overnight, do not move them for him; let him suffer the consequences when he wakes up and finds them sopping wet and smelling like mildew the next morning. He needs to learn to rely on himself to prepare for the real world. Likewise, if he chooses not to write a paper, do not provide him with an out, an excused absence, or even help him write it. Let him suffer the repercussions, even if it leaves a mark on his grades or he winds up unable to play in his basketball game due to academic problems.

### Unhealthy or nonexistent boundaries

Boundaries are important. That has been established already. However, those boundaries have to be healthy. Unhealthy boundaries, such as boundaries that are far too strict, or nonexistent boundaries, can actually prove to be emotionally harmful rather than beneficial. It can be difficult to mind the balance between them, and far too often, parents stray too far from that find line and into the territory of unhealthy boundaries.

When dealing with unhealthy boundaries, the parent may put far too much emphasis on the child listening to conversations that are inappropriate, such as about the parent's relationships, or other unreasonable topics of conversation. This can lead to a child feeling as though she must be the emotional support for her parent rather than the other way around. This is unhealthy and robs the child of innocence, forcing her to grow up far too early. If a child frequently listens to her mother complain about her father or other relationships, the mother is putting the child in a role where she feels obligated to emotionally support and care for her mother, even though that is none of her concern and likely inappropriate. This child learns to push away her own emotions in favor of other people's and never really learns self-regulation skills.

On the other hand, children whose parents have boundaries that are far too strict, such as a parent who does not wish to hear any emotional discussion, grow up feeling undervalued. A parent who puts up boundaries that are too strict leaves a child feeling as though they are missing parts of those close bonds typically developed with parents. Instead, the child feels the need to seek that bond out elsewhere, and may even engage in riskier behaviors seeking out the relationship that should have been developed with the parents. This child may seek out romantic relationships, even if they are unhealthy, just to feel close to someone if that role is not being fulfilled by parents. This can also lead to early exposure to all sorts of topics and things that children or teens have no business experimenting with. Likewise, this child is not likely to learn the skills necessary to self-regulate or to interact appropriately with other people. Because the child's parent instead prefers to keep the relationship within strict terms and may never allow the child to experiment beyond what the parent dictates, the child never learns how to interact with others or communicate when he may feel like needs are not being met.

### Too strict

Sometimes, parents try to parent but only manage to be too strict instead. Rather than creating a safe, controlled environment for their children to learn, they instead crackdown so there is never anything to learn. Their children may never be allowed to play with certain crowds due to misperceptions, or may not get the chance to go to sleepovers or parties due to their parents thinking they are inappropriate. They may be denied the ability to date during the teen years when children are learning all about their preferences and how to be in romantic relationships while still having the guidance of parents.

These children miss out on many aspects of social development that are crucial to learning all aspects of emotional intelligence. When they finally are old enough to break free into the real world, they are often severely emotionally stunted, and may even overcorrect, experimenting with everything they were denied in childhood. They likely lack control over themselves as being in control was never an option. Since their parents dictated everything, they never learned to make proper decisions or face the consequences of poor decisions as children when the long-term effects are typically minimal compared to having them happen in adulthood. Consider a teen who gets into a fight and impulsively punches someone—that will go on his record, and he may get in some trouble, but he is a minor and the criminal records of minors are typically considered confidential. However, if that same teen punches someone at age 19 shortly after moving out, that is considered a crime committed in adulthood and becomes public record, marring his background check for the next several years. By being too strict, you do your child a disservice. Your child needs to learn how to self-regulate and control himself while risks are still low. As a child and a teen, those risks are at the lowest they will ever be.

## CHAPTER 31

# Emotion Coaching
# Strategies

Emotion coaching is an integral part of raising emotionally intelligent children. It is the middle step between coaching elements and emotional intelligence.

Without emotion coaching, children do not receive the best foundations for building high EQs. While growing up in homes without emotion, coaching does not necessarily doom a child to failure as an adult; it certainly does not do the child any favors. He can grow to be quite emotionally intelligent despite his upbringing, but his upbringing is not what caused it unless he chose to be the exact opposite of what he was exposed to throughout life.

### What is Emotion Coaching?

Simply put, emotion coaching is a type of communication strategy. It is meant to support children and teens while they develop their own emotional intelligence and learn how to manage their own relationships. This parenting strategy teaches children to understand their own emotions, as well as how to manage them and cope in productive ways. Five steps come together to create effective, successful emotion coaching. These are:

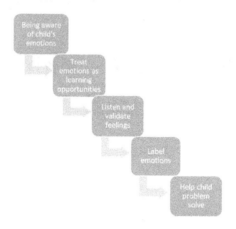

When all five steps come together, skillfully, a parenting style with an emphasis on empathy and developing higher levels of emotional intelligence is born. It is a very intensive parenting style and requires higher levels of patience and time, but that effort is well worth it when your child becomes more prepared for the adversities that will be faced in the future, as well as when you notice your own relationship with the child improving.

**Step 1: Be Aware of Your Child's Emotions (and Your Own!)**

Emotional intelligence is, as implied, all about emotions. Of course, the foundation is having a general knowledge of emotions. Just as the foundation to emotional intelligence is self-awareness, you must be aware of your child's emotions to be able to effectively emotion coach. An effective emotion coach must be a master at their own self-regulation. Pay attention to your own emotions first, no matter what they are, and understand them. Likewise, you should pay attention to your child's emotions, as well. Pay special attention to how your child expresses himself in various contexts with different emotions. You need to learn your child's emotional expressions if you hope to coach him. Watch for body language and facial expressions that can be helpful in the future to help you understand how your child is feeling at a glance. This will be crucial when you attempt to emotion coach.

If you are struggling with identifying your own emotions, it would be prudent to first work on strengthening your own self-awareness before proceeding. Remember, emotion coaching requires plenty of emotional intelligence from the parent's part to succeed; if you are struggling to identify your own feelings and emotional tells on the regular, you will struggle to accurately read your child's as well.

To see how this step might play out, consider this example: If you see your child in a tough situation, you may notice how his brow furrows in frustration, paired with a small scowl while his whole body tenses up as he stares intently at whatever happens to be frustrating him. You may notice how you can see the frustration in his eyes, and then you see him stomp his feet and clench his fists as he tries to figure out what to do to solve his frustration. His voice may be sharper when he talks, or he may whine and say he is stuck and needs help. The longer you focus on your child's body language, you may begin to identify smaller cues to their emotional state, such as the way he may bite his lip when scared or how one eyebrow may be quirked slightly when puzzled. Watch for patterns until you understand the ins and outs of your child's body language.

With a teen, this may be a bit more difficult. Teens are prone to sulking around by their nature and may even focus on hiding their emotions and coming across as cool and collected at all times. Even with teens, you may be able to notice emotional tells. Maybe her voice quivers slightly when she is upset, or she tends to play with her hair when nervous. Even teens who try their best likely have some emotional tells that you will be able to identify if you focus long enough on trying to discover them.

### Step 2: See Emotions as Teaching and Learning Opportunities

Remember how with emotional intelligence, learning opportunities come from failure? Well, they also come from emotions in general! Especially when emotions and tensions run high, you might make mistakes.

It takes a lot of self-management to be able to regulate your own reactions, especially if the emotions being felt are negative.

You likely will struggle with this step if you struggle with self-management for yourself. You need to be able to control your own emotions and reactions if you hope to be able to recommend ways to manage your child's, especially if your child's emotions are directed your way. It is easy to feel frustrated if your child is screaming, "I hate you!" over and over again in his anger about you refusing to allow him to eat dessert before dinner, after all.

Once again, within this step, you want to pay close attention to how your child is feeling. When emotions start running high, this is your cue to start a learning moment. You can identify your child's feeling to him, putting a word to those strong feelings that your child may not fully understand, depending on the age. You can provide your child with ways to cope with his strong emotions as well, guiding him through the steps one by one.

For example, if your six-year-old son is crying inconsolably because he dropped his Lego masterpiece that he spent all afternoon building and broke it, you have the perfect opportunity to guide your child through that disappointment and dismay. You should approach your child and get on your child's level. Put a hand on his shoulder and tell him that he looks very frustrated and sad right now, and ask if he wants a hug. Respect whatever his answer is to that question, and follow up with something along the lines of, "Are you frustrated?" Wait for him to answer. "Do you know what I do when I'm upset like you are? I like to take a deep breath, hold it in, count to five, and then breathe out as hard as I can. Would you like to try to do that too?" Gently urge your child to go along with your method. If he is reluctant, do not push, but stay there with your child and try offering another method to calm down. "What if you stomp three times? Would you feel better then?" If your child refuses to try, there is not much you can do other than be there for him. While you should not punish your child, suggesting that your child takes a private moment to compose himself is acceptable if what he wants to do is cry it out. The goal here is to guide your child to cope with emotions before he escalates from being upset into misbehaving or acting out. Crying on its own is not a form of acting out, and you should never tell your child not to cry or not to be a crybaby. If your child starts to calm down, you can ask him to talk about what happened and why he feels the way he does in order to encourage him to speak about his emotions.

With a teen, this step is often a bit more difficult. Teens are far more standoffish than children most of the time and maybe far more reluctant to speak about emotions with parents. Nevertheless, you should still seek to encourage it. If your teen comes home, seeming a little more reserved and brooding than usual, you can ask him what happened. Be prepared for the answer to be that nothing happened and everything is fine, and remember not to pry, no matter how much you may want to. Gently remind your teen that you are there if he wants to talk and move on. If his emotions begin to impact other people, such as snapping at people at the dinner table, gently call your child to the task and remind him that snapping is not acceptable, but that he is welcome to talk to you about whatever is bothering him. If he firmly refuses to speak to you, you can also encourage emotional expression through journaling or encouraging him to talk to friends, or even offering a therapist if you notice that his emotions are getting out of hand.

### Step 3: Listen and Validate Your Child's Feelings

Step 3 requires you to use two skills to better help your child: both empathy and listening skills. It takes a lot of effort to really listen and comprehend what someone else is saying, and that skill is something that many people have to go out of their way to strengthen. If listening skills are something you struggle with, work on those while also attempting this step. That is a skill that will serve you well, and will also benefit your child as well.

In order to validate your child's feelings, you must make it a point to take what she says seriously. Do not dismiss or criticize her emotions, as that only serves to make her feel invalidated, and misses the entire point of this step. Emotions, no matter what they are, are valid if they are being felt. There are no right or wrong ways to feel in certain situations, and you need to respect and remember that. If your child approaches you with specific feelings, you should always acknowledge and accept it. Further, you should make it a point to show your child that you are listening and even try to paraphrase what she says to you to ensure that you understand. By repeating back what she has said to you, you give her the opportunity to correct any misunderstandings.

Consider your 5-year-old daughter coming up to you and saying, "I'm really disappointed you didn't take me to the part today like we always do on Mondays." She might look up at you and pout. Your gut reaction may be to react defensively. Yes, you may typically take her to the park Monday evenings, but that particular day, you had had a late meeting at work, and then traffic had been horrendous on the way home, and you may have been an hour and a half late, eating into the time you would usually use for the park. Instead, you should seek to understand what your child is saying. Tell her that you understand and that you are also disappointed that you could not go to the park today, and ask if the two of you can go tomorrow instead.

Maybe your teenager comes up to you and says he is annoyed that you keep making him do chores and that he has to turn in his electronics by 10pm on school nights. He may try to make the argument that his friend has no curfew or chores, so he should not be required to do those things because it is not fair. He vents these frustrations to you and then asks you to eliminate the requirements.

This is a tricky situation, as disagreeing with him may come across as invalidating his emotions. This situation requires tact and skillful communication. You can respond saying that you were also frustrated by having to do chores as a child. Remind him that you are not his friend's parent and that your house rules stand, no matter how frustrating they may be for him. Acknowledge his feelings as valid and that he is more than welcome to feel that way, but those feelings do not obligate you to change your rules, no matter how unfair he may feel it is. Remind him that when he is an adult and in his own home, he is more than welcome to set his own rules, but for now, he has to live with yours.

## Step 4: Label Emotions

Step 4 returns back to the basics: self-awareness. Thus far, you have noticed your child's emotions, made it a point to acknowledge your child's feelings, and listened to what your child has had to say about his or her feelings without invalidating them, and now it is time to aid your child in identifying how she may feel. With this step, you should seek to name your child's emotions, identifying the emotions you can see present, and encouraging your child to use emotional vocabulary.

Putting a name to the feeling makes it less overwhelming and less intimidating. It allows your child to know exactly what she is dealing with. Much how knowing exactly what to expect is less frustrating or upsetting than being blindsided, your child being able to name exactly what she is feeling will take away some of the lack of control she may be feeling.

This step should also be followed for yourself: Name your emotions to your child as you feel them to set the example and help your child understand that emotions are normal and acceptable, while also helping your child develop a good vocabulary for the emotions she is likely to encounter.

Consider your four-year-old child throwing a tantrum over having gotten the wrong color plate. Perhaps he had asked for the pink one, but you did not hear him and gave the pink plate to his younger brother instead. This has set your four-year-old off, and he is crying about the color while insisting his brother gives him the plate, even though the two plates have entirely different food, with his brother's missing the foods that tend to upset his stomach that your four-year-old loves to eat.

Get down to his level and say, "I can see that you are very frustrated at the moment, aren't you?" He will probably nod his head angrily in response. "I'm sorry that I didn't hear you ask for pink—how about you take the pink plate for dinner? But for now, your brother is eating his food, and you can't take his plate away. I'm sorry you are so upset and frustrated, but frustration is not a good reason to make your brother stop eating. That would make him sad and frustrated, too." He may or may not agree to wait until dinner for the pink plate, but no matter the result, you have encouraged him to think about the word frustrated.

With a teen, things will probably be a bit more nuanced. If your teen comes to you and is acting out, snapping at everyone, you may ask why he is so irritated in the hopes of finding out what his problem is. He may shrug you off and not give you an answer, but at the very least, you have put a name to his feeling, or at least, what you are assuming is his feeling. You are far more likely to get results with internalizing good usage of emotional terms by dictating your own feelings: "I feel really frustrated when you snap at everyone like that. Can we use kinder words and tones instead?"

### Step 5: Encourage Problem Solving

This step is all about fixing problems before they get out of hand. You should correct your children's misbehaviors while making sure that you are emphasizing that the behavior is the problem, not the emotion. You can do this by explaining why the behavior is wrong. Emphasize that emotions should be expressed, but through words, not through acting out. This is a good time to start offering solutions for how to fix the problem as well. Keep in mind that it takes time to teach children to think critically about problems and begin identifying solutions, but it is a skill that is crucial to learn. It may be easier to tell your kid how to fix things, but that will not serve her as well in the long run. Instead, encouraging her to explore solutions with your supervision is a much better option. Further, when teaching your child to problem solve, make it a point to praise your child whenever she does something well or solves a problem on her own, so she knows she is on the right track.

Assume that your 6-year-old daughter is upset because her younger brother accidentally knocked over the big block castle she has been building. You hear her scream, "No!" and hear the sound of blocks flying, and your younger child comes running away, crying and clutching his head. Your daughter threw a block at him because he knocked down her castle.

In this situation, you should go to your child and identify that it is okay to be frustrated and angry, but throwing blocks is not safe and not acceptable under any circumstances. Point out how throwing the block hurt her brother and made him cry, and ask her if she knows what she should do next. At this point, she may apologize and say she can build it again, or she may dig in her heels and refuse to make any changes to her behavior. If she does not want to change her behavior, you could try sending her to time out until she is ready to behave, as children who are not ready to be nice do not need to be spending time with others.

Imagine that your teen has come home, upset about having failed a test. You know that the night prior to the test, he had spent the day playing video games, and then spent the night sleeping. He hadn't even attempted to study at all, and you know it. Upset, he tells you that he's so stupid and that he's never going to be able to go to the college he really wants to attend.

You ask him what happened with the test, and he says he does not know. You ask if he studied and see him look away sheepishly. You ask again, and he answers honestly; he did not think he needed to study because he had felt confident about the material. Then, you can ask him what he could do next time to make sure he has the appropriate amount of time to study, and you see the realization click. He seems to have gotten the idea.

## CHAPTER 32

# Emotion Coaching as Your Child Grows

**10 Tips for Being Aware of Your Child or Teen's Emotions**

1. Take a few moments every time you interact with your child to really study their expressions and put them in context with what is happening at that moment. Does she cross her arms when she is annoyed? Does he scrunch up his face when he smiles when he's ecstatic? Learn the subtle difference between both positive and negative emotions.

2. Notice how your child holds his or her body in a wide range of situations and seek to find patterns in posture based on emotions. Does he stand up straight and tall when proud or happy? Does she seem to try to shrink back when sad or frightened? Does he seem combatant when angry?

3. Listen to your child's voice and search for undertones that will let you cue into your child's emotional state. Does her voice waver when she is sad? Is there a squeal in her words when he is thrilled to be somewhere or doing something? Can you hear the uncertainty in his words when he doesn't know what to do next?

4. Look for little quirks or habits your child has when feeling certain ways, such as biting nails when nervous or twirling hair when restless. These can tell you far more than words, especially if your child happens to have a few telltale quirks, such as shifting feet back and forth or being unable to sit still when caught being dishonest.

5. Take the time to study your child's face when he or she is sleeping to get a clear idea of what the child's relaxed face looks like. Especially if your child has not slept with you for a while, it may look different than you remember! Take the few moments to really study that sleeping face and see how his features soften compared to what you are used to seeing during the day.

6. Learn to speak your teen's body language: Try to catch onto slightly different postures or expressions your teen may have that will help you cue into their emotional state. Teens are typically much more reserved with their emotions, so learning subtleties in your teen's body language is likely one of your best bets to understand how he is feeling.

7. Pay attention to whatever your teen is emphasizing at that moment. Some teens will journal or write obsessively during tough times, while others may play different types of video games depending on mood. Sometimes, they will play the music that closely relates to how they are feeling as well. Pay attention to how your teen is spending his time when at home.

8. No matter how tempting it may be, DO NOT try to take your teen's diary or journal, or otherwise invade your teen's privacy unless you have a good reason to do so. Yes, you would be able to learn what is happening and where your teen stands emotionally, but that is a significant betrayal of trust and will do far more damage than good.

9. Try to identify the undertones when your teen does open up with you. Listen to the language that is being used—is it self-deprecating, or is it playful and confident? Is it inherently angry or more positive and optimistic? You can learn a lot about people by hear-

ing the undertones behind the words, or paying attention to the context.

10. Watch how your teen interacts with peers (from afar, of course!). If your friend invites friends over, try to stay out of the way while paying attention to how she seems to interact with her friends. Are they happily chatting away, giggling, and enjoying each other's company? Do they seem upset or depressed? Do you see anything that is inherently worrying when she hangs out with her friends? This may be the most honest picture of your child's emotional states you will get, as she is bound to be more expressive with her friends than with her family at this stage.

## 10 Tips for Approaching Your Child or Teen's Emotions as Learning Opportunities

1. When something goes wrong when your child is trying to do something, ask her how she feels about that, and encourage him to be as expressive or descriptive as possible. You may need to add guiding questions in here, such as asking if angry is all she feels, or if there is more than one emotion bothering her at that moment. You want her to be as honest as possible with you, and you want her to practice using as many descriptive words as she can to foster communication skills.

2. Ask your child to think about how he could turn that negative event into something positive and productive instead. If his drawing does not quite look like a dragon, maybe he could turn it into something else and create a story about it instead of focusing on failing at attaining perfection. This reminds your child that imperfection can still be great or inspiring and that there is always light to find in a situation, even if it did not turn out the way your child may have expected. This also teaches your child to be flexible.

3. Make a cake with your child. Hype it up as being the most delicious cake and make it a point to let your child help you decorate.

When you give her the first slice, ask her to smash the cake with a spatula. When she does, ask her to take a bite of it, and then ask if it is still good, even though it was no longer exactly what she expected.

4. When watching a movie with your child, ask him to identify the feelings of other characters. Ask why they feel that way. Encourage your child to be as descriptive as he can be with the emotions in order to foster a wider emotional vocabulary. Encourage him to try this at key emotional points in the movie with a wide range of characters. Not only does this get him thinking about emotions, but it also encourages him to exercise his brain through analysis and comprehension.

5. Ask your child to imagine how she would feel if she were in another character's shoes when watching a TV show. This encourages her to think empathetically, imagining whether she would react similarly, or try an entirely different approach. Ask her to explain her reasoning as she does this as clearly as she can manage.

6. Encourage your teen to consider how his emotionally fueled actions impacted a friend or family member. You want him to identify how his own actions can impact many people around him as well, even if he did not intend to do so.

7. The next time you are upset at your teen, turn it into an empathy exercise. Ask her to identify your feelings, and to do her best to explain why you feel that way. Turn this into a discussion with you telling her how you actually feel and the reason behind it if your teen's guess was wrong.

8. Attempt to identify people's thoughts, feelings, and emotions at a glance to pass the time while driving or traveling with your teen. He has to look at someone, say how he is feeling, and offer up a reason for it, either humorous, or serious, and you have to decide whether it is realistic, and vice versa.

9. The next time your teen has a large outburst, encourage her to reflect upon it, judgment-free after tensions have fallen. Explain

that you are happy to listen, so long as your teen is mindful of her emotions and is not lashing out or hurting other people.

10. The next time you and your teen witness an altercation or argument, ask your teen what he would do to avoid being in a situation like that. He does not necessarily have to answer out loud, but you want him to start thinking about tough emotional issues.

## 10 Tips for Listening to and Validating Your Child or Teen's Emotions

1. Always make eye contact and put down distractions when your child or teen approaches you. Make it a point to give your child or teen your undivided attention. This teaches your child good listening skills while also proving that you care enough to put away any of the distractions and spend some good one-on-one time with your child. Your child deserves your full attention when she comes to you to talk about emotions, even if it may be at an inconvenient time.

2. Always paraphrase your teen or child's words back to him to ensure you heard him correctly. It can be difficult to fully understand what a child or teen is saying, especially if he is still young and struggles to fully articulate himself. If you did not understand your child correctly, he has the opportunity to correct you before the conversation progresses any further. If you have understood correctly, you proved to your child that you are actively listening.

3. When your child or teen approaches you to speak, make sure that you do not try to formulate rebuttals or pass any sort of judgment on what is being said. Your job is to listen to what your child or teen has to say, not judge it. Feel glad that your child chose to confide in you and make sure you do not betray that trust that was given through snarky asides or by spending so much time focusing on a response that you did not pay enough attention to the message your child was trying to convey.

4. Make it clear to your teen or child that he is more than welcome to feel any way he pleases, so long as he does not allow those feelings to spill over into his behavior in ways that are negative or unproductive. When his behaviors do become negative as well, make sure that you emphasize that the behaviors are what are being discouraged, not the emotion itself.

5. Try to relate to your child or teen when they approach you with negative feelings. Let them speak, and when they have, try to relate to them somehow. If your teen is upset about his first breakup, relate it to yours and how you felt as well. If your child is disappointed that his sandcastle fell down, tell him about a time that something you were working on did not go according to plan and how you felt. This makes them feel as though their emotions are legitimate.

6. Never tell your child or teen that she is overreacting, that she is okay, or say anything else that implies that her feelings are not accurate, justified, or acceptable. Your child or teen is free to feel however she pleases, and any feeling is legitimate.

7. After your child or teen has finished speaking, ask questions that further the conversation or that may help guide him toward a logical solution to whatever is triggering the emotions that were brought up in the first place.

8. Have an open-door policy—anything that is said to you is said in confidence unless you believe that your child or teen is breaking laws, at risk of being hurt, or someone else is at risk of being hurt. You want your child to be able to come to you with anything without fear of judgment, no matter what.

9. Never suggest to your teen, especially to daughters, that their emotions are actually just hormones and are an over-reaction. Your daughter's feelings are no less valid just because she is a girl, and implying that they are less trustworthy is sexist and unfair to her.

10. Never tell your child or teen that crying is unacceptable. Crying is a legitimate expression of emotion and is not a harmful behav-

ior to anyone around. It should not be belittled or discouraged, as doing so will only encourage your child to hide emotions altogether, rather than encouraging an open conversation about their emotions.

## 10 Tips for Labeling Your Child or Teen's Emotions

1. Make it a point to name your child or teen's emotion in conversations regarding them. This not only acknowledges and validates the emotion and shows that you are paying attention, but also allows children in particular to develop a wider vocabulary involving emotions. Every time you name your child or teen's emotions, make sure you use a handful of similar, but still different words that would describe the emotion to give your child or teen some variety and options.

2. Name your own emotions when talking to your child or teen about how something that directly affected you. If your child did not put away his Legos and you stepped on one, tell him that it made you very sad and angry to step on one because it really hurt. If your teen was out past curfew and did not answer his phone, tell him how afraid you were and how much you worried until you finally got a hold of him.

3. Find a picture of a feelings wheel online and print it out. Whenever your child or teen is getting overwhelmed or upset, encourage her to go to the feelings wheel and pick out a middle or outer level word to explain her feelings to you in a word that is more specific than angry, sad, or bad.

4. Give your teen the feelings wheel that you printed out for your younger child and encourage him to use outer words as well in a conversation. Turn it into a game—whoever can use the most specific language about their emotions wins.

5. Give the entire family copies of blank bingo sheets and have each person fill it out with outer level words from the feelings wheel. Set up a movie for movie night and try to identify the emotions

on your chart on characters in the movie. You must write down the context for each emotion on your chart as well for ease of remembering when it happened. The first person to bingo is the winner.

6. Encourage your child to identify how other children at the playground are feeling and to tailor her interactions with them accordingly. This gets her thinking about what emotions look like in other people, allowing her to practice some empathy.

7. Play emotional charades with your teen or child that can read independently. This gets the entire family involved and thinking about emotions. Take all of the outer emotions from the feelings wheel and put them in a basket or some other container. Take turns picking out one slip of paper and trying to act out the emotion written on the slip without using words. Whoever guesses correctly gets to keep that slip of paper. Whoever has the most slips by the end of the game is the winner.

8. Role-play or play dolls with your child and make emotions important. Make an annoyed face or gesture, or have your doll say, "Yuck!" in a disgusted tone and ask your child to identify the emotion she thinks your doll is feeling. Encourage her to keep trying until she guesses the right one. After your child identifies the emotion you were portraying, ask her to act one out and tell her that she will win if she can come up with one you cannot identify. Go back and forth, practicing the emotional exchanges.

9. Praise your child or teen any time they come to you to discuss their emotions unprompted, and offer even more praise if they use emotionally intelligent words or seek to be specific with their emotions. For example, if your child tells you he is frustrated, or your teen tells you that he is particularly livid today, those expressions would deserve extra praise compared to your child saying he feels bad.

10. Make emotions collage with your child. Give your child a bunch of old magazines, scissors, and glue, and have them find pictures of people showing signs of various emotions to paste in clusters

on their paper. Give her four or five categories of emotions to discover within the magazines. For children not yet reading, you can draw faces with the appropriate emotion to label each category. Put the completed collage up on the fridge, and encourage your child to run to point at whatever emotion she is feeling at any given moment.

## 10 Tips for Encouraging Your Child or Teen to Problem Solve

1. Ask your child or teen guiding questions when they feel stuck or otherwise unable to solve their problem. These guiding questions, such as, "what do you think would happen if I tried this?" help point the child in the right direction without necessarily giving them the right answer, especially if you make your suggestion just slightly flawed enough to not work, but close enough to the solution that they can figure it out with some more thought.
2. When your child or teen is overwhelmed, encourage him to identify the problem at hand. This problem could be something minor, such as being annoyed about not getting ice cream, or as major as struggling in class due to losing a parent. Once the problem is identified, solutions are easier to find. It is next to impossible to find the answer to questions you do not yet know.
3. Problem solving also entails making sure behaviors are not out of line. Emotionally charged behaviors can become a problem or make the problem worse. Remind children and teens that while all emotions are accepted, misbehaviors need to be managed and controlled. Reminders of consequences for adults may be appropriate, depending on consequences, such as losing a job if responsibilities are not met.
4. Remember, this is a work in progress. Do not expect your child or teen to suddenly be a master at emotional problem solving, especially if it is not something you have worked to strengthen much before now. Your child or teen will learn in time, so long as you

give her the time she needs. Your patience on the topic will make this step far more bearable.

5. Do not set your child up for failure! Children thrive in environments in which they are free to explore without fear of overstepping or being told no. If you can create an environment at home in which no is a rarely spoken word, your child will develop stronger problem-solving abilities simply due to not running into constant situations in which he is told no or has his creativity quashed for any reason at all.

6. Remember, teens are impulsive. The part of the brain that regulates impulses and weighs those impulses against risk is not yet developed and will not be until later in adulthood. Your teen may be likely to take risks that are not necessarily smart due to this. You should be prepared, especially if peer pressure gets involved. Teens may try to engage in risky behavior, which will only further get them into trouble. You should make sure they are armed with the knowledge they need prior to being in a dangerous situation.

7. Set up a code word that means your teen needs you to get them out of a risky or dangerous situation. Furthering the ideas in the previous section, setting up a safe word that your teen can text you provides your teen with an out for situations in which she may not feel comfortable or safe without her losing face to her peers. Because her peers will see her parent calling and demanding she comes home, she instantly has an excuse they will not argue with, and she is able to avoid a situation she wanted nothing to do with in the first place.

8. One of the best ways to develop problem-solving skills is to allow your child or teen to fail sometimes, especially if the situation is controlled. Allowing your child to fail and flounder a bit forces them to try to solve the problem on their own, forcing critical thinking skills, while you are still present if your child may need you. It is the best of both worlds, allowing for independence while also providing the safety net of a parent.

9. Both your teen and child should be encouraged to think up multiple solutions to any given problem. Ask her to think about the problem at hand and offer three or four solutions to it. Once those solutions have been brainstormed, ask her to weigh both the pros and cons for each solution. This then gives her a way to compare the various solutions against each other and discover the one that will have the best results for her.

10. Last, but certainly not least, you should encourage your child or teen to remain persistent. Failure is a part of life, and it almost certainly will happen repeatedly to him. He needs to be prepared to face that fact while also being willing to keep trying after a failure has happened. The only way to go after failing is up, and even if he continues to fail, he will be no worse off than he already was. This step may require extra encouragement—failing is hard, even for people who have finished developing!

## CHAPTER 33

# Recommended Children's Books to Help with Emotional Intelligence and Emotion Coaching

**Books for Toddlers and Preschoolers**

*Story of My Feelings* by Laurie Berkner: Paired with a CD with a song, popular children's music artist Laurie Berkner teaches children about their feelings and how all feelings are valid and have a purpose. Young children will love the music paired with cute illustrations and meaningful lyrics that will keep your child bouncing to the beat and fully engaged with the story. This is good for identifying basic emotions and teaching how emotions and behaviors are related.

*My Mouth Is a Volcano!* by Julia Cook: This book follows Louis, who always interrupts those around him. As soon as his thoughts pop into his mind, his mouth erupts, and he cannot help but tell those around him whatever has popped up with no regard to who was talking or if he was hurting someone else's feelings by interrupting them. Louis then gets interrupted, and he begins to understand the effect of interrupting people as they talk. He begins to think empathetically about the situation, and the child learns a fun technique for controlling his or her words until it is appropriate to chime in.

*Dealing with Feelings* Series by Elizabeth Crary: These books, aimed toward younger children, recognize the child's feelings, and guide the child through the process of dealing with them. It provides age-appropriate suggestions for coping with emotions and introduces children, and their parents, to the idea that there are better ways to deal with emotions than to react impulsively.

### Books for Children

*My Dragon Books* Series by Steve Herman: These books explore a wide range of feelings, from grief to anxiety, coping with change, and dealing with many more negative or powerful emotions. They follow a boy and his dragon, Diggory, through the various stages of emotions, as well as what your child can do to feel better, in easily understood language formatted with rhymes. With adorable illustrations and an idea that keeps a child's attention, this is a must-have series to coping with emotions, aimed toward kindergarteners-2nd graders.

*Angry Octopus* by Lori Lite: This story introduces your child to an octopus who feels angry about discovering his garden destroyed one morning. The octopus works through learning to manage his anger through a series of deep breaths and relaxing muscles, one by one. This book reads more like a guided meditation for your child and encourages him or her to follow along with the angry octopus and learn to relax on cue. It helps children understand the idea of anger, as well as emotional triggers while providing a coping mechanism for that anger to avoid lashing out unnecessarily, even in the face of anger that can feel almost overwhelming.

*Alexander and the Terrible, Horrible, No Good, Very Bad Day* by Judith Viorst: This book is a children's classic for a reason. Your child will follow Alexander as he has a day that just gets worse and worse. The ending offers little in terms of problem-solving or offering hope for the next day to be better, with the moral of the story being that sometimes, people just have bad days, and that is okay. This book is a fantastic stepping stone into conversations about Alexander's emotions, as well as how he could have behaved differently to see different results.

## Books for Tweens and Teens

*Conquer Negative Thinking for Teens* by Mary Karapetian Alvord and Anne McGrath: This book, aimed toward teens, helps teach them to identify patterns of negative thinking that could be negatively impacting their emotions, and therefore their behavior. Being able to control those negative thoughts is a crucial skill to mastering the self-management side of emotional intelligence, and this book will help teens focus on various types of negative thoughts while also teaching them the skills necessary to overcome those emotions. With easily understood language with an appropriate pace, assignments, and activities that are easily executed, and plenty of advice, this book will help motivated teens to manage their emotions and behaviors.

*The Feelings Book: The Care & Keeping of Your Emotions* by Dr. Lynda Madison: While this book may skew toward the tween end of this spectrum, there is valuable information that teens could learn hidden within these pages. A companion to the ever-popular *The Care & Keeping of You*, this book is primarily aimed toward girls, though the information within it could largely be applied toward boys.

*Don't Let Your Emotions Run Your Life for Teens* by Sheri Van Dijk: This book is a workbook aimed to teach your teen how to manage mood swings, anger, and other strong emotions. This book approaches emotions from a dialectical behavior therapy standpoint and guides your teen through the steps of becoming aware of thoughts and how to cope with them, along with plenty of examples included within.

## CHAPTER 34

# Conclusion

Congratulations! You have finished *Emotional Intelligence for Kids*! If you have made it this far, you likely have a pretty good idea of your strengths and weaknesses regarding your parenting style. You may be parenting in a style that you wish was different, or you may realize that your own EQ is not high enough for you to effectively emotion coach your child through their own emotions. No matter where you stand, hopefully, the information you found within these pages provided you with insight for where to go from here to better your own emotion coaching skills.

Regardless of whether your next step is to begin working on your own emotional intelligence or jumping right into emotion coaching your child, you should have found valuable information to help you on your journey. If you are planning to focus on yourself first to get your own EQ to a level that would be conducive to emotion coaching, try checking out Emotional Intelligence 2.0 and Emotional Intelligence Practical Guide. These two parts will provide complementary information to what was found in this one and will give you the guidance and skills you need to prepare to raise an emotionally intelligent child.

If you are ready to move on to emotion coaching your child, remember the key steps to emotion coaching: being aware of your child's emotions, seeing emotions as learning opportunities for your child, listening to and validating your child's feelings, labeling emotions, and helping your child to problem-solve. Each of these steps will help your child build up the foundations of emotional intelligence that will carry your child through life and help your child develop the skills to flourish socially.

Remember to avoid over- or under-correcting your own behaviors and parenting styles and creating unintended effects with your child. Remember, moderation is important in all things, and too much of any good thing can have unintended consequences. Overcorrecting can be just as bad as under-correcting, especially if you swing from too permissive to too controlling.

As you take your first steps in your emotion coaching journey, remember to keep in mind the most important part of the process: Being an involved, empathetic, and supporting parent. This will help strengthen your bond with your child, encouraging your relationship with him or her, and you may even find your relationship evolving into something better than you ever could have imagined as your child learns how to better communicate and regulate feelings. The end result will be a happier child, a happier parent, and less conflict overall. With less conflict and misunderstandings, both you and your child will be able to truly enjoy spending time together without worrying about meltdowns or arguments. Lastly, remember to keep moving forward, even if you run into hardships from time to time. There will be struggles and roadblocks, but you will get past them, and your child will learn from watching you persevere in the face of adversity.

CPSIA information can be obtained
at www.ICGtesting.com
Printed in the USA
LVHW010320140921
697767LV00003B/365

9 781914 456015